Primary Mathematics

Primary Mathematics

TEACHING FOR UNDERSTANDING

Patrick Barmby, Lynn Bilsborough, Tony Harries and Steve Higgins

Open University Press

Open University Press
McGraw-Hill Education
McGraw-Hill House
Shoppenhangers Road
Maidenhead
Berkshire
England
SL6 2QL

email: enquiries@openup.co.uk
world wide web: www.openup.co.uk

and Two Penn Plaza, New York, NY 10121–2289, USA

First published 2009

A catalogue record of this book is available from the British Library

ISBN-13: 978–0–335–22926–0 (pb)   978–0–335–22925–3 (hb)
ISBN-10: 0–335–22926–3 (pb)   0–335–22925–5 (hb)

Library of Congress Cataloging-in-Publication Data
CIP data has been applied for

Typeset by RefineCatch Limited, Bungay, Suffolk
Printed in the UK by Bell and Bain Ltd. Glasgow

Mixed Sources
Product group from well-managed
forests and other controlled sources
www.fsc.org Cert no. TT-COC-002769
© 1996 Forest Stewardship Council
FSC

The *McGraw·Hill* Companies

Contents

Illustrations

Figures

Tables

1

Introduction

I found it kind of weird that Rachel cannot learn numbers, because every time I go past her house with my little pony, she would come and she knows everything nearly about horses, so why can't she learn numbers really?

(Year 5 pupil)

This book has been written with the aim of promoting primary or elementary school teachers' understanding of mathematics, both those at the beginning of their careers and those who have been teaching for some time. In turn, we hope that it will indirectly enhance the mathematical experience of pupils in the classroom. The four authors of the book work as teacher trainers in primary mathematics education, and have a vested interest in improving the mathematical understanding of teachers. However, more than that, we also feel that we need to take a good look at what it means to understand mathematics. One of the existing problems we see with the subject, certainly here in England where we work, is that it is seen as having simple 'right' and 'wrong' answers. Therefore, in the classroom, teachers concentrate on making sure that children get the 'right' answer. However, we feel that this is too limited a view, which can all too often lead to only teaching procedures in mathematics. Instead, we should be concentrating on the various connections we can make within the subject. Being able to make more connections within and across different mathematical topics will help us to check the answers that we get for calculations, to reapply the knowledge in different situations and to make new connections that develop the way we think about the mathematics. Also, children come with their own prior experience to the classroom, so taking into account the possible connections that they can already make can help us render mathematics more meaningful for children. Therefore, before we present the mathematical topics that make up this book, we intend to clarify *our* notion of understanding and the implications it has for our mathematics teaching.

Our picture of understanding

This idea of 'making connections' is integral to our idea of understanding in mathematics, and one that many researchers in mathematics education have put forward in the past. For example, consider this quote from Hiebert and Carpenter (1992: 67):

> The mathematics is understood if its mental representation is part of a network of representations. The degree of understanding is determined by the number and strength of its connections. A mathematical idea, procedure, or fact is understood thoroughly if it is linked to existing networks with stronger or more numerous connections.

Also central to our notion of understanding, and stated above by Hiebert and Carpenter, is that these connections are made between the **mental representations** that we have concerning a particular mathematical **concept**. More specifically, Davis (1984: 203) defines mental representations as:

> Any mathematical concept, or technique, or strategy – or anything else mathematical that involves either information or some means of processing information – if it is to be present in the mind at all, must be represented in some way.

Goldin (1998) provides some specific examples of these mental representations, such as verbal representations, images, symbols, strategies and representations influencing our attitude towards the concept such as memories of past experiences. This last example of a mental representation is interesting in that it is not mathematical *per se*. However, it recognizes that our understanding of mathematics might also involve our broader experience, such as when to apply a procedure, or our experience of learning the idea in school. In our experience, when we talk to any student teacher about their understanding of a mathematical concept, it is not very long before they refer to their own school experience. Therefore, their understanding of the concept is inextricably linked with memories of learning that concept.

We can go further in developing this picture of understanding and ask how these connections are made. Sierpinska (1994) identified the 'process of understanding' as linking mental representations through **reasoning**. By reasoning, we do not just mean the formal, logical, deductive reasoning processes that we might associate with mathematics. Our reasoning might be quite informal; for example, we might do a multiplication calculation in a certain way (i.e. a representation that is linked to our idea of multiplication) because that was the way we were taught in school. That is the reason or explanation that links together our representations concerning multiplication. Over time, of course, we might want to develop our reasoning further. However, the important thing is that we recognize that our reasoning, whether formal or informal, constitutes part of our understanding.

Therefore, the overall picture of understanding that we have can be summarized in the model found in Figure 1.1. It is simply a model that we find useful when thinking about our understanding of mathematics. It makes clear that understanding is built up from connections between mental representations, the connections being made by the reasoning processes that we carry out. Based on this picture of understanding, we can put forward a number of implications for our teaching which we believe are important.

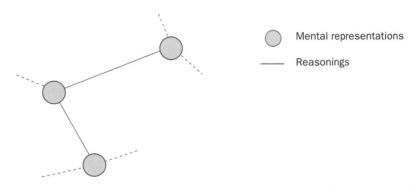

Mental representations

Reasonings

Figure 1.1 Picture of our 'representational-reasoning' model of understanding

Implications for understanding mathematics

The first implication is that because there is nothing to stop us from developing further links to concepts, and developing new links between concepts that we may not have connected together before, there is therefore no limit to our understanding. Conversely, it is unlikely that someone has no understanding or any links at all to a concept. Let us take an example – look at the word below:

compound

What do you understand by that word? It will depend on your background experience. If you have a business background, you might associate the word with 'compound interest', which is the interest that builds up on savings. If you have a musical background, it can mean a musical time in which the beats per bar is a multiple of three. If you are a scientist, then you might understand the word as

> **KEY POINT TO CONSIDER**
>
> Understanding is a continuum and is related to the meaning that the learner gives to representations of an idea. It is also the never-ending building up of connections between representations.

meaning a substance made up of more than one type of element. A compound can also mean living quarters. One of the authors remembers a science test that he gave when teaching in Kenya. To the question 'What is a compound?', the child answered 'A compound is where I live'. In the context of the science test, we could say that the answer was wrong, but it is not the case that the child had no understanding of the concept. They just did not display the understanding that we wanted them to have.

We therefore suggest that we view understanding of mathematics in a different way.

> Understanding is not a dichotomous state, but a continuum . . . Everyone understands to some degree anything that they know about. It also follows that understanding is never complete; for we can always add more knowledge, another episode, say, or refine an image, or see new links between things we know already.
>
> (White and Gunstone, 1992: 6)

We think that this view of understanding helps to make our teaching of maths more interesting – we are always looking for new links, and acknowledging what children bring to their learning of the subject.

Misconceptions in mathematics

The model also clarifies why children might have **misconceptions**. Young children develop their ideas about the world, and so develop their own personal or idio-syncratic meanings for their experiences both inside and outside the classroom. Therefore, one of the issues that we will highlight throughout this book will be children's misconceptions in particular areas of maths. However, let us begin by being a little more specific about what we mean by misconceptions.

Extensive research has been undertaken to identify patterns in children's beliefs, theories, meanings and explanations in mathematics, and can be characterized as research into learners' developing understanding or their changing conceptions. A number of terms have been used for these clusters of beliefs, including the following: children's arithmetic (Ginsburg, 1977); preconceptions (Ausubel, Novak and Hanesian, 1978); conceptual primitives (Clement, 1982); naive theories (Resnick, 1983); alternative conceptions (Hewson, 1985) and mathematics of the tribe (Steffe, 1988). When these conceptions are considered to be in conflict with the accepted meanings and understanding in mathematics, the term 'misconceptions' is commonly used (Nesher, 1987; Smith *et al.*, 1993). We have adopted this idea for misconceptions, though we would also argue that such evolving understandings in mathematics are essential and productive for the development of more sophisticated conceptions and understanding. As highlighted by Ryan and Williams (2007: 27):

> They are a natural outcome of intelligent mathematical development, involving connections, generalizations and concept formation . . . they signal a learning opportunity or zone, and so potential for development – for example, through targeted teaching. In general, we see the learner's underpinning knowledge (for example, the conceptions or misconceptions) as the object that teaching must expose and engage with.

Therefore, rather than dismissing misconceptions as 'wrong' answers, it would be far more constructive to look at the reasons why the child provides a given answer, and perhaps to acknowledge those reasons and tackle them. Teaching should therefore encourage children to make their understanding explicit.

In mathematics, these misconceptions often result from a number of different causes. Difficulties with language and informal meanings can lead to misunderstanding. If a child replied to the question 'What is the difference between 3 and 7?' with the answer '7 begins with an "s"', he would be correct linguistically but not mathematically. 'Difference' in mathematics has a particular meaning. If he replied to the same question 'minus 4' then his misconception would be of a different kind. As a teacher, you could infer that he knows a number of things about number **operations**, for example that difference and subtraction are related, and that you can subtract a larger number from a smaller, contrary to some young children's beliefs. However difference and subtraction are distinct concepts. Subtraction is not commutative so the order is important. Difference however has a property similar to **commutativity**. The difference between 3 and 7 is the same as the difference between 7 and 3.

Many misconceptions result from a limited understanding and the over-generalization of some aspects of this understanding. For example, multiplication of positive whole numbers results in a larger number as the product, so a child might infer that multiplication makes things bigger. However this 'rule' would not be true with **fractions** and negative numbers. Other kinds of misconceptions result from applying an idea or rule in the wrong situation. Faced with the addition of fractions for the first time, a legitimate inference might seem to be $\frac{1}{2}+\frac{1}{5}=\frac{2}{7}$. The arithmetic is correct if you interpret the numbers in a fraction as being separate, rather than the relationship between the two numbers being an important part of the fraction (see Chapter 5 for more details about fractions).

We therefore believe that misconceptions in mathematics are inevitable; in line with our picture of understanding, to develop a more complete understanding you first have to begin with a less complete conception. We also believe that misconceptions are largely predictable in that the patterns of experience from generation to generation are largely the same, and it is important for teachers to know how children's understanding of mathematics develops in order to build constructively on what children know and can do. Children's mistakes are rarely random and understanding why they get something wrong is therefore the starting point for helping them to correct it. We also suggest that misconceptions are productive. Identifying and building on incomplete or incorrect conceptions are important ways of developing coherent mathematical knowledge.

Representations and reasoning in mathematics

Another implication of our view of understanding is the importance of being able to access a range of representations for a given mathematical concept. Many researchers (for example, Krutetskii, 1976; Carpenter *et al.*, 1999; Thompson, 1999a) have all indicated the importance of representations in developing mathematical competence. Goldin and Shteingold (2001) suggest that representations are important for the learning of mathematics because of the inherent structure contained within each representation. This structure can shape or constrain learning. Furthermore, different representations emphasize different aspects of a concept, and so the development of an understanding of a particular concept comes from having a range of representations. As highlighted by Kaput (1992: 530) 'All aspects of a complex idea cannot be adequately represented within a single notation system, and hence require multiple systems for their full expression'.

When we talk about representations, it is necessary to distinguish between 'internal' and 'external' representations – external representations being words, graphs, numerals, diagrams, etc., whereas internal representations are the mental representations we possess at a personal level. For a given mathematical concept, both the internal and external forms may be similar, but not necessarily the same: the internal representations are always personally derived. However, we would hope that providing a range of external representations for a concept would develop the range of internal representations. For the purposes of teaching mathematics, we must be concerned with external representations, which may help pupils to develop flexible and powerful ways of working with concepts.

Although having access to a range of representations for a mathematical concept is important, we must be aware that it is not the only thing that we must consider. In our picture of understanding, we have two components – the range of mental representations *and* the reasoning linking them together. Therefore, we must also develop the reasoning that we can carry out between representations. Let us take an example of two symbolic representations for multiplication statements: 7×3 and 3×7. These two representations are linked together because the calculations both give the same answer of 21. Now, can we reason why? Let us provide some possible reasons below:

- The teacher said that you can always swap round the numbers in a multiplication question, and you still get the same answer.
- If I draw out 7 lots of 3 objects, I can see I get 21. If I draw out 3 lots of 7 objects, I can see that I also get 21. Therefore, the two calculations give the same answer.
- If we show multiplication as an array, then swapping around the numbers only changes the orientation of the **array**. Therefore, when multiplying together any two whole numbers, we can see that the answer must be the same.

KEY POINT TO CONSIDER

Reasoning is the process by which the learner articulates and demonstrates connections between representations.

All of the reasons given are valid; however, we would say that as we go down the list, the reasons provide more insight into the concept of multiplication. Therefore, by developing the reasoning we have in place, we also develop the understanding we have of the concept. Drawing out children's reasoning and developing the reasoning they use is therefore integral to developing understanding in mathematics.

Communicating mathematics

From the above discussion one of the implications for our teaching of mathematics is the importance of reasoning and accessing and developing children's reasoning. Implicitly linked with this idea of reasoning is the way in which we communicate mathematics. Children need to communicate their knowledge of mathematics through using relevant language to refine, consolidate and further develop their mathematical understanding (Association of Teachers of Mathematics, 1991). Likewise, in explaining mathematical concepts, teachers are trying to convey their understanding of a mathematical concept to children, using language as the essential mechanism for the process of communication. Therefore, the process of communicating mathematics is integral to our learning of mathematics.

There are two issues that we need to consider with regards to communicating mathematics. First of all, returning to our picture of understanding, because understanding is constructed by the individual, communicating mathematical ideas is not a simple matter of transferring concepts and understandings between individuals. The meaning contained within a particular piece of language or body of text is constructed by people so that they hopefully (but not necessarily) share an understanding of it. For example, while it is entirely possible for the teacher to explain the 'meaning' of a maths topic to children, this is rarely if ever effective on its own. Time needs to be provided for the children to engage in activities or to attempt **problems** related to the topic, so as to develop their ideas, explore their meaning and generally deepen their understanding of it. Classroom discussion along with classroom activities can therefore be thought of as an iterative process to develop and refine children's understanding, in order to arrive at a *shared* understanding.

Second, communicating mathematical concepts generally involves a language that is in part composed of words used more widely in 'everyday' language, and in part of terms that are confined to mathematics. Moreover, the language often includes domain specific symbols as well as words. These additional components of mathematical language reflect the nature of the subject in terms of precision. The way we use language in mathematics might therefore be quite different to the way we use language in other situations. We saw an example of this in the previous section on misconceptions. Pimm (1987) has likened children's growing acquaintance with mathematical terms and operations to the processes involved in learning a foreign language: both involve learning a new vocabulary and mastering a new grammar before the language can be used effectively. This new language is generally more tightly defined and formalized than everyday language. There is a greater emphasis on its appropriate and inappropriate use in mathematics, and a far smaller number of

> ### KEY POINT TO CONSIDER
>
> Pupil/pupil and pupil/teacher discussion is an iterative process which can help the pupil to develop and refine their understanding of a concept. The language used in discussion often includes domain specific symbols as well as words.

correct and a far greater number of incorrect applications than in the contexts referred to in everyday language. This can be new and strange for young children and they will typically need help in adjusting to this new language. Here, teachers and their use of language can be crucial in facilitating children's increasing familiarity with the new language. The wrong sort of approach or failure to take account of the child's own understanding as reflected in their use of language can cause greater confusion and set back mathematical learning appreciably. As we suggested for taking into account children's existing conceptions and understanding of mathematical concepts, we can draw upon children's own language and develop and refine this mathematically, rather than the teacher imposing a 'correct' but alien mathematical language on pupils. We can become acquainted with children's language and work with it, rather than ignoring or rejecting it and introducing something wholly foreign to children and outside their experience.

This importance of communicating mathematics therefore, both in terms of developing a shared understanding and also of developing mathematical language, again, has implications for the teacher. Teachers need to think of purposeful tasks and activities as a means of engaging children in reasoning and verbalizing about maths, rather than activities primarily determined by their suitability for assessment. In addition to thinking about appropriate tasks and activities, teachers need to consider the role of questioning. Skilled questioning has long been recognized as an effective pedagogic tool, but most questions are posed with a correct answer in mind. A typical scenario would be where a question is asked by the teacher, the child replies and the answer is accepted or rejected (Brissenden, 1988). In the latter case, this might be because the response is not the required one, or because time does not allow for further discussion. In any event, the child is left to worry about what the 'right answer' might be and how it differs from the one they have given. Instead, ideally, the teacher should give prior thought to drafting suitable questions, and the plan for the lesson needs to allow sufficient time for interpreting the question and thinking about it, and time for answering it, including scope for any discussion between pupil and teacher about the answer. Aiming for a freer discussion between pupils and teacher will also provide many more opportunities for assessing their progress and understanding in mathematics.

Structure of the book

We have provided a fairly extensive introduction to this book, not only to convey to the reader the perspective we are taking on 'understanding mathematics', but also to justify the structure that we have used. In the above discussion, we have highlighted the following important issues:

- understanding;
- representations;
- reasoning;
- misconceptions;
- communicating.

We draw on these issues as themes to focus on within each chapter and will look at a variety of ways of representing the concepts involved. As in the previous discussion, we will try to take a broad view of these representations; we may look at diagrams and symbolic representations, but we may also look at definitions of concepts and historical examples. We feel that this variety of representations will broaden the reader's understanding of the topic. We will then reason with the representations to make connections and to further develop our understanding. We will look at common misconceptions that children may have within the topic, either as an introduction to the ideas that we will discuss, or to reflect back on how what we have said in a chapter helps us to tackle misconceptions. We will also see how the concepts can be communicated in the classroom, both in terms of the language involved, and also opportunities for activities and discussion. We will end each chapter by providing the reader with opportunities for discussion, through questions for consideration and for reflection on the material in each chapter.

Finally, before we move on to the mathematical topics themselves, let us mention the 'mathematics' that we have included in this book. Clearly, our focus has been on looking at topics which are relevant for primary or elementary teachers. However, we have tried not to restrict our discussions to specifically covering any particular syllabus or curriculum. Of course, the topics that we have included have been influenced by the fact that we work with teachers in England; however, we have tried to include references to other countries such as the US so that we can look at the topics more broadly. Once again, we have done this in the belief that it will develop the reader's understanding of primary mathematics.

Questions for discussion

1 Do you agree or disagree with the view of understanding put forward in this chapter? What criticisms do you have of this view? Is it consistent with the view of mathematics in the curriculum for primary or elementary schools?

2 What are the implications of this view of understanding on the way that mathematics is learnt, taught and assessed in primary or elementary schools?

3 Is the view of misconceptions put forward in this chapter consistent with the view of misconceptions that you have seen in schools? What are the pros and cons of the view of misconceptions put forward here?

4 In your experience, how is mathematics 'communicated' in the classroom? What are the implications of the view of 'communication' put forward in this chapter?

2

Using numbers

The starting point for our examination of primary or elementary school mathematics is that of 'number'. Since a large part of the book will be looking at operations and concepts associated with number, we need to start with a clear understanding of this concept upon which we can build. We begin with what we actually mean by 'number' and we provide a range of representations upon which we can build our understanding of the topic, including both spoken and written numbers. We will also see the reasoning involved with the different representations, again seeing how understanding needs to develop in order for us to use numbers, and also the misconceptions that we can have with numbers. Finally, we look at how we can communicate number in the classroom, so we can ground our ideas in practical teaching contexts.

What is a number?

> **KEY POINT TO CONSIDER**
>
> There are a number of different ways in which we think about and use numbers – including cardinal uses, ordinal uses and as a measure.

A useful summary of different ways of thinking about 'number' is provided by Fuson (1988) in her research on children's counting and conception of number. First of all, we have **cardinal**, **ordinal** and **measure** numbers. Cardinal numbers refer to the number of objects or entities within a particular group or set. For example, we might state that there are three ping-pong balls in a packet. The 'three' in this case refers to the 'manyness' or the cardinality of the set of ping-pong balls. Cardinal numbers can be thought of as the answer to the question 'how many?' (Wilder, 1968) and usually involve positive whole numbers such as one and two, or zero. Ordinal numbers refer to the relative position of a particular entity with respect to other entities. A Formula One racing driver might be 'number three' on the starting grid, referring to their relative position at the start of the race. More commonly, we might use ordinal number words such as 'first', 'second' and 'third'. Ordinal numbers can be thought of as the answer to the question, 'In what order?' (Wilder, 1968). Finally, measure numbers tell us how many units there are of a particular quantity, for example 'three metres'. Measure numbers are related to cardinal numbers in that they can also refer to a number of entities (in this case, particular units) within a set (the particular quantity). However, measure numbers denote properties of objects rather than the actual number of objects.

Expanding on this concept of number, we can have 'sequential', 'symbolic' and 'non-numerical' uses of number. Fuson (1988) separates sequential uses into activities involving 'sequence numbers' and 'counting numbers'. Sequence numbers are simply numbers communicated in a particular order, but with no reference to any particular objects or entities. A child saying the numbers in order would be an example of this. Counting numbers involve the numbers being communicated while relating each number to a particular entity. A child pointing to different blocks in turn and saying the number sequence 'one, two, three . . .' would be an example. Note that the use of counting numbers does not necessarily imply that a cardinal use of number will result; the child would have to have developed an understanding of this use of a number. We will say more about this later when we discuss the principles that need to be understood by children for successful counting to take place. The symbolic use of numbers is representing numbers as symbols (1, 2 or 873). Often, the symbolic notation will imply other uses of the number (for example 4 apples or 1st January). However, this is not necessarily the case. We may have what Fuson terms as 'non-numerical' uses for using numbers as labels. For example, a car registration plate involves numbers that have no cardinal, ordinal or measure uses.

In addition to the categories provided by Fuson, we also include an additional category of 'abstract' approach or use of number (Lucas, 2000). This is in order to take into account number concepts that go beyond those already covered. For example, in a study carried out by Miller and Gelman (1983), looking at children's and adults' conceptions of number, they found that 'numerical applications of counting, adding, and multiplying appear to have a profound effect on the process of expanding children's conceptions of what numbers are' (p. 1478). Children might judge the numbers 2 and 4 as being similar because one is the double of the other or because they are both even numbers. Devlin (1998: 13) puts it this way:

> The counting numbers 1, 2, 3 . . . are a way of capturing and describing those patterns. The patterns captured by numbers are abstract, and so are the numbers used to describe them . . . There are still deeper patterns of number to be examined by the mathematician, patterns of evenness and oddness, of being prime or composite, of being a perfect square, of satisfying various equations, and so forth.

Lucas (2000) refers to the fact that 'we can formulate a rule for generating numerals to name new numbers quite apart from any cardinal or ordinal use we may have for them' (p. 154). This leads us to the range of different types of numbers that we encounter, both in primary mathematics and beyond:

- natural numbers: 0, 1, 2 and so on
- whole numbers or integers: . . . $-2, -1, 0, 1, 2$ . . .
- rational numbers or fractions: $\frac{1}{2}, 1\frac{3}{4}, -\frac{7}{8}$ . . .

- real numbers: $\sqrt{2}$, π, e . . .
- imaginary/complex numbers: $\sqrt{(-1)}$, $1 + 2i$ . . .

Representing numbers

In talking about the ways we can use numbers, we have indirectly touched upon two of the ways in which we can represent numbers. The sequential use of numbers involves a spoken representation whereas the symbolic use involves a written representation. Therefore, in looking at the different ways in which we can represent numbers, we can take these two categories as our starting point.

We begin by considering the number words. In English, we have the following for the first ten numbers:

one, two, three, four, five, six, seven, eight, nine, ten

Of course, there is no reason why these should be our number words. We could have the number words in Japanese or Swahili:

ichi, ni, san, shi, go, roku, nana, hachi, kyu, ju (Japanese)
moja, mbili, tatu, nne, tano, sita, saba, nane, tisa, kumi (Swahili)

These number words may be based on existing words. For example, Dehaene (1997) highlights the relationship between number words and body parts, with many words for 'five' being based on the word 'hand'.

Here are the next ten numbers in each of the above languages:

English	Japanese	Swahili
eleven	juichi	kumi na moja
twelve	juni	kumi na mbili
thirteen	jusan	kumi na tatu
fourteen	jushi	kumi na nne
fifteen	jugo	kumi na tano
sixteen	juroku	kumi na sita
seventeen	junana	kumi na saba
eighteen	juhachi	kumi na nane
nineteen	jukyu	kumi na tisa
twenty	niju	ishirini

Looking at these numbers, we start to discern patterns within the number words. Apart from 'eleven' and 'twelve', we can see that the 'teen' numbers are almost the numbers we used in the first ten numbers followed by 'teen'. Dehaene (1997) points out that all the words from eleven and twelve onwards are based on the constructions 'one and ten', 'two and ten', 'three and ten', etc., which in the past were clearer in how they were constructed than they are now. Likewise, 'twenty' is based on 'two tens'. This construction is much clearer in Swahili and Japanese. 'Na' in Swahili means 'and', so all the numbers up to nineteen make complete sense. Unfortunately, multiples of ten in Swahili are more difficult. In Japanese however, the number words, are completely logical, with the 'teen' numbers being 'ten-one', 'ten-two', 'ten-three', etc, and multiples of ten being 'two-ten', 'three-ten' and so on.

In all three examples given above, the representations for number words are based around the number 10. To count to 99 say, we do not need to learn 99 different words – we just need to learn ten words (if we ignore the irregularities) and then combine the

words in different ways to give us the other numbers. We call this structure the 'base' of the number system, and English, Japanese and Swahili are all **base-10** systems. The number system we use does not need to be base-10; some languages such as French and Danish are based on a base-20 system (and, as we shall see, the ancient Mayan system). In any case, the base of the number system provides a structure upon which to build up our numbers and number words.

Turning to written numbers, and taking a historical view of these, one of the earliest civilizations for which we have records was the Egyptians. They had a system for representing numbers as shown in Figure 2.1. One of the key aspects of this system is that there was no requirement for the development of the concept of zero. Thus 1004 and 1040 would be represented as seen in Figure 2.2. This was a base-10 system as the written numbers were based around introducing new symbols at multiples of ten.

Another ancient civilization with a different representation was the Mayans in South America. Their system, for smaller numbers at least, was in base-20 so that they needed symbols for all the numbers from 0 to 19. So, for example, the symbols for 0,

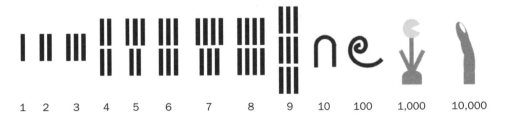

| 1 | 2 | 3 | 4 | 5 | 6 | 7 | 8 | 9 | 10 | 100 | 1,000 | 10,000 |

Figure 2.1 The Egyptian number system

Figure 2.2 1004 (left) and 1040 (right) in the Egyptian number system

Figure 2.3 Symbols in the Mayan number system

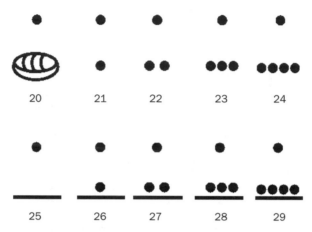

Figure 2.4 Place value in the Mayan number system

2, 5, 10, 15 and 19 are[1] as seen in Figure 2.3. After this, the Mayans used a system based on 20 so that the numbers from 20 to 29 were as in Figure 2.4, where the uppermost symbol indicated how many 20s and the lower symbol the 'extra bits'.

The Mayans therefore developed two important ideas: that of 'place value' where the position of the symbol determined its numerical value, and a symbol for zero to clarify the place value system (otherwise in their case a 20 would look just like a 1). One would expect now that for larger numbers, the top row would represent the number of 400s (20^2). But in fact in the Mayan system, the third group from the bottom represents the number of 360s (18×20), the fourth group represents the number of 7200s (18×20^2) and the next group the number of 144,000s (18×20^3). We can only speculate as to how this system evolved, but the Mayans appear to have developed quite a sophisticated calendar and it is thought that they made advanced astronomical calculations, including highly accurate calculations of the length of the solar year and the orbit of Venus. This may account for the use of 360 in their system. In any case, we can say that as a development to the number system used by the Egyptians, the Mayans used a positional system (i.e. place value) with a place holder (i.e. a symbol for zero) and therefore required fewer symbols to represent large numbers, thus making their number system more efficient.

The Babylonians developed their system of representing numbers from that of the Sumerians, possibly around the third millennium BC. They used a base-60

---

[1] One could say that within this base-10 system, the symbols have a 'semi-base' of five as well in order to build up the symbols.

system[2] in order to facilitate their number representations so that there were symbols for each of the numbers from 1 to 59 as seen in Figure 2.5. In this system we have two component symbols – one for 1 and one for 10. All other numbers are represented by groupings of tens and ones as above and then for larger numbers a place value system is used. Figure 2.6 therefore represents the number made up of 46 lots of 60 and 40 lots of 1, i.e. the number 2800. The problem with this system from our perspective is that it has no zero and hence we have no real way of knowing whether the above represents 46 lots of 60 and 40 lots of 1, or 46 lots of 3600 and 40 lots of 60, i.e. the number 168,000.

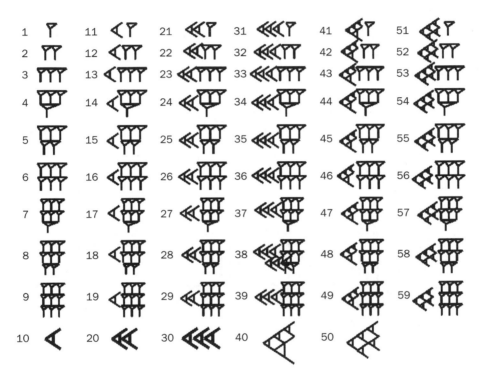

Figure 2.5 The Babylonian number system

Figure 2.6 2800 in the Babylonian number system

In China around the second century BC, a system was developed which consisted of symbols for the numbers 1 to 10 together with symbols for 20, 100 and 1000. This enabled the Chinese to represent large numbers without too much difficulty. This was

---

[2] Again, with a 'semi-base' of 10 to build up the symbols.

developed into a distinctive place value structure within which they used a system of rods which they could manipulate (see Figure 2.7). It would appear that this system of rods was developed as a calculating device for use by administrators and was a very quick way of doing physical calculations with numbers. They were set in columns which represented powers of 10 and the administrators used different coloured rods for positive and negative numbers. *Hengs* represented units, hundreds, etc., and *tsungs* represented tens, thousands, etc. Thus the number 45,698 would appear as in Figure 2.8. Alternatively, the number 60,390 would look as in Figure 2.9. As we can see, this system does not require a symbol for zero – just a space.

The number system we use today essentially developed from what is known as the Hindu-Arabic system. This system is often credited to two Indian mathematicians: Aryabhatta of Kusumapura who lived during the fifth century developed the place value notation, and Brahmagupta who introduced the zero symbol in the sixth century. In this system we have a base-10 structure. We require symbols for the

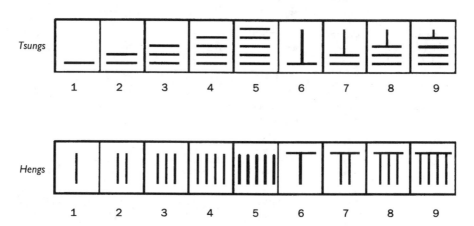

Figure 2.7 Ancient Chinese number system

Figure 2.8 45,698 in the ancient Chinese number system

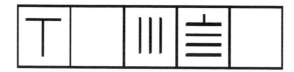

Figure 2.9 60,390 in the ancient Chinese number system

numbers 1 to 9 and then a place value system with a place holder of 0 takes care of the representation of larger numbers.

The base-10 structure and the place value system that we have allows for a very efficient way of working with numbers and performing a variety of operations on these numbers – provided that the user has a clear understanding of the nature of a place value system. Laplace summed up the achievment of the system as follows:

> It is India that gave us the ingenious method of expressing all numbers by means of ten symbols, each symbol receiving a value of position as well as an absolute value; a profound and important idea which appears so simple to us now that we ignore its true merit. But its very simplicity and the great ease which it has lent to computations puts our arithmetic in the first rank of useful inventions.
>
> (quoted in Dantzig, 2007: 19)

Reasoning with the representations for number

In the above discussion, we identified the base-10 structure and the place value property as being key aspects of the number system that we use. Let us emphasize this by showing how we can reason with the representations for number that we have.

As young children develop and extend their understanding of number words, the sequence, counting and cardinal aspects of number words become increasingly integrated (Fuson *et al.*, 1982; Fuson, 1988). Therefore, in order to use numbers, we need to be able to include these three aspects into our understanding – to be able to reason between these representations of number if you like. Starting with the first aspect of number, we can see that the base-10 structure of our number system enables us to reason the words for other numbers. For example, recognizing the structure within 'twenty-one' and 'twenty-two' enables us to reason that the next numbers are 'twenty-three', 'twenty-four' and so on. The structure therefore helps us to build up our number words. This is even clearer in Japanese where the base-10 structure is clearer.

When mistakes occur in the use of sequence numbers, these are usually related to children's developing skills rather than particular misconceptions. For example, inaccurate 'counting' in very young children is usually related to their knowledge and production of the sequence of number words. The pattern of development tends to be that children recite words as an unbroken chain (e.g. 'wuntoofreeforefive'), often as a performance for parents or older relatives. This

> ### KEY POINT TO CONSIDER
>
> Making sense of the characteristics of the different representations of numbers is an important element in the development of understanding the structure of the number system. These characteristics are the key to being able to reason between representations of numbers.

recitation cannot really be considered to be counting (Steffe and Cobb, 1988). The sequence of number words that children can say increases in length with age and usually has a 'stable' and an 'unstable' portion until the counting sequence is completely mastered. Mistakes here are usually where a number is missed out or two numbers in the **sequence** are reversed. The stable portion is what a child regularly produces, the unstable part is where this varies with number names said in the wrong order or with a number or numbers missed out. It is very rare for words other than numbers to be included in the counting sequence (Gelman and Gallistel, 1978; Fuson *et al.* 1982), though the stable portion of the sequence can be incorrect (e.g. a child regularly missed out seven). Also, although our base-10 system can support the development of larger number words, there is some evidence that the structure of number names in English causes some difficulties, particularly with irregularities in the numbers between ten and twenty and at the decade transitions (e.g. twenty-nine to thirty). This problem at the decade transitions persists for older children when counting backwards (Fuson *et al.*, 1982). Mistakes in words are often inventions based upon conflations of number words (e.g. eleventeen) or reasoned extensions of the counting sequence (e.g. twenty-ten, twenty-eleven).

Moving on to the written representation of number, the base-10 structure and the place value system also enable us to build up our written number system. Once we know the ten symbols for 0 to 9, then we can write 10, 11, 12 . . . 19, 20, 21 . . . 100, 101, and so on. Understanding the place value property also enables us to imply from our written number that it is made up of a certain number of units, tens, hundreds and so on. So 435 will be composed of four hundreds, three tens and five units. As we shall see, this in turn helps us to carry out operations on these numbers (addition, subtraction, etc.) because we can break down numbers using the place value property. We will say more about this in the next chapter, but one can see the potential of our number system for 'the great ease which it has lent to computations' as highlighted by Laplace in the previous quotation.

Reasoning about the use of number

Following on from developing the spoken representation, i.e. the sequential use of number, children then need to understand the counting and cardinal uses of number. When children start to count collections of objects or other things different types of mistakes occur related to the coordination of saying number words and pointing or touching the objects being counted. Fuson (1988) details the patterns of mistakes that occur during this stage, such as 'skim' and 'flurry' errors where children either skim over objects and do not say enough counting words or produce a flurry of words as they point to an object or objects. Skim errors result in a count which is smaller than the set counted, whereas with flurry errors the child's total is greater than what is being counted. A further difficulty can arise in keeping track of the objects being counted, particularly if the collection of items is disordered or in a random arrangement, with the result that some objects are missed out or counted twice. Therefore, children need to reason between the number words they are saying and the objects they are counting. These objects can also be varied in character. Steffe and Cobb (1988) argue that the development in counting competence progresses through understandings of what can be counted, from

- objects that can be touched, through to
- pictures (in which some items may be partially obscured) to

- verbal counting of objects which cannot be touched (though pointing or nodding actions are often used to keep track) to
- abstract items.

Therefore, the link between the spoken words and the objects being counted needs to incorporate this variety in the objects.

Moving on to the cardinal use of number, a further misconception that can occur in early counting is confusion between the ordinal and cardinal properties of number. One of the authors observed a 4-year-old child counting a collection of coloured plastic bears. In answer to the question 'How many bears?', she correctly touch-counted and

> **KEY POINT TO CONSIDER**
>
> For young children a key element of reasoning is making the link between the spoken words and the objects being counted.

replied 'seven'. But, on being asked 'Show me five bears', she pointed to a red bear (which was the fifth bear she had counted) and said 'There, that's five bear'. Munn (1994) argues that an essential aspect of the development of counting is children's perceptions of the purpose of counting. Her work on young children's beliefs about counting suggests that as children enter school, they see counting as playful rather than as purposeful or enabling you to find out about quantity. Making the reasons for counting explicit is therefore an essential ingredient in successful teaching of early number. A link that children therefore need to make is that between the counting and counting aspects of number. The cardinal property of a group of objects, i.e. the final number we get to in a counting sequence, is somehow an important property that we need to recognize. Children also need to recognize that the cardinal property of a group of objects does not change if the objects are counted in a different order. However, this can be challenging as children make inferences about features of counting from their own observations (Briars and Siegler, 1984; Fuson, 1988). These inferences can result in beliefs that some common features of counting are essential (Briars and Siegler, 1984), such as the need for 'adjacency' (a consecutive count of objects next to each other) and a requirement to 'start at an end' (usually with the counting moving from left to right).

Therefore, bringing together the reasoning processes required by the use of numbers, specifically spoken numbers, Gelman and Gallistel (1978) suggested that five counting principles underpin the understanding of counting for young children:

1   The stable order principle – each counting word must be said in the same place in the counting sequence.

2   The counting or one-to-one principle – each item counted needs a unique counting word.

3   The abstraction principle – anything can be counted.

4   The cardinal principle – the last number word said is the number of items counted.

5   The order-irrelevance principle – the items in a collection can be counted in any order.

Gelman and Gallistel suggest that once children have particularly grasped the final principle, then they know how to 'count'. A diagnostic task that we can use to see whether children can indeed 'count' is to put out a collection of objects, such as seven coloured cubes in a row, and ask them to make the middle cube number six. Alternatively, for any of the counting principles, Thompson (2008) suggests that using a toy ('Naughty Teddy') or a puppet ('Miss Count') can be an effective way to help children identify counting mistakes in a playful setting. With this approach, the teacher or other adult has the toy or puppet make specific counting errors for the children to correct. The teacher can therefore identify which counting principles are parts of the children's understanding of the use of spoken number, and which are not.

Communicating numbers

> ### KEY POINT TO CONSIDER
>
> Young children bring a great deal of knowledge about numbers with them to the classroom. It is important that this knowledge is built upon in classroom activities.

Since children will already have some familiarity with number before starting school, it is important that teachers take advantage of this, and relate informal number learning from home to the school experience in order to develop mathematical communication. For example, children will have encountered numbers as the number of a house (their own, friends' or relatives'), the number of a bus, or the number on a football shirt. In all these instances, the number is used as a label, a non-numerical use of number. Children may even be able to recite numbers in sequence, perhaps based on experience of counting up and down stairs. They may have also encountered number in terms of quantity – for example, when setting the table, you place four plates, four knives and four forks. However, as we have seen in the section on reasoning about the uses of number, such verbal use does not imply a more complete understanding of number. Accordingly, it is important that teachers recognize the need to translate these informal understandings of number, which may have limited use in formal maths, into a more accepted way of thinking and communicating mathematically. It is therefore very important that children are given every opportunity to experience numbers in the contexts of situations that occur naturally in the classroom. So, for example:

> How many pencils do we need in the pot?
>
> How many paint brushes do you need on your table?
>
> Are there sufficient straws for everybody?
>
> How many children have dinner money?

Nursery rhymes and songs also provide the opportunity for working with simple numbers:

> Baa Baa Black Sheep
>
> Old King Cole

Ten Green Bottles

Ten Little Monkeys

Five Currant Buns in the Bakers Shop

Activity 2.1 One more

We can even introduce the idea of 'one more' with the following rhyme:

One little rabbit wondering what to do;

One more came along and then there were two.

Two little rabbits sitting down to tea;

One more came along and then there were three.

Three little rabbits knocking at the door;

One more came along and then there were four.

Four little rabbits going for a drive;

One more came along and then there were five.

Five little rabbits getting up to tricks;

One more came along and then there were six.

Moving on to the written numbers, according to Skemp (1989), in the early stages in children's development of language 'connections between thought and spoken word are initially much stronger than between thoughts and written words or thoughts and mathematical symbols' (p. 103). Accordingly, it is of fundamental importance that children develop an understanding of the language associated with number *and* an awareness of how language is connected to the notation. To promote this, they should be encouraged to explore connections between them rather than just learning and using the correct vocabulary, for communicating mathematically (with numbers) is more than this. So it is not sufficient to adorn the classroom with words associated with number as part of the displays; the teacher needs to ask the children questions, encouraging them to communicate and explain their reasoning through the skilful use of appropriate questions that offer a range of answers and so promote discussion. The aim is to develop real understanding of number rather than just number manipulation, where children have uncritically accepted and learned the correct vocabulary. This latter situation often leads to the correct vocabulary being used in 'typical' contexts and operations, but the children then have difficulty in generalizing it, and adapting their knowledge to even slightly unfamiliar contexts.

Simple games like Bingo or card games can therefore be used to encourage one to one counting and also links to symbolic notation (see Activity 2.2).

Activity 2.2 Bingo

1	4	6
2	5	3

The children take it in turns to roll a dice, then count the correct number of counters to place on the correct number of their grid. The cards can be adapted for larger numbers:

2	10	6	8
11	5	7	12
3	9	4	2
6	7	11	5

The children throw two dice, count all the spots on the dice together and then cover the correct number. The winner is the player who is first to cover his or her card.

Tasks like these not only promote children's understanding of the initial stages of counting, but also develop the confidence required to underpin the successful handling of more advanced concepts of number at later stages of mathematical education. They can also highlight misconceptions with larger numbers. As identified by Fuson *et al.* (1982) and Fuson and Kwon (1991), our number system can cause difficulties for children, particularly the numbers 10 to 20, where there are problems relating the number word to its value – for example eleven and twelve. In other languages such as Japanese, as we have seen, it is less complicated since the number words correspond more closely to the value of the number. Sometimes, rather than addressing this problem directly, what we do in the classroom is to spend a lot of time learning to count by rote. This of itself does not determine children's understanding of the concept of number but parents are often convinced that their children are mathematically proficient because they can 'count to a hundred'. Instead, for appropriate understanding, children have to be given opportunities to communicate using numbers either verbally or symbolically.

Questions for discussion

1 How might a historical perspective of number help pupils to develop a sense of number as a dynamic rather than a static concept?

2 Is an understanding of the way that we represent or see numbers an important prerequisite for being able to work with numbers?

3 How might these ideas of representing or seeing numbers influence the pedagogy of the classroom?

4 What examples of 'principles of counting' or not understanding these can you draw on from your own experience of young children's counting?

3

Addition and subtraction

On the face of it, one might expect addition and subtraction to be one of the simpler areas of mathematics that we look at in this book. Surely, addition is just the process of changing and increasing a given group of objects, perhaps by combining it with another group, and subtraction is the reverse. However, this is a very limited view of addition and subtraction, and Fuson (1992) has specifically criticized text books for taking such a view: 'Textbooks rarely provide children with an opportunity to consider different meanings for the +, −, and = marks, and the meaning ordinarily given in textbooks are the Change meanings' (p. 245). The need to consider this variety of meanings becomes more important when we consider that the way children approach addition and subtraction calculations can, at a young age, depend on the situation presented to them. Therefore, if we are to support children in these calculations, then we need to have an insight into these various meanings. In this chapter, we begin by examining the different situations that result in addition and subtraction calculations, and then go on to look at how these are related to the way that children approach the calculations.

Different addition and subtraction situations

Summaries of the various addition and subtraction problems that occur are given in a variety of references (e.g. Carpenter and Moser, 1983; Carpenter *et al.*, 1988; Fuson, 1992). Carpenter and Moser (1983) proposed four broad classes of addition and subtraction problems: change, combine, compare and equalize problems. We will examine each of these in terms of how they differ from one another. Fuson (1992) identified a number of characteristics that we can look at, the first being whether the problem is an 'active' situation (i.e. involves some proposed action) or is a 'static' situation.

> ## KEY POINT TO CONSIDER
>
> There are four broad classes of addition and subtraction problems: change, combine, compare and equalize problems.

Secondly, is the problem a **unary** situation, where one quantity is added on to give an answer? This is as opposed to **binary** situations where two distinct quantities are brought together in a problem. Finally, a problem can vary with which is the unknown quantity. We usually deal with 'result-unknown' problems ('Patrick has three biscuits and is given four more biscuits. How many biscuits does he have altogether?' Alternatively, using shorthand notation, $4 + 3 = ?$). However, it may be that we do know the result, but do not know one of the addends ($? + 3 = 4$ or $3 + ? = 4$). We need to take all these characteristics into account when looking at addition and subtraction situations. We will use diagrams to represent the different situations based on those provided by Fuson (1992). We will also provide examples to highlight the differences between different problem types.

Change situations

Change situations are active, unary situations which can involve adding to (change add to) or taking away from (change take away from) an initial quantity (see Figure 3.1). Examples of change situations are:

> *Patrick has three biscuits and is given four more biscuits. How many biscuits does he have altogether?* (Change add to, result unknown)

> *Tony has some biscuits and gives four biscuits to Patrick. Tony then has seven biscuits. How many biscuits did Tony have to begin with?* (Change take away from, start unknown)

> *Patrick has four biscuits and is given some more biscuits. Altogether, he then has seven biscuits. How many biscuits was he given?* (Change add to, change unknown)

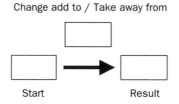

Figure 3.1 Diagram of change situations

Combine situations

Combine situations are active, binary situations with two separate quantities or parts being brought together (see Figure 3.2). However, the unknown in the problem can

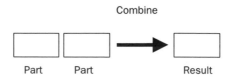

Figure 3.2 Diagram of combine situations

determine whether addition or subtraction is used to solve the problem. Examples of combine situations are:

> *Lynn has three plain biscuits and five chocolate biscuits. How many biscuits does she have altogether?* (Combine, result unknown)

> *Lynn has eight biscuits, three of them are plain and the rest are chocolate. How many chocolate biscuits does Lynn have?* (Combine, part unknown)

Compare situations

Compare situations are static, binary situations, looking at the difference between two quantities (see Figure 3.3). However, the unknown in the problem can again determine whether addition or subtraction is used. In some cases, the phrases 'how many more' or 'how many less' may cue the appropriate solution of carrying out addition or subtraction. In some cases however, the phrase might cue the opposite of what is required. Examples of compare situations are:

> *Steve has four biscuits and Lynn has six biscuits. How many more biscuits does Lynn have than Steve?* (Compare, difference unknown)

> *Steve has four biscuits and Lynn has two more biscuits. How many biscuits does Lynn have?* (Compare, difference known and cues solution)

> *Steve has four biscuits. He has two more biscuits than Lynn. How many biscuits does Lynn have?* (Compare, difference known and cues opposite to solution)

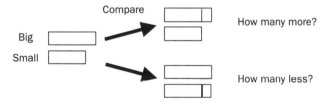

Figure 3.3 Diagram of compare situations

Equalize situations

Equalize situations are active, binary situations, again looking at the difference between two quantities, but this time calculating what change is required to one of the quantities to make the quantities the same (see Figure 3.4). Once again, the phrases 'how many more' or 'how many less' may cue the appropriate or the opposite solution depending on the structure of the problem. Examples of equalize situations are:

> *Steve has four biscuits and Lynn has six biscuits. How many more biscuits does Steve need to have the same as Lynn?* (Equalize, difference unknown)

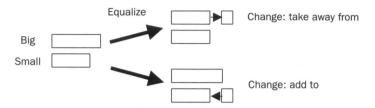

Figure 3.4 Diagram of equalize situations

Steve has four biscuits and gets two more biscuits. Now he has the same number of biscuits as Lynn. How many biscuits does Lynn have? (Equalize, difference known and cues solution)

Steve has four biscuits. If Lynn gets two more biscuits, she will have the same number of biscuits as Steve. How many biscuits does Lynn have? (Equalize, difference known and cues opposite solution)

The problem examples given above do not cover all the possible combinations. We could extend the problem types further by considering all the combinations of unknowns as well as the problem types. Carpenter and Moser (1983) provide the following list of possible combinations for addition/subtraction involving two known quantities (which we call a and b):

$a + b = ?$ $? = a + b$

$a + ? = b$ $b = a + ?$

$? + a = b$ $b = ? + a$

$a - b = ?$ $? = a - b$

$a - ? = b$ $b = a - ?$

$? - a = b$ $b = ? - a$

It is an interesting exercise to match up the above combinations with the possible problem types. However, what we have done in this section is to simply highlight the fact that there are many types of problems that involve addition and subtraction calculations. In the next section, we will examine the different ways that children represent addition and subtraction situations themselves, and what implications this has for how they carry out calculations.

Representing addition and subtraction – direct modelling

An initial way in which young children will model addition and subtraction situations is through direct **modelling**. By direct modelling, we mean that children use concrete objects to represent the objects in the situation. Two possible examples of concrete objects used by children are shown in Figure 3.5. Fuson (1992) proposes that children go through three developmental stages for representing addition and subtraction. Direct modelling is involved in the first of these stages, what she calls the 'single representation of an addend or the sum'. Here, children need to match each

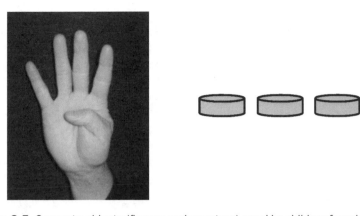

Figure 3.5 Concrete objects (fingers and counters) used by children for addition and subtraction

item in the addition/subtraction situation with one of their concrete objects. For example, for the problem 'Patrick has three biscuits and is given four more biscuits. How many biscuits does he have altogether?', the child might count out three counters, then count out four more counters, then count all the counters together. Carpenter and Moser (1984) also identified three levels in children's use of addition and subtraction strategies, again their first level being the use of direct modelling. The different strategies that they identified within this level are:

- *Count-all (addition)*: Represent both quantities with physical objects, put them together and count all.

- *Separate from (subtraction)*: Represent the initial quantity with physical objects, remove the required quantity and count the result.

- *Adding on (subtraction)*: Represent one quantity with physical objects, add on a set of elements until the required total is obtained, count the set of elements that needed to be added.

- *Matching (subtraction)*: Represent two quantities with physical objects, then do a one-to-one matching until there are some remaining objects. Count these remaining objects.

What is interesting here is that there are a variety of direct modelling strategies that researchers have observed, in particular for subtraction. In fact, the choice of strategy made by children using direct modelling is dependent on the type of addition/subtraction situation that is presented to them.

> The results of a number of studies consistently show that young children have a variety of strategies available to solve different subtraction problems and that the strategies used generally tend to be consistent with the action or relationships described in the problem.
>
> (Carpenter and Moser, 1983: 23)

Therefore, for example, with a compare situation result unknown, we might expect a child to directly model the problem using a matching strategy. With a change add to change unknown problem, we might expect an adding on strategy. We can therefore start to see the importance of recognizing the different addition or subtraction situations that we can have, and how they might influence the initial approach taken by children in solving these problems.

Representing addition and subtraction – counting strategies

The second of Fuson's developmental stages involves 'abbreviated sequence counting procedures'. Here, rather than directly modelling each part of the addition or subtraction problem, the child moves on to recognize that the number words within the problem already represent the quantity of the objects concerned, and counting can be used to model the problem. Therefore, children move from using actual objects to counting as representing the objects. Carpenter and Moser have as their second level 'counting strategies' which make use of counting sequences. For example:

- *Counting-on from first (addition)*: The counting begins from the first number in the problem. For example, for the problem 'Lynn has three plain biscuits and five chocolate biscuits. How many biscuits does she have altogether?', the children would start counting up from three: 'three . . . four, five, six, seven, eight'.

- *Counting-on from larger (addition)*: The counting begins from the larger number, in recognition that less counting-on is required.

- *Counting down from (subtraction)*: The counting begins from the first number, and children count backwards from this number. For example, for the problem 'Patrick has eight biscuits and gives three biscuits to Tony. How many biscuits does Patrick then have?', the children would start counting down from eight: 'eight . . . seven, six, five . . . it's five'.

- *Counting up from given (subtraction)*: Alternatively, for subtraction, rather than counting down from the first number, one can count up from the second number to achieve the first number, the answer being the number of counts required to do this. For the previous problem: 'three . . . four, five, six, seven, eight . . . it's five'.

To these examples from Carpenter and Moser, we can add another example from Thompson (1999b):

- *Counting down to (subtraction)*: This is the reverse of the previous counting up from given example. Again for the previous example: 'eight . . . seven, six, five, four, three . . . it's five.' Here the child is counting down from the first number to the second number, and finding the number of counts required to do so.

Representing addition and subtraction – number facts

The final stage described by Fuson and also by Carpenter and Moser uses **derived fact** and **known fact** procedures. Here, children take the numbers given in the addition and subtraction problems, and redistribute them to make number facts that are already known (i.e. derive number facts). Alternatively, the problem may already involve a number fact that is known to the child. The extensive list of these strategies, as provided by Thompson (1999b, 2000a), is given below:

> **KEY POINT TO CONSIDER**
>
> Counting strategies lead to the use of known facts and derived facts. These include the use of doubles, subtraction as the inverse of addition, bridging through tens and compensation.

- *Use of doubles (addition and subtraction)*: Known facts, such as 18 − 9 is 9 because of doubles.

- *Use of near-doubles (addition and subtraction)*: Derived facts, such as 13 + 15 is 28 because of the 13 + 13 double.

- *Subtraction as the inverse of addition*: Using known addition facts for subtraction, for example for 7 − 3, knowing that one adds 4 to 3 to get 7.

- *Using fives (addition)*: Derived number facts, separating out the fives and adding them first. For example, rearranging 6 + 7 as 5 + 5 and 1 + 2.

- *Bridging through tens (addition and subtraction)*: Derived facts, adding or subtracting to stages of ten as points at which to split up the quantities to be added or taken away. For example, 8 + 7 as 8 + 2 and 5, or 14 − 6 as 14 − 4 and taking away a further 2.

- *Compensation (addition and subtraction)*: Derived facts, altering the numbers to be added or subtracted to simplify the problem, and then 'compensating' for the alteration. For example, 14 + 8 could become 14 + 10 and then take away 2, or 13 − 8 could become 13 − 10 and then add 2.

- *Balancing (addition and subtraction)*: Derived facts, similar to compensation, but balancing out both parts of the sum to allow for any alterations. For example, again, 14 + 8 could become 12 + 10, or 13 − 8 could become 15 − 10.

- *Partitioning (addition and subtraction)*: Derived facts, splitting up both quantities into units, tens, etc. For example 18 + 17 as 10 + 10 and 8 + 7, or 24 − 11 as 20 − 10 and 4 − 1.

- *Sequencing (addition and subtraction)*: Derive facts, splitting up one of the quantities into tens and units, and then adding or subtracting these split quantities in sequence. For example, again, 18 + 17 as 18 + 10 + 7, or 24 − 11 as 24 − 10 − 1.

- *Mixed method (addition and subtraction)*: Derived facts with a combination of **partitioning** and sequencing, splitting both quantities into units, tens, etc., adding or subtracting the higher numbers but sequencing the smaller numbers. For example, 18 + 17 as 10 + 10 and 8 and 7, which becomes 20 + 8 and then add 7. For subtraction, 24 − 11 would become 20 − 10 and then add 4, then subtract a further 1.

Another way of categorizing some of the procedures is given by Beishuizen (1993). The partitioning strategy is referred to as a '1010' procedure, since the tens in the calculation are split off within the calculation to begin with. The sequencing strategy is referred to as the 'N10' procedure, since the first number is not split up and tens are added to or subtracted from that first number.

Representing addition and subtraction – visual representations

We have related the stages in children's understanding, put forward by Fuson and by Carpenter and Moser, to different ways of representing addition and subtraction, from direct modelling with concrete objects through to using derived number facts. We can also use visual representations to help develop this understanding (see Figure 3.6). We can move from representations similar to concrete objects that we can use, for example the counters representation at the top of the figure, through to more abstract representations such as the empty number line at the bottom. Gravemeijer (1994a) argues that the empty number line supports children in using their own informal strategies in addition and subtraction, and also to develop more efficient methods of calculation. In the example of the empty number line in Figure 3.6, we can see an example of bridging through ten, presented for 8 + 5. In Figure 3.7 three further examples are given of

> **KEY POINT TO CONSIDER**
>
> Different representations show different characteristics of addition/subtraction and can encourage different ways of working – counters and number blocks encourage working discretely with tens and units whereas the number line encourages more flexible ways of working.

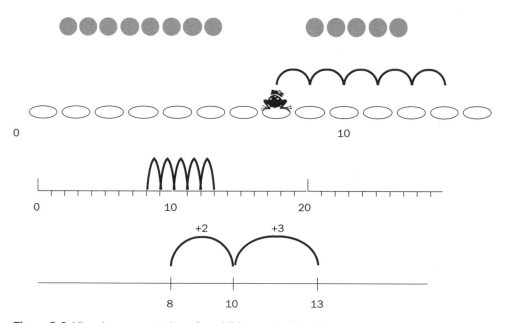

Figure 3.6 Visual representations for addition and subtraction

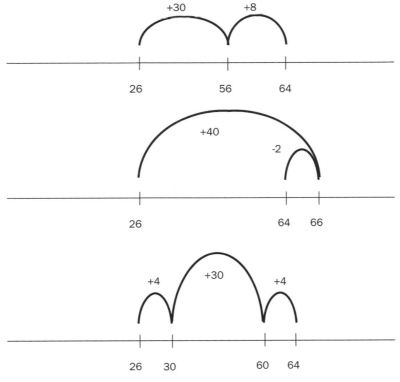

Figure 3.7 Using the empty number line – sequencing strategy (top), compensation strategy (middle) and bridging strategy (bottom)

using the empty number line with the calculation 26 + 38. We can see the flexibility of the representation from the variety of strategies. This is in contrast to the place value representations which we will discuss below (which emphasize the partitioning strategy), and a representation such as the number square which emphasizes the sequencing strategy (see Figure 3.8).

1	2	3	4	5	6	7	8	9	10
11	12	13	14	15	16	17	18	19	20
21	22	23	24	25	26	27	28	29	30
31	32	33	34	35	36	37	38	39	40
41	42	43	44	45	46	47	48	49	50
51	52	53	54	55	56	57	58	59	60
61	62	63	64	65	66	67	68	69	70
71	72	73	74	75	76	77	78	79	80
81	82	83	84	85	86	87	88	89	90
91	92	93	94	95	96	97	98	99	100

Figure 3.8 Using the number square with the sequencing strategy

Representing addition and subtraction – place value

In addition to those given above, we can also examine a number of representations (both concrete and visual) that represent addition and subtraction incorporating the idea of place value. As the traditional written methods of addition and subtraction depend on place value, these other representations can be used to support the use of and an understanding of these methods (see Figure 3.9).

As we highlighted above, these representations specifically encourage children to work with partitioning or 1010 procedures, reorganizing the calculation in terms of units, tens and so on. For example, using the Dienes blocks, for $26 + 38$ see Figure 3.10. Representing this in a symbolic form would be $26 + 38 = 20 + 6 + 30 + 8 = 50 + 14 = 64$. We can even do this in a more traditional, vertical format:

$$
\begin{array}{rcl}
26 & = & 20 + 6 \\
+38 & = & +30 + 8 \\
\hline
& & 50 + 14 \quad = \quad 64
\end{array}
$$

We refer to this as extended number notation, where the units, tens, etc., are specifically shown by splitting them up in the vertical format. The advantage of using these

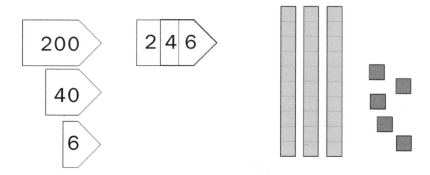

Figure 3.9 Representations for number incorporating place value: arrow cards and Dienes blocks

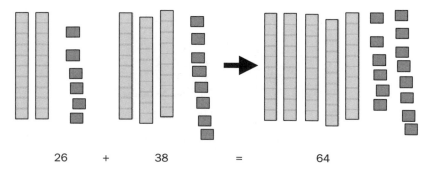

$$26 \quad + \quad 38 \quad = \quad 64$$

Figure 3.10 Representing $26 + 28$

representations in this way is that they enable us to see more clearly how the traditional vertical method for addition works.

$$
\begin{array}{ccc}
& 26 & \text{or} \quad 26 \\
& +38 & +{}_138 \\
\hline
& 14 & 64 \\
& 50 & \\
\hline
& 64 &
\end{array}
$$

Using these different representations is perhaps more important for explaining the more difficult traditional methods for subtraction. Figure 3.11 shows the Dienes blocks once again, this time for the calculation $34 - 18$. Representing this symbolically in a vertical format:

$$
\begin{array}{rcrcr}
34 & = & 30 + 4 & = & 20 + 14 \\
-18 & = & -10 + 8 & = & -10 + 8 \\
\hline
& & & = & 10 + 6 & = & 16
\end{array}
$$

The extended number format again helps to explain traditional 'decomposition' method for subtraction.

$$
\begin{array}{c}
{}^{2}\;{}^{1} \\
\cancel{3}4 \\
-18 \\
\hline
16
\end{array}
$$

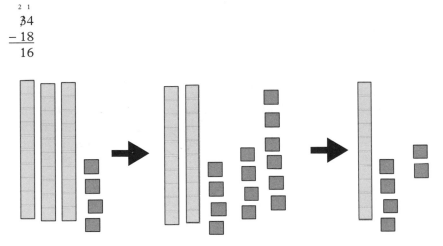

Figure 3.11 Representing $34 - 18$

Reasoning the properties of addition and subtraction

In addition to using representations to explain the methods of calculation we use for addition and subtraction, we can also explain and reason the particular mathematical properties of these operations. Research from Canobi (2005) considered pupil understanding of different concepts which are important within addition and subtraction. The concepts explored were:

- Commutativity, i.e. a + b = b + a.
- Subtraction complement; i.e. a − b = c implies that a − c = b.
- Inversion principle, i.e. a + b = c implies that c − a = b and c − b = a.
- Three term inverse property, i.e. a + b − b = a.

Points noted in the research were that properties were based on the idea of a number triple (i.e. a + b = c) which gives rise to a number of possible calculations. These are all related to the types of addition/subtraction problems that pupils are required to engage with given earlier in the chapter. For instance, let us look at the example of the change take away from, start unknown question that we looked at earlier.

> Tony has some biscuits and gives four biscuits to Patrick. Tony then has seven biscuits. How many biscuits did Tony have to begin with?

Symbolically, we can write this as ? − 4 = 7. The inversion principle allows us to change this to 7 + 4 = ? which we can then easily calculate. Therefore, it is important that children have a grasp of these properties since they will help them make sense of the different addition and subtraction situations. Another point noted in the research was that part–whole relationships was a key concept to understand. We will explain this idea further shortly.

Let us then demonstrate how representations can be used to explore and reason these important properties of addition and subtraction. All the properties can be investigated using a blocks representation, and we shall do this specifically for the combination 9 + 7 = 16. Looking first of all at commutativity, Figure 3.12 shows that 9 + 7 gives the same result as 7 + 9. Essentially, in any number triple such as *a + b = c*, we have two parts brought together to make a whole. So 9 and 7 above are bought together to make 16. Understanding which are the parts and which are the whole allows us to explain commutativity. For addition, whichever way round we bring together the parts, the same parts are being brought together. Therefore, the same whole will be obtained. Addition is therefore commutative. However, if we consider subtraction we have a whole with a part being removed. For example see Figure 3.13

Figure 3.12 9 + 7 is the same as 7 + 9

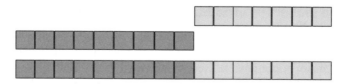

Figure 3.13 16 − 7 = 9

for $16 - 7 = 9$. 16 is the whole from which the part (7) is being subtracted. The two numbers are fundamentally different in character. If we swap the numbers around to $7 - 16$, we are implying a completely different total and a completely different part. Therefore, subtraction does not commute.

However, the subtraction compliment property does apply to the operation. Instead of $16 - 7 = 9$ which we represented above, let us show $16 - 9 = 7$ (see Figure 3.14). In the two situations, we have the same whole and we swap the parts we are subtracting. Because the two parts are the same in character (i.e. they are both parts!), then this swapping over works. And in fact the part–whole picture we are using also helps to explain the inversion principle and the three term inverse property. Bringing two parts to give a whole implies that we can start with the whole and remove a part. If we bring together two parts and then remove one of the parts again, we end up with the other part. Thus using the representation and the notion of parts and wholes allows us to reason all the important properties for addition and subtraction.

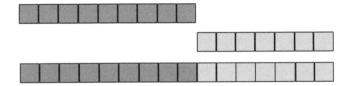

Figure 3.14 $16 - 9 = 7$

Communicating addition and subtraction

A structured approach to teaching and learning mathematical vocabulary to promote children's ability to use correct terminology as early as possible is an important component of any effective maths strategy. For example, for addition and subtraction, there is guidance provided for teachers in England and Wales with regards to the vocabulary to which children need to be introduced (DfEE, 2000):

> add, more, make, total, sum, altogether
> score, double
> one more, two more . . . ten more . . .
> how many more to make . . .?
> how many more is . . . than . . .?
> take away, leave
> how many are left/left over?
> how many have gone?
> one less, two less . . . ten less . . .?
> how many fewer is . . . than . . .?
> difference between
> is the same as.

Following on immediately from this, 'plus', 'subtract' and 'minus' are introduced, along with the introduction of the equals sign (=), and later the terms 'increase' and 'decrease'. However, of course, this vocabulary by itself will not have a significant impact on children's understanding of the **concepts** of addition and subtraction. Besides introducing children to appropriate language and familiarizing them with its use, in communicating addition and subtraction in the classroom, we need to link the possible situations that we might have for addition and subtraction to words. We must provide children with a range of activities that allow *them* to do this, so reinforcing the connections and developing understanding, rather than just being taught strategies or correct mathematical vocabulary. There is indeed evidence that using problems and contexts as a basis for teaching addition and subtraction is more successful than teaching computational skills first and then trying to apply them to solve problems (Carpenter and Moser, 1983). There is also evidence from the Netherlands that making explicit connections between the two approaches is beneficial (Gravemeijer, 1994b; Treffers and Beishuizen, 1999), especially by encouraging pupils to model their calculations on paper, such as by using an empty number line.

Discussion-based activities related to real-life situations are therefore an essential component of activities from the outset, and lesson plans should make full provision for them. They are also key to relating the 'informal' mathematical knowledge that children bring to school with the formal mathematics of the classroom. This might be done not only to make sense of addition and subtraction situations, but also in developing knowledge of number facts as well.

Creating contexts where children have to use reasoning language about calculations (but, if, then, so, because) ensures that their thinking is connecting aspects of their mathematical knowledge and an important indicator of their understanding.

Activity 3.1 Exploring simple addition and subtraction

Give the pupils a set of five counters. Tell them to gently throw the counters onto the paper.

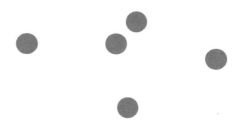

Ask them to discuss the result and the arrangement of the counters.

In Activity 3.1, what can we see on the paper? We might just see five counters. Or we can see 2 and 1 and 1 and 1 counters. Or 2 and 2 and 1 counters. Or 1 and 4 counters. The exploring and discussing of this informal knowledge can then lead to the introduction of words such as 'add' or the symbol '+' and eventually use of the = sign. So, what calculations do we see?

$2 + 1 + 1 + 1 = 5$
$2 + 2 + 1 = 5$
$1 + 4 = 5$

We might also notice that removing two counters from five gives us three. This leads on to a discussion of subtraction. Of course, with very young children there is a natural tendency for responses to 'wander' and not necessarily be totally focused on the activity so that the discussion may not directly relate to the counters on the paper. Because of this, and perhaps because of the reluctance on the part of teachers to encourage children's discussion, such activities may appear time consuming. However it is crucial to create time for children to explore these concepts individually so that they can generate meanings that make sense to them.

This type of approach is also used by Hughes (1986), working with children on early addition and subtraction (see Activity 3.2).

Activity 3.2 Cubes in a box

A number of cubes, say 5, are placed in a box and counted.

Cubes can then be removed and the children asked to decide,

　　　how many cubes remain in the box?

This leads on to calculations such as:

$5 - 2 =$
$3 + 2 =$

If there are ten cubes, then this can also be preparation work for number bonds to ten. By asking the question 'How many ways can 10 cubes be sorted?', children can construct number bonds to ten for themselves rather than teaching the bonds as can be seen in many maths workbooks.

Moving on to more cubes, children can start to work on more complicated addition and subtraction calculations. Some children may continue using cubes as a means of maintaining their confidence, while others may move on to pencil and paper, and there will be those children who are beginning to develop mental strategies for addition and subtraction. The next step is then to make the link between the place value properties of the numbers and how this supports addition and subtraction. In representing these operations, we have already discussed some forms of representations such as Dienes blocks that incorporate place value. Once again, children need to reason and develop their understanding of using tens and units. They therefore need to spend time on activities such as using Dienes blocks before moving onto the algorithms. As shown earlier, Dienes blocks can provide a structural representation that allows children to physically carry out both addition and subtraction calculations:

$26 + 38$

Adding:

2 ten rods	+	3 ten rods	=	5 ten rods
6 cube units	+	8 cube units	=	14 cube units

10 cube units can be exchange for 1 ten rod leaving = 6 ten rods and 4 cube units.

This physical representation of addition and subtraction promotes the development of children's real understanding of the calculations, while also providing opportunities for discussion, ensuring that they both experience and communicate the mathematical process before moving on to written **algorithms**. The use of Dienes blocks is of particular value to children struggling with mathematical concepts, and ample time should be incorporated in lesson design to allow for their use. Moreover, Dienes blocks can also provide greater challenges for more able children, who can be asked to investigate the strategies for addition and subtraction, and to demonstrate and explain each strategy to their partner using the blocks.

The danger of not allowing this discussion is exemplified by Yackel (2001) who cites an instance from first and second grade children in the US. As a class, pupils were asked to work out the total of 16 + 9 cookies, written as a horizontal problem. Strategies were discussed in class and all pupils came up with the answer 25. However, Yackel then found that when confronted with a vertically arranged but otherwise identical exercise from a page in a textbook:

$$\begin{array}{r} 16 \\ +\,9 \\ \hline \end{array}$$

this was perceived by the pupils as a different task. While some pupils reached the correct answer, some came up with 15 while others had 115. Yackel's example underlines the need to provide activities which develop understanding through allowing pupils to effectively reason, so that they can make sense of the methods that they use.

However, while it is appropriate to stress the importance of discussion-led activities for developing children's mathematical thinking and understanding of addition and subtraction, this is not intended to imply that recall of number facts or practice of written algorithms are of less importance. What *is* crucial is to help children develop a flexible and fluent use of addition and subtraction strategies. They need to be able to calculate accurately and efficiently and explain their methods and reasoning using correct mathematical terminology.

Misconceptions with addition and subtraction

Let us end this chapter by considering the misconceptions that can arise with addition and subtraction, and how these relate back to the issues we have so far discussed. Misconceptions with addition and subtraction usually relate to one of the following areas:

- The language being used and how this relates to the mathematical calculation, particularly in terms of the categories of problems described earlier in the chapter.

- Systematic errors related to counting or tallying strategies with small numbers.
- Misunderstanding the symbols or layout of a calculation (formal representation).
- Seeing multi-digit numbers as composed of separate numbers (place value).

One of the key challenges at this stage of learning mathematics is that children make mistakes in relating the signs used (+, – and =) to the various ways that these symbols relate to contexts or situations they can understand from their experience (Baroody and Standifer, 1993). As we highlighted at the beginning of the chapter, children need to be exposed to a large variety of addition and subtraction situations (e.g. compare, combine, equalize, change add to, and change taken from) and given opportunities to consider different meanings for the +, – and = symbols.).

In addition, early calculation problems often relate to the use of incorrect counting strategies. We highlighted earlier that one of the more basic representations that children can use for addition and subtraction are counting strategies. However, one of the commonest problems occurs through tallying with fingers or when using a number line where the first number (or finger) is counted, rather than counting on: 'Seven, eight, nine, ten; seven plus four is ten'. Therefore, children have to be aware of how to use the representations.

The above sources for problems may explain why children usually find subtraction more difficult than addition. Fuson (1992) argues that this is because most children use counting down strategies which are more likely to lead to mistakes, so errors in counting might be one reason. It is also possible that the situations in which subtraction is the mathematical operation have more potential for misunderstandings than addition situations (e.g. 'take away' and 'compare' problems are both represented by the same mathematical operation). For example, when 9 – 3 = 6 represents the situation 'Steve has 3 cars. Patrick has 9 cars. How many more cars does Patrick have?', the minus sign means compare rather than take away. Another typical error might be a response to the problem 'Tony gave away 15p to Lynn. He now has 42p. How much does he have to begin with?' Children may give the answer '27p' through interpreting the problem as a subtraction calculation. A number of things might have happened here. There is potential for misunderstanding in the language. 'Tony gave away' implies taking away. Therefore, as we emphasized in the section on communicating addition and subtraction, children need to be given the opportunities to tackle and explore different situations so that they can link the words involved to the different situations.

Research has also shown how children use their own strategies to 'chunk numbers using thinking strategies' (Fuson, 1986) or use derived fact strategies based on known facts (Carpenter and Moser, 1984; Thompson, 1997). These strategies evolve over time and generally become more sophisticated, though they can contain mistakes or 'bugs'. In continental Europe, the teaching of arithmetic has traditionally been based on developing competence at mental calculation

KEY POINT TO CONSIDER

Working with the various representations can help to explore misconceptions in addition and subtraction, such as the structure of numbers, and the language of the number system.

(Blöte *et al.*, 2000) whereas in the US and in England, at least until the introduction of the National Numeracy Strategy in 1998, more paper-based and formal teaching based on algorithmic procedures was used at an earlier stage. Pupils make a variety of mistakes in multi-digit addition and subtraction calculations (Brown and Van Lehn, 1982). Patterns of mistakes suggest children interpret and treat multi-digit numbers as single-digit numbers placed adjacent to each other, rather than using place-value meanings for the digits in different positions (Fuson, 1992). Yet, with specific teaching, 6- and 7-year-olds are able to understand place value and to add and subtract four-digit numbers more accurately and meaningfully than 7- and 8-year-olds taught normally (Fuson, 1992). In this chapter, we have put forward representations for place value that may aid this process.

However, primary school pupils in general may have a limited understanding of place value (Sowder, 1992). By the end of primary schooling, most pupils are able to identify the place values of the digits that appear in a number, but they cannot use the knowledge confidently in context (for example, pupils have trouble determining how many boxes of 100 chocolate bars could be packed from 48,638 bars). Thompson (2000b) argues that this is due to an overemphasis on place value rather than the 'quantity value' of numbers (he argues that it is more important to see 45 as 40 and 5 than to be able to say it is four tens and five ones). This has significant implications for teaching in early primary or elementary schooling where pupils should identify the value of the digits based on their quantity (seeing them as parts of a whole number) rather than looking at columns or spending time grouping cubes into tens and units (seeing them as separate numbers). We would argue that using extended number notation for addition and subtraction may help in this, but we must still be aware of the potential problems that may arise.

Questions for discussion

1   Based on the ideas present in this chapter, how would you approach the teaching of addition and subtraction in the primary or elementary classroom? What is the place of written algorithms in your approach?

2   How can we incorporate the same ideas to develop our approaches to teaching mental calculations?

3   In light of what we have discussed in this chapter, how would we assess pupil understanding of addition and subtraction, both with mental and written calculations?

4   In this chapter, a link was made between the direct modelling strategies used by children and the addition/subtraction situation presented to them. Suggest likely strategies that children would use for each of the addition and subtraction situations given.

4

Multiplication and division

In Chapter 3, we examined addition and subtraction: what these operations entail, how we can represent these operations and how we communicate the ideas involved. Moving on now to multiplication and division, one might expect (perhaps drawing on the concepts that we already have, or what we learn in school) that we will draw on many of the ideas presented in Chapter 3. This is because we commonly represent multiplication as **repeated addition** and division as **repeated subtraction**. For example, Kouba (1989) looked at pupils' strategies for tackling word problems involving multiplication and division situations. She found that the repeated addition method for multiplication and the repeated subtraction method were commonly used by children, although 'sharing by dealing' was also used by children for some division problems. However, we must recognize that difficulties occur if we rely only on these common representations for multiplication and division. For example, how can we explain what is happening when we multiply fractions or **decimals**? In doing the calculation $\frac{3}{4} \times \frac{1}{2}$ does it make sense to repeatedly add $\frac{3}{4}$ a 'half' number of times or vice versa? Also, we will show in this chapter that restricting our representations of multiplication and division to just repeated addition and subtraction hinders our ability to recognize and explain some of the properties of these operations. In order to reason with multiplication and division, we need to broaden the range of representations that we use. We will deal with these issues later on in the chapter. However, first of all let us take a careful look at what we mean by multiplication and division.

What do we mean by multiplication and division?

To explain this let us examine the different situations in which these concepts can arise. We draw on some of the work done by researchers in the past in categorizing these different situations: namely, Vergnaud (1983), Greer (1992), Nunes and Bryant (1996) and Carpenter *et al.* (1999).

Multiplication

We begin with multiplication. The first situation we look at is intuitively the most obvious example of multiplication, what Greer (1992) refers to as 'equal groups' and Nunes and Bryant (1996) refer to as 'one-to-many correspondence situations'. Both these terms highlight a different property of what Carpenter *et al.* (1999) call 'grouping' situations. Using Figure 4.1 as an example, we have equal groups of tangerines – each packet corresponds to a group of three tangerines. Using mathematical terminology, we have a **multiplicand** (whatever is being multiplied, in this case the group of three tangerines) and a **multiplier** (the number of times we multiply the multiplicand).

Related to this initial concept is another situation identified by Greer, that of equal measures. The example he gives is:

> 3 children each have 4.2 litres of orange juice. How much orange juice do they have altogether?

The concepts of equality and one-to-many are still in place, except in this case, the 'many' does not have to be a whole number. Intuitively, we are still grouping things together (i.e. we clearly have a multiplicand and a multiplier), and it is easy to see how the repeated addition model applies to this situation.

The next category that we identify is what Nunes and Bryant (1996) refer to as 'situations that involve relationships between variables'. This includes problems involving rate: 'Peter walks at 2 miles per hour. How far does he walk in 1½ hours?';

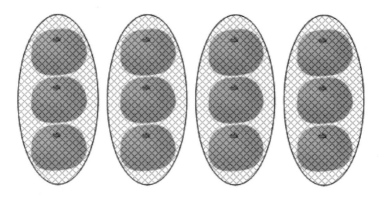

Figure 4.1 Equal groups of three tangerines in each packet

price 'Potatoes cost 60 pence per kg. How much will 4kg of potatoes cost?'; and converting measures 'an inch is 2.54cm. How long is 5 inches in cm?' Although we are no longer dealing with tangible groups, we can reframe the relationship by splitting up one **variable** in terms of the other (so, 2 miles in each hour, 60 pence for each kilogram, 2.54cm for each inch). It then becomes clearer that this is a multiplication situation (with multiplicand and multiplier) which again can be modelled by repeated addition. However, a difficulty that can arise is that the situations can involve decimals or fractions. Therefore, even if pupils recognize the situations as involving multiplication, they need to use methods other than simple repeated addition to carry out the calculation.

Similarly, we can consider what Greer (1992) calls 'multiplicative comparison' and 'multiplicative change' situations. Examples of each are given below:

Anne has 3 times more sweets than her younger brother Robert. If Robert has 5 sweets, how many sweets does Anne have? (Multiplicative comparison)

The apple tree in our garden has grown to 2.2 times its height that it was five years ago. If the tree was 1.5m tall five years ago, how tall is it now? (Multiplicative change)

With situations involving whole numbers, if a pupil recognizes the word 'times' to denote multiplication, then the situation can be modelled with repeated addition. If the situation involves decimals or fractions, then other methods of calculation are required. Related to multiplicative comparison situations are 'part–whole' or **proportion** situations, for example:

In a school, 4/5 of the teachers are female. If there are 20 teachers in the school, how many female teachers are there?

Here, the 'part' situation is being compared to the 'whole'. We can easily recognize the multiplicand (20 teachers) and the multiplier (4/5). However, the difficulty here is that these situations will always involve multiplying by a number less than one. Therefore, again, we cannot simply use repeated addition to do the calculation.

The final category we consider is what Vergnaud (1983) terms as 'product of measures' and Carpenter *et al.* (1999) call 'symmetric problems'. In this broad category, we include Greer's classifications of 'rectangular area, product of measures' and 'Cartesian product'. Examples of each are given below:

A garden measures 10m by 4m. What is its total area? (Rectangular area)

What is the weight of an object if its mass is 5kg and the acceleration due to gravity is $10m/s^2$? (Product of measures)

A crisp manufacturer produces crisps with three different flavourings, and sold in two different sizes of bags. How many types of bags of crisps does the manufacturer produce? (Cartesian product)

These types of situations differ from the previous ones in that it is now unclear what are the multiplicand and the multiplier in the scenarios. In the case of a Cartesian product, which is where multiplication is used to find all the possible combinations for a given situation, we could choose either characteristic as the multiplicand and the other as the multiplier. For rectangular area and product of measures however, multiplication is used more by definition rather than grouping of any quantities (e.g. area is defined as length times width; weight is defined as mass times acceleration due to gravity). All these situations are termed 'symmetric' as it does not matter what we consider to be the multiplier and the multiplicand. Because we cannot readily identify these, these situations are more difficult to identify as multiplication problems.

Division

By contrast to the range of multiplication situations that we have identified, the situation for division is much simpler. We have two main categories that are identified in the literature: **sharing/partitive situations** and **grouping/quotative situations**. We illustrate each of these in Figures 4.2 and 4.3 respectively.

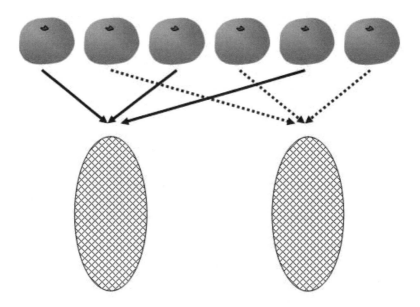

Figure 4.2 Sharing tangerines one at a time into two packets

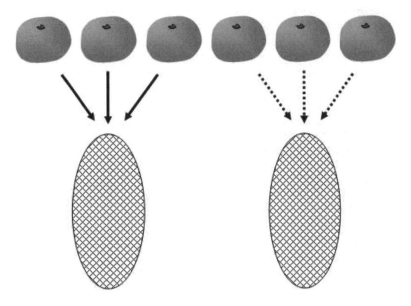

Figure 4.3 Grouping tangerines three at a time into two packets

In the sharing model of division, we allocate or 'deal' objects one at a time into each of the groups required (solid line first, then dashed line in Figure 4.2). In the grouping model, we allocate a collection of objects at a time to the groups required (all the solid lines first, then the dashed lines in Figure 4.3). We can see that both of these correspond to the intuitive models of division identified by Kouba (1989), where the grouping model is repeated subtraction. Another way of thinking about these models is provided by Greer (1992). In the sharing model, we divide the objects by the number of final groups to obtain the number of objects in each group (in the case of Figure 4.2, 6 divided by 2 is 3). What we are doing is *division by the multiplier*. In the grouping model, we divide the objects by the number of objects in the final group to obtain the number of groups (in the case of Figure 4.2, 6 divided by 3 is 2). Here, we are *dividing by the multiplicand*. This explains why we only have two main models for division; we have either the multiplier or the multiplicand to divide by and we cannot divide by anything else.

What happens though in the situations where it is difficult to identify the multiplier or the multiplicand? It is important to recognize that we also carry out division when it is simply the inverse of multiplication. For example, modifying the previous example for product of measures:

If the weight of an object is 50N and the acceleration due to gravity is $10m/s^2$, what is its mass?

We cannot identify the multiplier or the multiplicand in these types of situations. However, because weight is mass times acceleration due to gravity, we use division to go from mass to the other two measures. Therefore we add 'division as inverse of multiplication' as another situation to consider. Of course, this is also implicit in the other division situations, and is a property of multiplication/division that we learn to apply to all situations. However, until we learn this property we will not recognize certain situations, like the one involving product of measures, as involving division.

How can we represent multiplication?

KEY POINT TO CONSIDER

Key ideas within multiplication are replication, the binary nature of multiplication, commutativity for multiplication but not division and distributivity. The key representation for multiplication is the array as this shows all the above characteristics.

Having looked at the different situations in which multiplication and division can arise, let us now examine how we can represent these operations. According to Nunes and Bryant (1996: 144), a commonly held view of multiplication and division is that they are simply 'different arithmetic operations ... taught after they have learned addition and subtraction'. However, they also suggest that in actual fact, 'multiplication and division represent a significant qualitative change in children's thinking' (p.144). While addition and subtraction can be thought of as the joining of sets, multiplication is about replication. Anghileri (1989) agrees with these ideas, and suggests that one of the problems for pupils when they work particularly on multiplication is that they view it as a unary operation. What that means is that pupils operate on just one number in the calculation, the second number involved being just the number of times you repeat the operation. Repeated addition results from this way of thinking about multiplication. For division, we just repeatedly subtract a particular number. Anghileri however suggests that pupils need to view multiplication as a binary operation with two inputs. The first input represents the size of a set (the multiplicand) and the second represents the number of replications of that set (the multiplier). Thus the two numbers represent distinct elements of the multiplication process.

There are a number of important aspects of multiplication discussed by Anghileri (1989) including:

- Replication (rather than joining as in addition/subtraction).
- The binary rather than unary nature of multiplication, and the notion of two distinct and different inputs.
- Commutativity for multiplication but not division.
- **Distributivity**.

When considering ways of representing multiplication visually, we need to consider how the representation might both show the above characteristics and also aid the calculation process.

Let us therefore begin by examining different ways of representing multiplication, and then extend our ideas to division later. A popular representation of multiplication is shown for 3×8 in Figure 4.4. Now, let us consider some questions which relate to the important aspects of multiplication.

Figure 4.4 Plate of strawberries – a representation for 3×8

Does the representation show replication and the binary nature of multiplication?

There are 3 plates of strawberries with 8 strawberries on each plate. The idea of replication seems to be a clear characteristic. There are also two inputs – the number of strawberries on a plate and the number of plates in the picture. The binary nature of the operation is evident.

Does the representation show commutativity?

If we look at a similar representation for 8×3 (see Figure 4.5), the diagram is clearly very different to 3×8. So this representation does not clearly illustrate the fact that multiplication is commutative.

Figure 4.5 Plate of strawberries – a representation for 8×3

Does the representation show distributivity?

This particular representation does not show the distributive nature of multiplication. For example, it does not show that 3×8 can be viewed as $(2 + 1) \times (5 + 3)$.

Does the representation aid calculation?

Yes, as the number of strawberries can be counted either in 8s or in 1s. However, whereas these methods are probably acceptable for small numbers, it will be more difficult when large numbers are being multiplied.

The 'plates of' representation therefore only illustrates some of the important aspects of multiplication and only helps with multiplication of small numbers. Some other common representations for multiplication are shown in Figure 4.6. As before, we can ask questions of each of the representations to see whether they highlight the important aspects of multiplication and aid calculation. However, it is our contention that the array is a key representation for multiplication in the same way as the number line is for addition. To illustrate why this is, let us ask the questions specifically of the array representation.

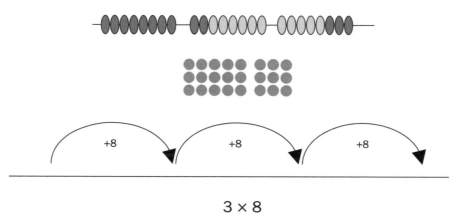

$$3 \times 8$$

Figure 4.6 Other possible representations (beads, array, number line, symbols)

Does the representation show replication and the binary nature of multiplication?

The array illustrates the replicative nature of multiplication in that rows (or columns) are being replicated. It also illustrates the binary nature of multiplication where the inputs are the number of counters in a row and the number of rows.

Does the representation show commutativity?

The commutative nature of multiplication can be shown by the array (Figure 4.7). By re-orienting the array, we can show that 6×7 is equivalent to 7×6.

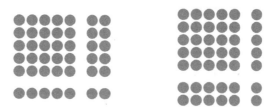

Figure 4.7 Array representation for 6×7 and 7×6

Does the representation show distributivity?

The distributive nature of the operation can also easily be shown through the structure of the array. In the right hand diagram above, from the horizontal spacing we have placed in the array, we can see straight away that 7×6 can be rewritten as:

$$7 \times 6 = (5 + 2) \times 6 = (5 \times 6) + (2 \times 6)$$

The vertical spacing in the diagram shows that:

$$7 \times 6 = 7 \times (5 + 1) = (7 \times 5) + (7 \times 1)$$

Considering both the horizontal and vertical spacing shows that:

$$7 \times 6 = (5 + 2) \times (5 + 1) = (5 \times 5) + (5 \times 1) + (2 \times 5) + (2 \times 1)$$

This means that the seven times table – which is generally thought of as the most difficult times table for pupils – could be viewed as the $(5 + 2)$ times table.

Does the representation aid calculation?

In the examples in Figure 4.7, the counters in the array can be counted in 1s, in 7s and also in 6s. Furthermore, the reason we have spaced out the array at intervals of 5 (rather than having one dense block of counters) is that we can use the structure of the representation to find the total number of counters. Let us look at the example of 14×12 given in Figure 4.8: Because of the spacing within the array, we can recognize groupings of counters that are multiples of 5. We are then left with the bottom right-hand corner counters that we can count. We can quickly total up the parts of the array to find that $14 \times 12 = 168$. Of course, we could space out the array at an interval other than 5 (10 might seem logical). However, using this spacing means that only multiplication tables up to 5×5 need to be learnt.

Using this array representation also provides a clear progression, starting from real-life examples of multiplication and working towards written methods for

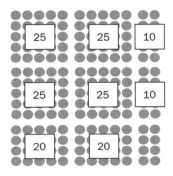

Figure 4.8 Array representation for 14×12

multiplication that are used in schools. In particular, we can make a clear link between the array and the grid method (see Figure 4.9). Linking the array representation to the grid method shows why we can split up the numbers being multiplied into a grid. Furthermore, we can also see that we do not have to split the grid into tens, units and so on. One teacher we know, who has used the array to explain multiplication to his pupils, uses the grid method split up into fives. That way, lower ability pupils do not have to rely on number facts beyond 5×5.

From the grid method, we could then progress onto more formal written methods for multiplication. Let us examine different written methods for 146×84 (see Figure 4.10). The right-hand calculation in Figure 4.10 is what we would associate with a traditional, long multiplication method of calculation. However what we are doing in long multiplication can best be explained by referring back to the array representation and the grid method. We know from the array representation that we can split up the numbers we are multiplying according to the distributive law. In the grid method we have split 146 and 84 into hundreds, tens and units. Multiplying the separate parts and adding the totals together provides the overall answer. In fact, in long multiplication, this is exactly what we are doing. When we start with 'six times four is 24 . . .' it is implied that we have separated the six and the four from their numbers. The reason we start off with a zero in the second row of the long multiplication is that we are multiplying not by eight but by 80. We can illustrate this link between long

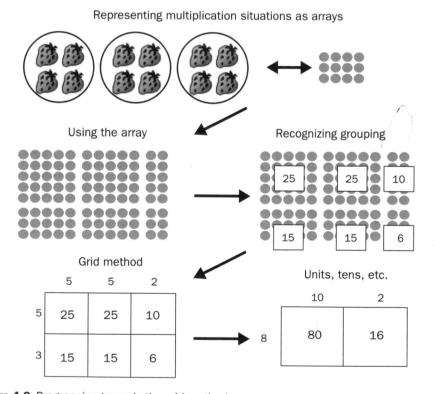

Figure 4.9 Progression towards the grid method

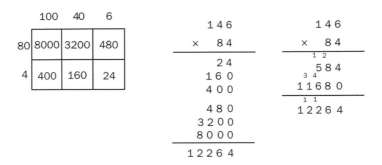

	100	40	6
80	8000	3200	480
4	400	160	24

```
        1 4 6              1 4 6
   ×      8 4         ×      8 4
   ───────────        ─────────────
          2 4              1 2
        1 6 0              5 8 4
        4 0 0            3 4
                       1 1 6 8 0
        4 8 0          ─────────────
        3 2 0 0          1 1
        8 0 0 0          1 2 2 6 4
   ───────────
        1 2 2 6 4
```

Figure 4.10 Linking the grid representation with formal methods of multiplication

multiplication and the grid method more clearly by writing down the total from each stage of the long multiplication, as shown in the middle representation in Figure 4.10. We get the same numbers as the grid method, the parts of which total up to the same numbers as in the long multiplication. The advantage of long multiplication is that it is a quick, concise way of doing multiplication. The drawback is that it provides no explanation for why we do what we do. To gain this understanding, we have to make these links back to the array representation and the grid method. In the same way, we can gain understanding of other written methods of multiplication, such as the Gelosia method given in Figure 4.11.

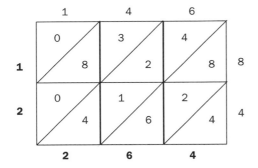

Write down the two numbers you are multiplying on the top and right of the grid. Multiply the numbers associated with each square, writing the resulting units in the bottom right of the square, and the resulting tens in the top left. Add all the numbers along each diagonal, moving from the right-hand diagonal to the furthermost left, writing the result on the bottom or the left of the grid. If there are tens in each addition, these are carried across to the next diagonal.

Figure 4.11 The Gelosia method of multiplication

Representing division using the array

Having chosen the array as an important way of representing multiplication, to maintain consistency between the operations, we would like to also use it to represent division. We can use the fact that division is the inverse of multiplication in order to adapt the array representation for division (see Figure 4.12). Whereas for multiplication it was the total of the array that we were trying to find, for division, what we are calculating is what the unknown dimension must be. However, does this representation explain the important properties of division? The properties we identified at the beginning of the chapter were:

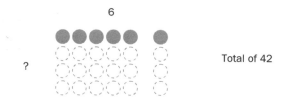

Figure 4.12 Array representation for 42 ÷ 6

- Division as sharing.
- Division as grouping and repeated subtraction.
- Division as the inverse of multiplication.

Also, we would ideally like the representation to explain other mathematical properties of division:

- Why is division not commutative (e.g. 24 ÷ 3 is not equal to 3 ÷ 24)?
- Why can we swap the **divisor** and the answer (e.g. 24 ÷ 3 = 8 and 24 ÷ 8 = 3)?
- Why can we partition the number we are dividing (which we call the **dividend**) but not the number we are dividing by (the divisor)? (e.g. 24 ÷ 3 = (18 ÷ 3) + (6 ÷ 3) but we do not carry out 24 ÷ (2 + 1)).
- Why can we factorize division calculations (e.g. 24 ÷ 8 = 12 ÷ 4)?

As for multiplication, the representation should also aid calculation and explain more formal methods of division. Therefore, let us ask these questions of the array representation.

Does the representation show division as sharing?

Looking at Figure 4.12, we can view the known dimension as the number of groups we are sharing the total over. Therefore, division can be seen as sharing.

Does the representation show division as grouping and repeated subtraction?

An advantage of the array is that we can view grouping of objects in the rows *or* the columns of the representation. We can therefore just as easily see the division as grouping property in Figure 4.12, where the known dimension is the size of the group. To find how many groups we would have from the total, we simply need to find how many times we subtract the size of the group from the total. Alternatively, we can use repeated addition to build up to the required total.

Does the representation show division as the inverse of multiplication?

By keeping the same representation as for multiplication, we make the link between multiplication and division explicit.

Does the representation show why division is not commutative?

Let us refer to a complete array once again (see Figure 4.13). In the last chapter we stated that subtraction was not commutative because we were taking a 'part' away from a whole – the two numbers were fundamentally different in character, and so would completely change the situation when swapped over. We can put forward a similar argument here for division. Unlike swapping the two dimensions of the array in multiplication, we

can see that swapping either dimension of the array with the total would not result in a correct total. This is because we are swapping numbers which are different in character (we have the dimensions and we have the total). Therefore, we can see why division is not commutative.

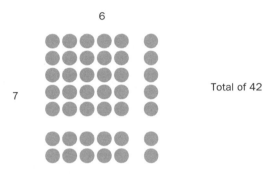

Figure 4.13 Array representation for $42 \div 6 = 7$ or $42 \div 7 = 6$

Does the representation show why we can swap the divisor and the answer?

Figure 4.13 shows that if one of the dimensions of the array is the divisor, then the other dimension is the answer to the division calculation. As in multiplication, the representation shows why we can swap round these two dimensions and for the resulting division calculation to still be true (we can see that in this case the numbers that are being swapped are the same in character).

Does the representation show why we can partition the dividend but not the divisor?

Let us draws lines through the array representation for division (Figure 4.14). In the left-hand diagram, what we have effectively done is by splitting the array (total 42), we split the answer of the division calculation (7). Therefore, the calculation becomes $(24 + 18) \div 6 = (24 \div 6) + (18 \div 6) = 4 + 3$. Therefore we can split up the dividend as long as we add up our separate answers at the end. However, when we split up the divisor as in the right-hand diagram, we get $42 \div (4 + 2) = 28 \div 4$ or $14 \div 2$. We get

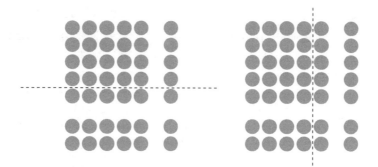

Figure 4.14 Splitting up the array representation for 42 ÷ 6 = 7

the answer to the calculation from either part, not added together. However, we can see that if we partition the divisor then the dividend changes as well. Therefore, we cannot split the divisor without affecting the totals that we are working with.

Does the representation show why we can factorize division calculations?

Following on though, if we split the right-hand diagram into two equal parts, then we would halve the dividend and halve the divisor without changing the answer to the calculation. Similarly if we split the array in to three equal parts. We are effectively factorizing the different parts of the calculation.

Does the array aid calculation?

Representing a division problem using the array does highlight what is happening in the process of division. For calculations involving small numbers therefore, the representation proves useful. As we move to bigger numbers, as for multiplication, we need to move on to more concise methods of calculation. However, we can link the array representation directly to repeated subtraction or addition (see Figure 4.15). This shows repeated addition on the left-hand side, like building up the array one row at a time until we get the required total. We then see how many rows are needed. Alternatively, we can subtract a row at a time from the total, to see how many rows made up the array. This corresponds to the repeated subtraction method in the centre of the figure. Rather than subtracting one row at a time, we can subtract a number of rows instead. This leads naturally to the **chunking** method, illustrated in the right-hand calculation in Figure 4.15.

We may then move on to short division. The example of 65 ÷ 5 is given in Figure 4.16. In the short division method, we start by seeing how many times the divisor goes into the left-hand numeral of the dividend, 'carrying' the remainder as 'tens' for the next numeral, and repeating the process. In fact, what we are doing here is splitting the dividend into convenient multiples of tens and units (and hundreds, thousands, etc. if the dividend was bigger). Therefore, the sum becomes (50 + 15) ÷ 5 = 10 + 3. We saw previously from the array representation why the division calculation can be split up in this way.

1	6			42			42
1	+ 6		1	− 6		5	− 30
	12			36			12
1	+ 6		1	− 6		2	− 12
	18			30		7	0
1	+ 6		1	− 6			
	24			24			
1	+ 6		1	− 6			
	30			18			
1	+ 6		1	− 6			
	36			12			
1	+ 6		1	− 6			
7	42			6			
			1	− 6			
			7	0			

Figure 4.15 Repeated addition and subtraction for 42 ÷ 6

$$5\overline{)65} \quad \Longrightarrow \quad 5\overline{)6\,{}^15} \;{}^1 \quad \Longrightarrow \quad 5\overline{)6\,{}^15}\;{}^{1\,3}$$

Figure 4.16 Short division method for 65 ÷ 5

We might finally move on to long division, an example of which is given in Figure 4.17. In long division, as in short division, we start by finding out how many times the divisor 'goes into' the left-hand numerals of the dividend. In the above case, 23 goes into 87 three times with some remainder. We then find out what is left over from this calculation by subtracting the multiple of the divisor that we found (3 × 23 = 69) from the part of the dividend we were looking at. We then 'drop down' the next numeral of the dividend, in this case dropping down a 1 to get 181 with the previous remainder. We then see how many times 23 goes into this number and the process is repeated.

What actually does all this mean though? Why do we carry out this process? We can explain long division by comparing it to the chunking method we highlighted

$$23\overline{)8717} \quad \Longrightarrow \quad 23\overline{)8717}^{\;3} \quad \Longrightarrow \quad 23\overline{)8717}^{\;37} \quad \Longrightarrow \quad 23\overline{)8717}^{\;379}$$

	69	69	69
	18	181	181
		161	161
		20	207
			207
			0

Figure 4.17 Long division method for 8717 ÷ 23

```
                      8717 ÷ 23
          300       − 6900
                        1817
           70       − 1610
                         207
            9       −  207
          379            0
```

Figure 4.18 Chunking method for 8717 ÷ 23

previously (see Figure 4.18). We first of all find the multiple (in hundreds) of the divisor we can subtract from the total. In finding what remains using subtraction, we are doing the same as we did in the long division. However, we do not complicate matters by 'dropping down' numerals of the total number one at a time; rather, we find what is left over altogether. Then we repeat the process, finding the further multiple (in tens and then in units) of the divisor that we can subtract from what we have left. Therefore, the chunking method makes explicit what we are implying in long division.

These methods then provide more concise methods of carrying out division calculations. However, starting off with the array representation provides a possible teaching sequence that we can move through, as well as clearly explaining the properties of the division operation.

Communicating multiplication and division

Turning our attention now to how multiplication and division are communicated in the classroom, teachers need to consider the range and variability of the language associated with the operations, and how this is to be addressed through planning for multiplication and division topics. Some words and phrases are shared with addition and subtraction, but children also need to learn about and understand a new set of number meanings related to multiplication and division (Nunes and Bryant, 1992). Just as we have a range of situations and representations associated with multiplication and division, so we need to develop children's language in referring to these.

As for addition and subtraction, there is guidance on the language required for multiplication and division for teachers in England and Wales (DfEE, 2000). For example, words and phrases required for Year 2 (ages 6 to 7 years) children are:

> lots of, groups of;
> ×, times, multiply, multiply by, multiple of;
> once, twice, three . . . times;
> times as (big, long, wide);
> repeated addition;
> array;
> row, column;
> double, halve;

share, share equally;
one each, two each, three each . . .;
group in pairs, threes . . . tens;
equal groups of;
divide, divided by, divided into;
left, left over.

This is a formidable list, especially when compared with that for the final year of primary schooling (Year 6 – ages 10 to 11 years) where little new is incorporated save for 'multiplication' and 'product'. It is therefore important to construct a strategy for developing mathematical language and communication that is consistent throughout primary school. Recognition of the need to revisit

> ### KEY POINT TO CONSIDER
>
> There is a range of language associated with multiplication and division and there is a need to develop activities which allow the young learner to acquire competence in the use of this language.

mathematical language development in the different year groups of children, rather than merely providing a 'simple maths vocabulary', is an essential element of a successful language strategy for multiplication and division.

An essential preliminary is to consider children's very early acquisition of mathematical language that in turn influences the mathematical knowledge and skills they bring into school. These predominantly informal experiences of the world influence children's understanding and awareness of language, and need to be borne in mind when introducing mathematical vocabulary if confusion is to be avoided. An example of an activity that can be carried out early on with children is a sharing activity where the words 'lots of', 'each' and 'equally' are repeatedly used (see Activity 4.1).

Activity 4.1 Sharing with the teddy bears

In play, children can share sweets or biscuits between their teddy bears at the teddy bears' picnic, where they will be repeating the language of sharing with lots of sweets, giving one at a time to each teddy and knowing each teddy has the same number of sweets or biscuits.

Moving on, primary children can then be introduced to different types of situations for multiplication. To develop the key language associated with these situations, one can provide discussion opportunities for each situation *and* practical activities in the real world. For example, we can draw on the questions exemplifying all of the multiplication situations at the beginning of the chapter. Representations such as arrays can provide an essential visual support to demonstrate the language of multiplication and its link with the associated processes (e.g. rows, columns, lots of, etc.) Real-life examples of arrays can also be used, such as a large block of chocolate with individual squares, jelly cubes and bundles of wall fixing plugs. However, experience of different representations is also essential for developing children's familiarity, confidence and imagination in mathematical operations. In addition to being given 'problems' and practical activities associated with different representations, in order to develop class discussion and provide assessment opportunities, children can be asked to write their own stories allowing them to use the different models they have for multiplication. This approach also provides the teacher with invaluable insights into their understanding of mathematical processes. Likewise, specific discussion-based activities such as Activity 4.2 can again be used to assess understanding.

Activity 4.2 Always, sometimes, never

Give pupils a series of statements and ask them to say whether they are always true, sometimes true or never true and to give an example or to explain why this is the case. These can be about operations, or numbers or shapes.

Multiplying makes things bigger

An even number that is divisible by 3 is also divisible by 6

You can't divide a smaller number by a larger one

When you multiply an odd number by an odd number you get an even number

You can multiply a number by 4 by doubling it twice.

For division, we need again to provide a broad range of situations and activities in order to develop children's language and reinforce the linkages between language and process. In this respect, it is important to recognize that the 'typical' situation of equal sharing (e.g. share 27 sweets between 3 children) is only one such division situation, and it can cause difficulty later for children if the language of sharing ('one for Janet, one for you and one for me . . .') is overemphasized at the expense of other language and imagery associated with division. Therefore, the situations and activities that we devise need to place equal emphasis on grouping (quotitive) approaches as well as the more usual sharing (partitive) situations, allocating objects one at a time. Examples of problems for grouping situations might be:

To organize the school trip for 150 children, how many 30-seater buses will be required?

A shopkeeper sells carrots in bags holding 10 carrots. If he has 80 carrots, how many bags will he need?

The class will be running in the relay race on school sports day. Each team has 4 runners. If there are 24 children in the class, how many relay teams will there be?

For sharing situations:

There are 24 biscuits in a packet to be shared equally between 4 children. How many biscuits does each child get?

I have 30 daffodil bulbs to be placed in 5 flower pots. How many bulbs in each pot?

Teachers also need to familiarize children with the notion of division as inverse multiplication and to naturally make connections between the two operations to reinforce the links between them. For example:

How many groups of 3 sweets are there in 27 sweets?

Other examples of division as the inverse of multiplication include the interrelationships of length, width and area, or distance, time and speed. Further examples of division as the inverse of multiplication can be demonstrated using money:

8 pencils cost 96 pence in total. If I have 60 pence, how many pencils can I buy?

Again, arrays can be used to demonstrate division as both grouping and sharing, as demonstrated earlier in the chapter. The same real life examples such as a chocolate bar, jelly or a bunch of wall fixing plugs can be a helpful practical tool in explaining concepts via the array. In order to include as many examples as possible from their own experiences to represent as an array, the children should be encouraged to provide their own examples and/or discover other instances from home, school or their everyday activities. When *both* multiplication and division are treated in this way, the links between multiplication and division as its inverse should become clearer to children.

Challenges in teaching multiplication and division

To conclude this chapter, let us examine some of the challenges that one might face initially when teaching multiplication and division, and how using the array representation might help. The introductory language of multiplication, detailed in the previous section, presents a number of particular difficulties. First, there is the confusion of 'times' and 'multiplied by'. When children visualize 'four times five' do they see four sets of five objects? What about four multiplied by five? Do we picture the same thing? If we are being precise, 4×5 indicates four (things) repeated or multiplied five times, so it might be better to say it is 'four, five times' rather than 'four lots of five'. As we saw earlier in the chapter, the use of representations such as 'groups of' or a number line can maintain this confusion, because they highlight that 'four times five' for example is different to 'five times four'.

Of course, the commutative law means that the answer to a multiplication calculation or its 'product' is the same whether it is four, five times or five, four times. But the confusion about what it is we mean and the way we are expecting pupils to visualize this is not often discussed. One of the key advantages of the array representation is that it illustrates this commutativity by displaying the relationship in two dimensions. The other ways of showing this relationship are less flexible, and require us to understand the relationship as a process (i.e. we will see that answers are the same when we have completed the calculations). Therefore, a key teaching point initially is that when we are talking about square numbers with children (see Chapter 7 for examples), even before they begin to investigate multiplication, they can begin to get acquainted with the array representation which we will use later to illustrate multiplication.

KEY POINT TO CONSIDER

Teaching activities for multiplication and division need to give young learners the opportunity to explore different representations of multiplication and division and to reason about the connections between these. They also need to spend time exploring the array as this both helps to gain an understanding of the concept of multiplication and develops techniques for performing calculations.

Another advantage of the array is that it builds understanding of the grid method for long multiplication – a key challenge for learners. This builds development of understanding of the distributive law or how we can chunk multiplication. Again this will help children to develop flexibility in mental calculation and encourage them to see that even if they do not know the solution to a multiplication or division calculation, they can break it down or chunk it into smaller parts. An important teaching point is to encourage them to visualize the problem so that they can work out an alternative solution through this breaking down into smaller parts.

The most common misconceptions for both younger learners (Anghileri, 1989; Kouba, 1989) and adults (Graeber *et al.*, 1989) are that 'multiplication (always) makes numbers bigger', the opposite that 'dividing (always) makes numbers smaller', and in division that 'you can't divide a smaller number by a larger'. These misconceptions can be hard to overcome and need to be tackled directly and explicitly. Use of the array to show the relationship within a quantity has a number of significant advantages. Children do not have to see multiplication and division as repeated addition or subtraction of a quantity (which naturally lead to these misconceptions). They can rather use the array to show how the numbers in a multiplication or division calculation are related. We will tackle some of these specific issues related to the multiplication and division in the next chapter on fractions. For now, we need to be aware that viewing multiplication and division *only* as repeated addition and subtraction can result in challenges for children's learning.

Questions for discussion

1   How would you incorporate the ideas presented in this chapter into your teaching of multiplication and division? What activities would you do with different year groups? What are the implications for classroom pedagogy and for assessment?

2   Although the array representation has been highlighted as important in the chapter, what limitations do you think it has?

3   Explain the Gelosia method given earlier, based on the ideas developed in this chapter.

5
Fractions

In the preceding chapters, we have examined the mathematics concerning whole, positive numbers. We now move on in this and the next chapter to look at the domain of rational numbers, which are numbers that can be expressed by one number being divided by another, for example $\frac{3}{4}$ or 0.75. We begin in this chapter by looking at fractions. However, the topic of fractions is one of the most challenging parts of the number curriculum in primary or elementary schools (Brousseau *et al.*, 2007). To see why children find them so difficult, we begin the chapter with a discussion of the misconceptions that children have about fractions.

Misconceptions of fractions

The misconceptions that children have about fractions relate particularly to the way in which fractions are represented as numbers, and the standard ways that we use to represent fractions in diagrams and pictures in mathematics teaching (Kerslake, 1986). A further series of challenges arise as teaching moves from fractional parts of a single whole to fractions of quantities. **Improper fractions** (e.g. $\frac{10}{7}$) and mixed numbers (e.g. $3\frac{1}{2}$) also cause particular difficulties. In terms of representations, Hart (1981) reported that although diagrams sometimes help with the solution of fractions problems or were used as a checking procedure, the actual process that children used with diagrams did not necessarily support conceptual understanding. For example, interpreting a part–whole diagram might simply involve counting the shaded pieces, counting the total number of pieces, and then just writing one whole number on top of the other (see Figure 5.1).

The result is that when asked to give the fraction *not* shaded, after pupils had just correctly worked out the fraction shaded in a part–whole diagram, Hart found that few subtracted the fraction shaded from the whole to work out the amount unshaded. They resorted to counting again. It might be inferred that although pupils gave the correct fractions after counting, they did not see the connection between the fraction

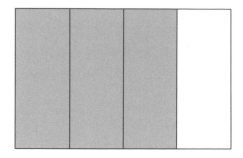

Figure 5.1 Part–whole representation for fractions

represented and the whole number 1, or the complementary addition, for example $\frac{3}{4}+\frac{1}{4}=\frac{4}{4}=1$. The counting technique does not require the application of any concept of fractions as parts of a whole. The fraction is interpreted as a pair of separate whole numbers. Similarly with a number line, pupils have difficulties in placing a fraction (e.g. Kerslake, 1986; Hannula, 2003). A common error is to place the fraction $\frac{1}{3}$ at a third of the distance along a number line, however long the number line happens to be (for example, 0 to 2).

Other issues arise with operations involving fractions, specifically addition, subtraction, multiplication and division, usually due to the application of an algorithm to solve these calculations. The commonest error in addition and subtraction of fractions is for pupils to add the **numerators** and the **denominators** (so $\frac{1}{2}+\frac{2}{3}=\frac{3}{5}$ would be a common mistake). This might start from pupils seeing each fraction as representing two separate rather than interrelated numbers. However, even when children have been taught about the concept of equal parts and also about the concept of a common denominator before adding or subtracting, the error is surprisingly stubborn. This may be because the separate number concept then works again with multiplication (where $\frac{1}{2}\times\frac{2}{3}=\frac{2}{6}$), so even when they have overcome one misconception, it is resur-

rected by overextending the application of a subsequent algorithm.

Division is the most challenging of operations with fractions (Ma, 1999). Errors made in division of fractions have been classified as falling into three broad categories (Tirosh, 2000). Pupils make algorithmically based errors (with mistakes made in the computation process); intuitively based errors due to misconceptions associated with division; and errors based on formal knowledge about the nature of fractions. In terms

---

KEY POINT TO CONSIDER

Young learners experience many difficulties with making sense of fractions – both in terms of fractions as numbers and how to operate with fractions. They need to experience different representations of fractions, to make explicit the connections between them and to have opportunities to reason in order to develop their understanding.

of algorithmic errors, the most common 'bugs' (Ashlock, 1990) include inverting the dividend instead of the divisor or inverting both (i.e. applying the rule 'turn upside down and multiply', but not remembering what to turn upside down). The actual operation is also difficult to understand intuitively. Conceptions of division as partition depend on the divisor being a whole number, so the idea of dividing with a fraction does not make sense (Fischbein *et al.*, 1985). Mistakes may also arise from related misconceptions, for example, a pupil's belief that $\frac{1}{4} \div \frac{1}{2} = 2$, resulting from an intuitive belief that the dividend should always be greater than the divisor, therefore $\frac{1}{4} \div \frac{1}{2} = \frac{1}{2} \div \frac{1}{4} = 2$ (Tirosh, 2000).

What does emerge from the research is that pupils need to experience different representations of fractions, to make explicit the connections between them and to have opportunities to reason in order to develop their understanding, not just with fractions, but also by relating them to decimals, percentages and ratios. Furthermore, we bear in mind the warning provided by Nunes and Bryant (1996: 228):

> The disconnection between pupils' understanding of division of discontinuous and continuous quantities developed out of school and their learning of fractions might come about exactly because pupils do not think of fractions as having anything to do with division, and only relate fractions to part–whole language.

We need to ensure that children have a broad understanding of fractions. Therefore, we begin by taking a broad look at what we mean by rational numbers before considering how we can specifically represent fractions.

What are rational numbers?

Behr *et al.* (1983) put forward seven sub-categories within this category of 'rational number':

- Fractional measure
- Linear coordinates
- **Quotient** (i.e. an indicated division)
- Decimals
- Ratio
- Rate
- Operators.

Already, looking at the variety of interpretations and sub-categories that we need to consider in order to understand rational numbers, we can see why 'complete comprehension of rational numbers is a formidable learning task' (Behr *et al.*, 1983: 92–3). Let us describe each of these sub-categories before we consider those directly related to the concept of fractions.

Fractional measure is defined by Behr *et al.* as how much there is of a particular quantity in terms of a particular unit of that quantity. This includes not only the part–whole picture of fractions (e.g. $\frac{3}{4}$ being 3 parts out of the whole unit that is made up of 4 parts), but also the idea of proportions and percentages (how much we have of a subset of a quantity out of the total set of the quantity). **Linear coordinates** are the use of rational numbers to describe numbers between whole units on a continuous linear measures (e.g. on a ruler) or on a representation such as a number line. Quotient is the idea that $\frac{3}{4}$, for example, can indicate a division operation, i.e. 3 divided by 4. The result of such a division can alternatively be expressed as a decimal by extending the base-10 system described in Chapter 2. **Ratio** is a measure of the comparative relationship between two different quantities (we might have three of one type of object to one of another type). **Rate** also describes the relationship between two quantities but is used then to define a new quantity. For example, the mass of an object divided by its volume defines its density (note that rate here does not necessarily involve time). Finally, we have the rational number as an **operator**, where the number is a transformation. We will see this when we look at enlargements in shape and space.

> ### KEY POINT TO CONSIDER
>
> There are three basic ways of thinking about fractions: fractional measures, linear coordinates and quotient. We need to recognize and consider these different meanings for fractions in order to develop understanding.

In this chapter on fractions then, we will concentrate on the first three sub-categories, namely fractional measures, linear coordinates and quotient. We will also examine ratio and relate it to the ideas of proportions and percentages that are part of the fractional measures sub-category. In fact, what we find is that how we represent fractions is actually determined by which of the sub-categories we are trying to convey. Therefore, let us turn our attention to the various representations we have for fractions, so that we can begin to discuss the different meanings for fractions.

How can we represent fractions?

It is interesting to look at how fractions were represented historically, in order to get an idea of how they were used. In Figure 5.2 we see how Menninger (1969) describes the

Babylonian half   Egyptian half   Egyptian quarter

Figure 5.2 Babylonian and Egyptian symbols for fractions

visual symbols used by the Babylonians and the Egyptians. The use of fractions for these cultures was developed from their use of measures. Therefore, the Babylonian half is clearly half a vessel. The Egyptian half represents one half of the whole and the Egyptian quarter represents four parts. We can see that the representations are closely allied to a part–whole picture of fractions. Figure 5.3 shows that Egyptians also had ways of expressing unit fractions (Ifrah, 1985). The sign for 'mouth', meaning 'part' in this context, is placed above the representation for the number for the unit fraction (5 or 10 in the above example). Again, we see that the idea of 'part' is integral to the representation of the fraction.

The way we write fractions today, with one number written above another, was used by the ancient Greeks and in India in the seventh century (Flegg, 1983). The line in the middle was introduced by Arab mathematicians. Therefore, the modern symbolic representation for a fraction that we commonly use today is as shown in Figure 5.4. From a part–whole perspective, the number denoting the units making up the whole is the denominator, on the bottom of the fraction. The number denoting the parts of the whole is the numerator, on the top of the fraction.

It is important that we do not simply work with symbols, but that we can draw on other representations for fractions as well. Mack (1993), in her study which aimed to develop understanding of fractions in 11- to 12-year-old American students, found that: 'In instruction I frequently had to move back and forth between problems represented symbolically and problems in the context of real-world situations before students successfully related fraction symbols and procedures to their informal knowledge' (p. 23).

Therefore, real-world representations need to be provided to pupils so that they can understand fractions more fully. Two common visual representations that are used for

> ### KEY POINT TO CONSIDER
>
> Fractions can be represented in a number of different ways and the different representations illustrate a variety of characteristics of fractions.

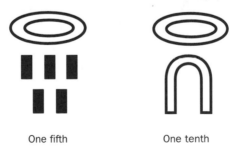

One fifth   One tenth

Figure 5.3 Examples of Egyptian symbols for unit fractions

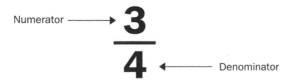

Numerator ⟶ $\dfrac{3}{4}$ ⟵ Denominator

Figure 5.4 Modern symbolic representation of a fraction

fractions related to real-world contexts are the circular and rectangular (see Figure 5.5). We can relate these to real life contexts such as cutting up pizza, cake or bread. Each representation shows three parts highlighted out of a whole of 4 parts, i.e. $\frac{3}{4}$. However, as we saw from the earlier discussion on rational numbers, and also from the historical look at fractions, we have to be careful that we do not restrict our view of fractions to that of 'parts of a whole' only. We can use the real-life representations to illustrate fractions as a quotient. For example, taking the pizza representation, if we have the situation of three pizzas being divided between four people, one way of dividing might be as shown in Figure 5.6. Each $\frac{3}{4}$ is the same amount as in the part–whole representation, but we have arrived at that amount in a quite different way.

Behr *et al.* (1983) also differentiated between continuous and discrete representations of fractions. For example, the circular and the rectangular representations shown are continuous representations in that we are dividing up a continuous material (e.g. a pizza or a cake). We could also represent a fraction with discrete objects as shown in Figure 5.7. The 'whole' here is a set of discrete objects such as coloured balls, and the 'part' is a subset of that. Again, we are presenting a view of fractions that is different to the traditional partitioning of some continuous whole. We can also present a fraction on a number line as in Figure 5.8. This presents the linear coordinate nature of a fraction, representing a position somewhere between those indicated by the whole numbers. It also represents fractions as numbers between whole numbers.

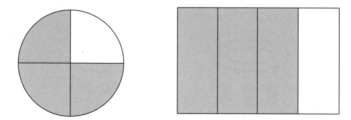

Figure 5.5 Circular and rectangular (continuous) visual representations for fractions

Figure 5.6 Quotient representation of three divided into four parts

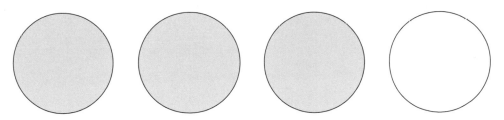

Figure 5.7 Discrete visual representations for fractions

Figure 5.8 Linear coordinate representations for fractions

Reasoning rules for operations with fractions

We have identified a number of representations of fractions in the above discussion. However, for reasoning how we carry out operations with fractions – addition, subtraction, multiplication and division – there is one particular representation that we find useful: the rectangular or square part–whole representation. We will demonstrate the usefulness of this representation by using it to explore key ideas with fractions, namely **equivalent fractions** and reasoning the 'rules' that we have for the operations.

> ### KEY POINT TO CONSIDER
>
> Using the rectangle representation of fractions, we can illustrate each of the operations. This allows the young learner to visualize the operations and to work on their own generalizations of the way in which the operations work. A key idea that the learner needs to make sense of is that of equivalent fractions.

Equivalent fractions

Equivalent fractions is the idea that the same quantity can be symbolically represented in different ways. For example, let us take the fraction $\frac{1}{3}$. Using the square representation, we would show this as in Figure 5.9. With this representation, we can change the size of the denominator – the number of parts if you like – and again show this visually. The split can be performed vertically or horizontally, although the horizontal split possibly makes the fraction easier to see (see Figure 5.10). For each of the representations above, we can see that the actual quantity (the shaded portion) remains the same. Therefore, although symbolically these fractions look different, they are equivalent. We can see from the diagrams that if we decide to split the denominator (the total number of parts) then we also change the numerator (the

Figure 5.9 Square representation of $\frac{1}{3}$

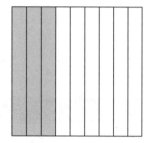

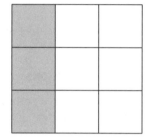

Figure 5.10 Square representations of $\frac{3}{9}$

parts out of the total) without changing the fractional part. We could have split $\frac{1}{3}$ in many different ways: into $\frac{2}{6}$, into $\frac{4}{12}$, and so on.

Addition and subtraction

These ideas on equivalent fractions can now be used to show how we can add fractions together if the denominators are different. Let us begin with a simpler example of $\frac{2}{3} + \frac{2}{3}$.

Using our square representation, this would appear as seen in Figure 5.11. The first key point to note is what constitutes a whole: in this case it is one square. From the diagram, we can quickly see that we have two parts within each whole, each part being 'one third', added to two more parts which are again 'one thirds'. In total, we have four of these parts, namely four thirds or $\frac{4}{3}$. We can also see that this would be the same as one 'whole' square with one third left over, or $1\frac{1}{3}$.

 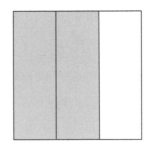

Figure 5.11 Representation of $\dfrac{2}{3}+\dfrac{2}{3}$

Let us now look at $\dfrac{2}{3}+\dfrac{3}{5}$ (see Figure 5.12). Here, the parts we are bringing together are very different, so we cannot simply add them together in a straight-forward way. However, let us try and use the idea of equivalent fractions. If we split each part of the left-hand diagram into a further five pieces (i.e. the number of parts on the right-hand side), and split each part of the right-hand diagram into a further three pieces (i.e. the number of parts on the left-hand side) we get the representation seen in Figure 5.13. Changing the orientation of the second representation has simply

Figure 5.12 Representation of $\dfrac{2}{3}+\dfrac{3}{5}$

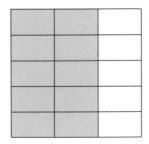 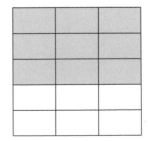

Figure 5.13 Representation of $\dfrac{10}{15}+\dfrac{9}{15}$

helped us to do this (imagine the two grids being placed over each other). We have converted our calculation to $\frac{10}{15} + \frac{9}{15}$ which is equivalent to the original addition $\frac{2}{3} + \frac{3}{5}$. The whole is still the square but now each of the little cells is $\frac{1}{15}$. Now we can add these fractions together as they both involve 'fifteenths'. Counting the parts or completing the whole, we can see that the answer would be $\frac{19}{15}$ (see Figure 5.14). Summarizing this symbolically:

$$\frac{2}{3} + \frac{3}{5}$$
$$= \frac{10}{15} + \frac{9}{15} \quad \text{(Making the denominator the same through equivalent fractions)}$$
$$= \frac{19}{15}$$

Symbolically, the procedure that we carried out was to multiply the top and bottom of each fraction by the other denominator. We did this, then we added the numerators. Therefore, we have obtained a 'rule' for adding fractions.

We can do the same for subtraction, as seen in the example $\frac{3}{4} - \frac{2}{5}$ in Figure 5.15. As in the case of addition, the parts we are dealing with can be different – here we have quarters and fifths. We use the same process as before for obtaining equivalent fractions, namely split each part of the left-hand diagram by the other denominator which is five, and split each part of the right-hand diagram by the other denominator which is four (see Figure 5.16). We now have 15 'twentieths' on the left-hand side and 8 'twentieths' on the right-hand side. Subtracting the right-hand parts from the left

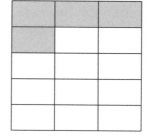

Figure 5.14 Representation of $\frac{19}{15}$ or $1\frac{4}{15}$

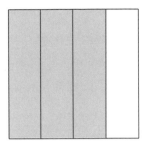

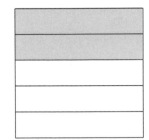

Figure 5.15 Representation of $\dfrac{3}{4} - \dfrac{2}{5}$

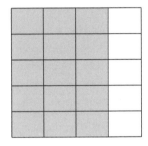

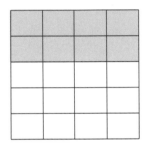

Figure 5.16 Representation of $\dfrac{15}{20} - \dfrac{8}{20}$

gives 7 'twentieths' or $\dfrac{7}{20}$. Summarizing this symbolically:

$$\dfrac{3}{4} - \dfrac{2}{5}$$

$$= \dfrac{15}{20} - \dfrac{8}{20} \quad \text{(Making the denominator the same through equivalent fractions)}$$

$$= \dfrac{7}{20}$$

For subtraction then, we can say that we make the denominators the same for each fraction by multiplying top and bottom by the other denominator. Then we subtract the numerators. Thus in addition and subtraction, using the representation and then working with or reasoning with this representation has provided us with 'rules' for working with fractions. Furthermore, and more importantly, the representations provide meaning to what we are doing.

Multiplication and division

We now try to apply a similar process to the operations of multiplication and division. Starting with multiplication, what does it mean to multiply $\dfrac{2}{5} \times \dfrac{3}{4}$? In this case, this is where the notion of multiplication as repeated addition starts to break down. It does not mean anything to add $\frac{2}{5}$ by $\frac{3}{4}$ times. Going back to the previous chapter, one of the ways of viewing multiplication is as groupings. In this context, it makes more sense to say that we have $\frac{3}{4}$ groups of (or lots of) $\frac{2}{5}$ or visa versa. Now, when we considered multiplication of whole numbers, we suggested that the two dimensional array was the best representation for making sense of multiplication. Therefore, we will adopt a similar two dimensional picture of multiplication of fractions, but combine it with the square representation we have used above for fractions.

We start with $\frac{2}{5}$ as seen in Figure 5.17. If we consider exactly what we are showing here, we have a unit (a whole), and we have shown $\frac{2}{5}$ of this whole along one of the dimensions of the square. If we now wish to find $\frac{3}{4}$ of this, we can find this along the other dimension of the square (see Figure 5.18). We have applied the $\frac{3}{4}$ on the other dimension of the square. This is equivalent to what we did in the last chapter, having so many counters or units in one direction and then repeating the groupings a certain number of times in the other direction. We can see that the answer to this calculation is $\frac{6}{20}$. We can also notice something else. With this two dimensional picture for multiplying fractions, we have the denominator of one fraction splitting the whole in one direction, and the other denominator splitting the whole in the other direction. Therefore, the resulting denominator, i.e. the resulting number into which the whole is split, is given by the two denominators multiplied together. Likewise, of the pieces that the whole is split into, we are initially only interested in a fraction of these given by the first numerator. When we split the whole in the other direction, we are again interested in a fraction of these given by the second numerator. The number of resulting pieces that we are interested in is therefore given by the two numerators multiplied together. Therefore, we have established a rule for multiplying fractions – multiply the

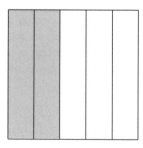

Figure 5.17 Representation of $\frac{2}{5}$

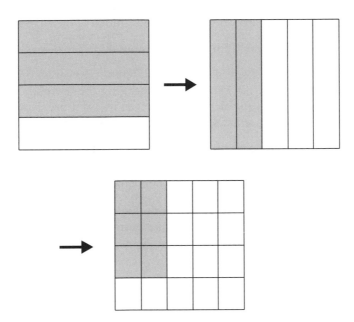

Figure 5.18 Representation of $\frac{3}{4} \times \frac{2}{5} = \frac{6}{20}$

numerators together and multiply the denominators together. The two dimensional representation of the calculation enables us to see why this is.

As we mentioned in the section on misconceptions, the most difficult operation with fractions is division. For example, what does $\frac{2}{3} \div \frac{1}{2}$ mean? If we go back to the case of whole numbers, and look at the example of 6 ÷ 2, one of the meanings is how many 2s there are in 6. Can we apply this view of division to fractions? In $\frac{2}{3} \div \frac{1}{2}$, we would need to ask ourselves how many $\frac{1}{2}$s there are in $\frac{2}{3}$. We can show this as in Figure

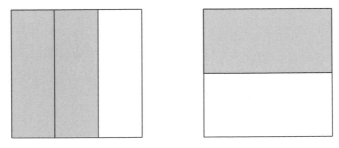

Figure 5.19 Representations of $\frac{2}{3}$ and $\frac{1}{2}$

5.19, where the question becomes how many or how much of the shaded section from $\frac{1}{2}$ will fit into the shaded section from $\frac{2}{3}$. As with subtraction previously, this is difficult to do as the parts in each fraction are quite different. However, using equivalent fractions we can change the diagram without changing the fractions. We apply the same process for obtaining equivalent fractions that we used previously (see Figure 5.20). Now we can ask the question again: how much of the right-hand shaded section will fit the left-hand shaded section? From the diagram, the answer is $\frac{4}{3}$ or the whole section plus a third of it. That is, the answer to the question is $\frac{4}{3}$ or $1\frac{1}{3}$.

Looking back at the process we have been through, what we did was effectively to make the two denominators of the fractions the same, then divide the numerator of the first fraction by the numerator of the second fraction. Symbolically, this process is:

$$\frac{2}{3} \div \frac{1}{2}$$
$$= \frac{4}{6} \div \frac{3}{6}$$
$$= \frac{4}{3}$$

By trying other fractions in the division calculation, we can see that this process always works. Therefore, we have derived a 'rule' that we can apply: make the denominators the same through equivalent fractions and then divide the first numerator by the second. Interestingly, this is quite different from another rule for dividing with fractions we might have learnt at school, namely 'turn the second fraction upside down and multiply the fractions'. This other rule can be derived using algebra, but not so easily derived using visual methods. Therefore, we prefer this alternative rule that we can actually reason and explain using visual representations.

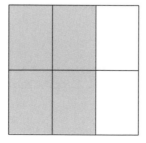 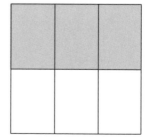

Figure 5.20 Representations of $\frac{2}{3}$ and $\frac{1}{2}$ as equivalent fractions

Other representations for fractions: proportions, percentages and ratios

Returning to our initial discussion on representing fractions, we extended our conception of fractions by examining the different representations and situations which can involve fractions. We can also make further links to other symbolic ways of representing fractions and other conceptions of rational number. For example, in looking at the discrete representation in Figure 5.7 (page 67), rather than describing the situation as $\frac{3}{4}$ or $\frac{1}{4}$, we might say we have 'three out of four' shaded counters or 'one out of four' unshaded. We can therefore describe the discrete situation in terms of 'proportions', where we define proportions as 'relative magnitude or extent' (*Collins English Dictionary*, 2004). The 'three out of four' describes the number of shaded counters relative to the total; what we are describing here is a part–whole relationship, where the parts and the whole are made up of discrete objects. Of course, we could just as well describe continuous quantities using proportions – three out of four parts of a circle are shaded for example. Therefore, implied in the fractional measure concept is this idea of proportion, this relationship between the parts and the whole, whether we are dealing with continuous or discrete objects.

This concept of proportion is useful because it indeed describes the relationship between the parts and the whole, rather than actually depending on the size of each. For example, all the situations in Figure 5.21 have the same proportion of shaded counters. In each case, we have 'three out of every four' counters shaded, or 'one out of every four' counters unshaded. We also see that we can express the same proportion in different ways – 'one out of every four' or 'two out of every eight' or 'three out of every twelve'. We can see that this parallels our discussion of equivalent fractions previously, and we have this equivalence because we are describing parts relative to the whole or the total. This in turn brings its own problems, as how can we agree on a way of describing proportions so as to make comparisons between situations easier? In fact, one agreed way of doing this is by expressing proportions of a hundred. So in the above case, if we had a hundred counters, we know that seventy-five of them would be shaded. We can write this symbolically as 75% where the % symbol implies 'out of one hundred'. This is the percentage format for proportions and we can make a direct link between fractions and percentages using equivalent fractions:

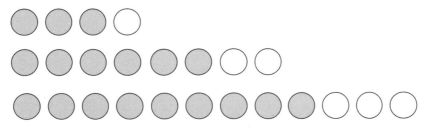

Figure 5.21 Discrete situations with the same proportions

$$\frac{1}{2} = \frac{50}{100} = 50\%$$

$$\frac{3}{4} = \frac{75}{100} = 75\%$$

$$\frac{1}{8} = \frac{100}{800} = \frac{12\frac{1}{2}}{100} = 12\frac{1}{2}\%$$

$$\frac{1}{3} = \frac{100}{300} = \frac{33\frac{1}{3}}{100} = 33\frac{1}{3}\%$$

Note that because we always denote percentages as 'out of one hundred', the proportion might not be a whole number. For example, 'one out of three' implies '33⅓ out of one hundred'.

The above description of proportions has highlighted the part–whole conception of proportions. However, if we take proportions as being 'relative magnitudes', we could also express one part relative to another part, rather than the whole – i.e. express a 'part–part relationship'. For the above discrete objects therefore, we could have 3 parts to 1 part or 3:1. This introduces the idea of ratio, another way of conceptualizing rational numbers. And like the part–whole relationships, the part–part relationships or ratios can be expressed in different ways. The ratio 3:1 is equivalent to 6:2 which is in turn equivalent to 9:3; in each case the relative magnitude of one part to another remains the same. Ratios can also express more complex part–part relationships; for example, if the ratio of red, blue and green counters in a box is 1:3:6, this implies that there is 1 red counter for every 3 blue counters and every 6 green counters.

Whether we express fractional quantities as fractions, percentages or ratios depends on the situation. For example, are we more concerned with part to whole relationships? Do we want a common basis for comparison? Are we more interested in part to part relationships? Of course, we can easily convert between each symbolic representation. We have seen already how to move between fractions and percentages. To move between fractions and ratios, we have to be clear about the implied number of parts and the total. Going back again to the discrete counters shown in Figure 5.21, saying that we have a fraction of $\frac{3}{4}$ shaded counters implies that we have 'three out of four' shaded and 'one out of four' unshaded. The ratio is therefore 3:1. Alternatively, in the above example of the coloured counters in a box, the ratio of 1:3:6 implies that for every 10 counters 1 will be red, 3 will be blue and 6 will be green, and therefore a fraction of $\frac{3}{10}$ or a percentage of 30% will be blue.

Communicating fractions

In terms of communicating rational numbers in the classroom, as we have highlighted in the chapter so far, there is recognition that they are difficult both to understand and to teach because of the variety of meanings included within the concept. The Primary Strategy Framework (DfES, 2006b), which underpins the teaching of primary mathematics in England and Wales, suggests that successful teaching effect-ively links the key concepts of fractions, decimals and percentages, each with its own mathematical vocabulary. However, without appropriate language to make these connections, understanding of the relationships between the three strands and also of the other meanings associated with rational numbers becomes a very difficult exercise.

Children come to the formal classroom study of fractions with earlier, informal experience of dealing with parts of a whole (e.g. familiarity with the principle of equal sharing, as with cakes, chocolate, pizzas, etc.). In other words, they have developed an informal use of some of the language of fractions – particularly that associated with sharing situations – but without necessarily understanding it. So they usually possess a degree of prior knowledge from real-life experiences that allows them to make *some* connections with the formal language of the maths curriculum, but there is a need to strengthen and consolidate connections between the two bodies of knowledge for a deeper understanding of the relationships (Mack, 1993). In this regard, when intro-ducing fractions, it is important to spend time on the teaching and understanding of the use of the term 'parts of a whole' and the concepts associated with this. We can illustrate this with objects familiar to the children:

- parts of a whole apple;
- parts of a whole pizza;
- parts of a whole chocolate bar.

However, difficulties often arise from the imprecise use of language. For example, problems can arise from children's natural confusion when they encounter homo-phones (e.g. a 'whole' is different from a 'hole' (Haylock, 2006); or their familiar-ity with colloquial uses such as: 'A whole half of pizza', 'Can I have a big half?', 'I have eaten a whole half'). Also, we have the fact that a single fractional 'part–whole' concept can take on different appearances so that the *same* fraction from an identical whole *looks* different – as, for example, dividing a block of chocolate into halves horizontally, vertically or diagonally (see Figure 5.22). One possible activity that can be used to help with this is to present the children with a flag (see Activity 5.1).

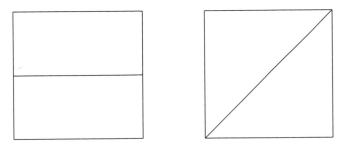

Figure 5.22 Different appearance of the concept 'half'

Activity 5.1 Flags

Design your own flag with patterns cut up into quarters. How many different designs can be made?

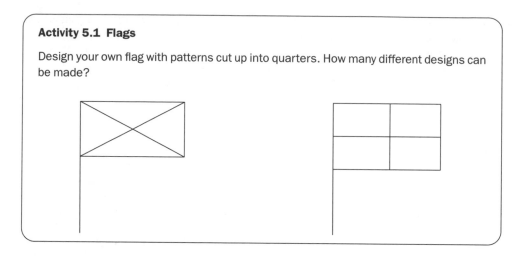

A related difficulty can occur when children encounter the same fractional concept across different wholes; e.g. half an apple does not resemble half a bar of chocolate, yet we emphasize the importance of 'equal' or equivalent parts when discussing fractions. It is therefore important to bear such issues in mind when introducing them to children, and advisable not to spend too much time on a single shape because children become too familiar and may then only associate fractions with particular objects – chocolate cake, pizza, apple, toffee bar or whatever. That is, they focus on the part of the specific item rather than the general notion of fractional parts. It is important therefore to use a range of objects for comparison, for instance comparing a variety of fruits which can be cut into relevant fractions and the fractional parts compared.

We need to emphasize the importance of 'equal' in terms of fractions and be explicit and precise in the use of language, to differentiate between equal and unequal fractions. It can be helpful, as suggested by Skemp (1989), to use the term 'parts' to mean equal fractions and 'bits' when they are unequal, and to be very clear in explaining the difference between these to the children. Then, according to Skemp (1989), the children should experience lots of practical hands-on activities involving things that can be easily cut up to ensure deeper understanding of equal and unequal fractions. For example, use a range of different shapes in card which the children can cut up into relevant parts, or plasticine sausages which also can be cut, or they can construct shapes using multilink where the fractions can be presented in different coloured cubes to demonstrate equal and unequal parts of a whole.

A clear, sound understanding of the term 'parts' to mean equal parts of the whole is essential before the concept moves on and children are introduced to the term 'equal' as in 'equivalent to', as we saw in equivalent fractions. We need to recognize the significance of the terminology and ensure children have sufficient hands-on experience of activities which demonstrate that equivalent means equal in value, rather than providing paper and pencil exercises where:

$$\frac{4}{8} = \frac{2}{4} = \frac{1}{2}$$

Multilink provides an effective tool for demonstrating equivalent fractions (see Figure 5.23). Likewise, a fraction chart can also be constructed on graph paper (Bailey *et al.*, 1990). See Activity 5.2.

$$\frac{3}{12} = \frac{1}{4}$$

Figure 5.23 Using multilink for equivalent fractions

Activity 5.2 A fraction chart

The children draw a rectangular grid 18cm × 10cm with ten 1cm rows. They then calculate the lengths of the sections in each row.

Fraction	Length of each sections mm
1 whole	180mm
1/2	90mm
1/3	
1/4	
1/5	
1/6	
1/8	
1/9	
1/10	
1/12	

Once the lengths have been recorded, the children can complete and label each fraction. The chart can then be used for children to find a number of equivalent fractions, for example, all equivalent to $\frac{1}{2}$.

The notion of equivalence further highlights the problem of using words borrowed from general speech, and of attributing mathematical meaning to them without reference or understanding of what has been done. Algorithms for equivalent fractions are rich in ill-defined, unhelpful phrases such as 'cancel out' and 'top heavy' which are words that often get in the way of understanding the concept. Children's understanding of 'equivalence', their knowledge of equivalent fractions, and of the process of reducing fractions to the lowest form all need to be securely established for them to be able to apply these concepts in a range of situations involving addition, subtraction, multiplication and division.

KEY POINT TO CONSIDER

In order to be able to communicate about fractions, the learner needs to develop an appropriate language. This language can be developed by focusing on a variety of representations of fractions and using these as a focus for discussion and reasoning.

In addition to children experiencing the part–whole conception of fractions, we emphasized earlier in the chapter that children need to experience the multiple, varied aspects of fractions, and we need to introduce them to a range of models that both facilitate and deepen their understanding of them and develop their use of the language associated with the key concepts and processes. Despite the potential difficulties (e.g. time in the classroom), much recent research has shown that children find fractions easier to work with when they are presented as fractions of *something*, rather than being presented with abstract numbers and symbols (Clausen-May, 2005). Also, as we did earlier in the chapter, fractions, alongside proportions, percentages and ratios, can be introduced in the classroom through the use of different representations, providing the opportunity for discussion of concepts, not only making the links between the various aspects of fractions but also developing the children's mathematical language. Particular activities can also be used to highlight different properties of fractions. For example, with the quotient picture of fractions as shown in Activity 5.3. For a challenge, the number of bars can be decreased or the number of people at the table increased depending on the ability of the children.

Activity 5.3 Dividing up a chocolate bar

Here are three chocolate bars on the table. How can we divide the bars between the four people on your table so that all get an equal part?

This activity allows for a discussion about fractions which is other than the simple part–whole picture of fractions. Another issue, related to that of the linear coordinate or number line picture of fractions, is that the concept of 'fractions' necessarily involves the notion of order, so a range of activities enabling children to *discover* which is larger and which is smaller is a valuable part of any teaching strategy. Children have difficulties in understanding the order involved in symbolic representations, for example that $\frac{1}{4}$ is larger that $\frac{1}{8}$. We saw previously that this issue be can be discussed through representations such as the part–whole pictures, but practical activities can also be used for discussion around the symbolic representation. For example, we have dice fractions as shown in Activity 5.4. This activity can promote children's learning whether working alone or in pairs. When in pairs, the activity provides an ideal opportunity for discussion which also develops the children's understanding of a range of fractions and, by adapting the activity, can extend the terminology to include further associated concepts such as equivalent/improper/proper factions.

Activity 5.4 Dice fractions

Roll the dice and fill in one of the squares. After each throw fill in another square. Try to make the left-hand fraction greater than the right-hand one.

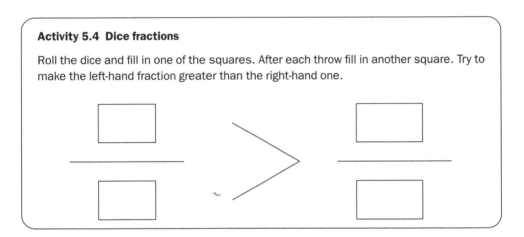

We also saw from the misconceptions that children often find 'rules' associated with fractions complicated and confusing. They are usually expressed rather formulaically in words and numbers which are often either learned by rote – usually without understanding – after which children move on to other topics too quickly. Perhaps we need to consider whether we need to teach *all* the terms and 'laws' relating to calculations using fractions – for example, numerators, denominators, proper, improper and mixed fractions for deeper understanding. Or we can use more informal language, so that children can engage on their own terms, which could lead them to a greater understanding of the concepts and processes involved? For instance, let us take the example of the cancelling rule where we 'divide the numerator and the denominator by the same number'. How do we teach this cancelling rule? It is a convenient technique but does not relate clearly to the concepts involved. Too often it is taught by rote, and we assume that children will have absorbed and understood the concepts because they are confident in using the phrases, but this will frequently not be the case. The approach we used earlier in the chapter would be to provide opportunities for children to reason with the representations for fractions. There is also a need for much discussion of the language used if children are to develop a full understanding of the concepts involved. For instance, 'cancelling' in general speech does not relate to what is happening when a fraction is cancelled. Relating this language directly to a visual representation of equivalent fractions will hopefully help to clarify the mathematical process and the language that we use to describe it. Above all, the approaches used to teach fractions need to make the most of the interconnections between the components of fractions, as highlighted at the beginning of the chapter, and to incorporate different models for calculations to provide the basis for discussing why particular methods are applicable to particular problems. In other words, the approach should not simply be about practising the rules, but rather using varied approaches to stimulate and deepen children's understanding of fractions.

Questions for discussion

1 Why do you think that fractions is one of the most difficult topics in primary mathematics for pupils to understand?

2 What are the key ideas that underpin the notion of fraction?

3 How do the ideas on representations in this chapter really help the pupils to give meaning to these key ideas?

4 A child uses a discrete representation for $\frac{2}{3}$ as shown in Figure 5.24. In calculating $\frac{2}{3} + \frac{2}{3}$ therefore, the child concludes that the answer is $\frac{4}{6}$ (see Figure 5.25). Where has the child gone wrong? What can we learn from this mistake?

Figure 5.24 Discrete representation for $\frac{2}{3}$

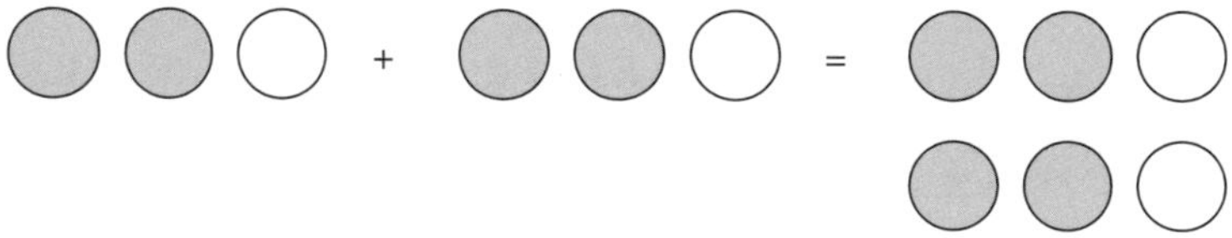

Figure 5.25 Discrete representation for $\frac{2}{3} + \frac{2}{3}$

6

Decimals

We now move on to examine one of the types of rational numbers that we did not cover in Chapter 5, namely decimals. As we mentioned previously, this form of rational number comes about through extending the number system so that rational numbers can be represented as well as whole numbers. However, this means that decimals can be difficult to understand because we need to have understanding of both the number system and of fractions:

> To operate effectively with decimal fractions thus requires both the ability to understand and use the notational conventions of the place value system of recording decimals, and the more basic ability to grasp the underlying concept, of say 'three tenths'. This latter ability involves being able to operate with the various meanings of a fraction . . .
>
> (Dickson *et al.*, 1984: 284)

We saw in the last chapter that we needed different representations in order to capture the different meanings of fractions. Likewise, we will need to draw on different representations for the meanings we can associate with decimals. However, before we do that, let us examine what misconceptions children can have with decimals.

Misconceptions with decimals

The first challenge pupils have is with recognizing decimal numbers. A number of researchers have noted that pupils are confused by the range of symbols in mathematics. Swan (1983) noted that some students appeared to confuse the decimal point with the 'r' in division remainders (9 r 2), the dot in 3.59pm or the comma in the coordinates

(5,2). Students similarly confuse fractions and decimals identifying 1.4 as being the same as $\frac{1}{4}$ (Markovits and Sowder, 1991). Hiebert observed this inappropriate 'conversion' between decimals, arguing that the main reason for this is that pupils struggle to make sense of the decimal point (Hiebert and Wearne, 1986).

When asked to order decimals, two main patterns of error occur (Steinle, 2004) which can be broadly identified as 'longer is larger', where the more decimal places there are the larger the number is thought of (so 0.345 is identified as larger than 0.54), and 'shorter is larger' where the fewer the number of decimal places the larger the number is believed to be (so 0.6 is identified as larger than 0.75). The 'longer is larger' misconception is more prevalent, but declines with age. The 'shorter is larger' is rarer, but more persistent. There are different reasons why these misconceptions develop and it is necessary for pupils to explain their thinking in order for the teacher to identify the underlying misunderstanding. For example, the belief that the number after the decimal point represents tenths works fine for 0.1, 0.2 and so on, up to 0.9, but what about 0.10 and 0.11? Is 0.11 equal to eleven tenths and therefore larger than 0.9? Aspects of everyday language may maintain the confusion as 'nought point eleven' (rather than point one one) sounds larger than 'nought point nine'.

When it comes to the operations of addition, subtraction, multiplication and division of decimals, most errors occur with the application of algorithms either inappropriately or incorrectly. Brown (1981), for example, asked students to multiply 5.13 by ten. For some pupils, their strategy was to overgeneralize the 'add a nought' rule for whole numbers and answer 5.130. Others were not happy with this procedure and modified the rule giving the answer 50.130. This is an example of pupils (incorrectly) inventing or repairing a rule to deal with a situation where their current rule does not provide them with a satisfactory answer. Belief that 'multiplication makes things larger' might lead to a reasoned solution of 0.6 for 0.3 × 0.2; however, it may also be the case that the pupil simply ignored the decimal point in their calculation. Corresponding errors occur with the belief that division makes things smaller (e.g. 12 ÷ 0.6 = 0.2; Graeber and Tirosh, 1990). Unless the reasons for errors are explored, the underlying misconception may remain.

Some of the clear implications from the research in this area are that the teaching of decimals is challenging and teaching directed to overcome misconceptions is necessary. It is not helpful to have a staged introduction (such as by dealing with numbers with one place of decimals first, then two places) as this may avoid rather than confront errors. As the causes of pupils' misunderstandings are complex and diverse, it is essential that learners are asked to explain their thinking and reasoning so that the causes of their difficulties can be identified and addressed (Ryan and Williams, 2007). However, in what follows in this chapter, we will try and specifically address the areas of misconceptions highlighted above, namely the meaning of the decimal point, the ordering of decimals and operations with decimals. We will do this by drawing on different representations for decimals and reasoning with these.

What are decimals?

We saw in Chapter 2 that our number system is a base-10 system, where as we move from column to column to the left, we go up in powers of ten. For example, see the number 273 in Figure 6.1. Conversely, if we move to the right through the columns, then we are dividing by ten each time. Moving right from the hundreds, we divide by 10 to get tens. Moving right from tens, we divide by 10 to get ones. What would therefore happen if we moved right from the ones or units column? Well, if we divide one by ten, we get one tenth. Therefore, the position to the right of the ones would represent tenths. Moving to the right again, dividing tenths by ten would give us hundredths. So, two places to the right of the ones represents hundredths. And we could continue indefinitely to the right, as we could continue indefinitely to the left (see Figure 6.2).

2 hundreds   7 tens   3 ones

Figure 6.1 The base-10 number system

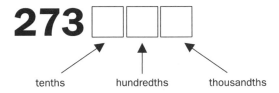

tenths   hundredths   thousandths

Figure 6.2 The decimal system

However, if we put numbers into those places, how would we know that there are tenths, hundredths, thousandths and so on? In other words, how would we keep track of the ones or units place? Historically, different approaches have been used to identify the ones place. Flegg (1983) provides the approaches seen in Figure 6.3 used by European mathematicians from the sixteenth century onwards. The position of the ones has been shown with a '0' over it with other numbers for the decimal numbers, or with lines, or with a point after it as we use today (in some European countries, a comma is used instead of a point). Therefore, in the way we use decimals today, we need to recognize that (a) the ones or units are positioned just to the left of the decimal point, and (b) the numbers after the decimal point become smaller by factors of ten as we move to the right, i.e. tenths, hundredths, thousandths and so on.

Therefore, we have an agreed symbolic way of representing decimals. However, what

> ### KEY POINT TO CONSIDER
>
> Decimals are the way in which fractional parts are represented within the place value system. The keys ways of looking at decimals are as a part of a unit, as a point on a number line and as a result of a division operation.

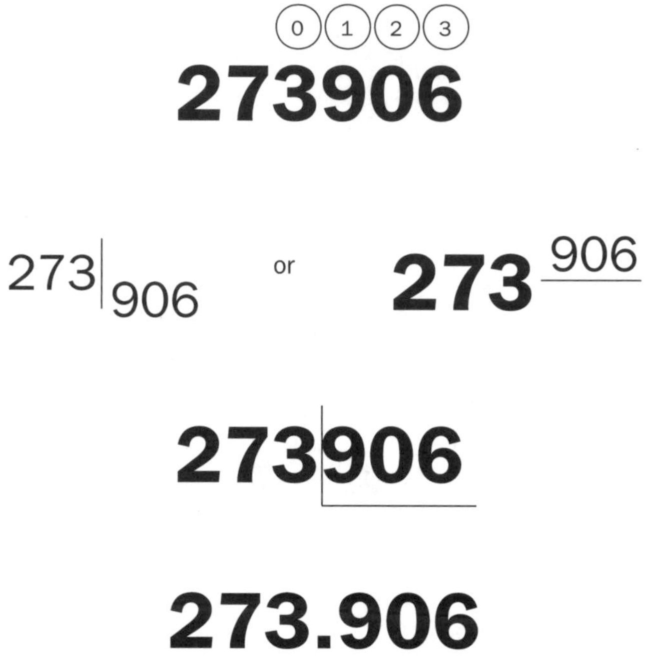

$$(0)(1)(2)(3)$$

273906

$$273 \Big| 906 \qquad \text{or} \qquad \mathbf{273}\frac{906}{}$$

273|906

273.906

Figure 6.3 Alternative representations for decimal numbers

do we actually mean by decimals? From the way that decimals are constructed we can see their relationship with fractions. In fact, the various meanings we highlighted for fractions in the last chapter also apply to decimals. The three main meanings we examined with relation to fractions were

- fractional measure;
- linear coordinates;
- quotient (i.e. an indicated division).

Dickson *et al.* (1984: 287) similarly highlighted the three main meanings of decimals to be (a) decimals as sub-areas of a unit region; (b) decimals as points on a number line; and (c) decimals as the results of a division operation. These are shown diagrammatically in Figure 6.4. From the diagrams, we can clearly see the different meanings for decimals. However, we discussed in the previous chapter that we can use continuous or discrete objects to represent fractions. The above diagrams, particularly (a) and (b), show more the continuous picture for decimals (i.e. a continuous object split into parts). Therefore, we might add a further meaning for decimals, involving discrete objects (see Figure 6.5). In particular with this last representation, but also with the part–whole picture given in (a), we can see that decimals can also be used to describe proportions as we did with fractions and percentages. In fact, we will examine the equivalence of fractions, percentages and decimals a little later on.

It is, however, informative to consider a little further the continuous view of decimals. Looking at the number line representation in (b), what would happen if we

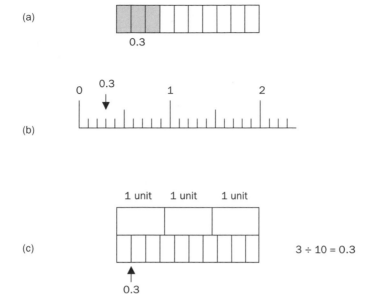

(a)

(b)

(c)

Figure 6.4 Meanings of decimal numbers

0.3

Figure 6.5 Discrete meaning of decimal numbers

shifted the arrow slightly, by one tenth of the separation between marks? What number would that represent? Magnifying the above picture gives us Figure 6.6. The separation between the large marks is 0.1 or a tenth. Therefore, one tenth of this separation will be a hundredth or 0.01. So the arrow will have moved an additional

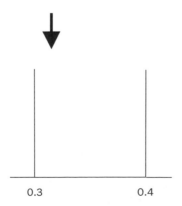

Figure 6.6 Magnifying the number line of the linear scale

distance of 0.01 from a position of 0.3 to a new position of 0.31. Alternatively, if we had moved an even smaller distance of one hundredth of the division between the marks, this would have resulted in an additional distance of 0.001 from the original position of 0.3 to a new position of 0.301. What do we notice from this? First of all, 0.31 is bigger than 0.301 because we have added a distance of 0.01 (one hundredth) rather 0.001 (one thousandth). Second, we could have moved as small a distance as we wished – there is no limit to how small this could have been. This 'number density' property of the number line emphasizes the continuous nature of decimals, and more generally our number system. Third, when we wrote 0.3, we could have specified that this contained no hundredths or thousandths, i.e. we could have written 0.300. However, we imply by leaving these further zeros out that there are no more smaller increments to consider. Some of the common numbers that we come across everyday in fact have no end to their decimals, for example, π (pi) or the square root of 2.

$$\pi = 3.14159265358979323846264338327950288419\ldots$$
$$\sqrt{2} = 1.41421356237309504880168872420969807856967\ldots$$

These are called irrational numbers because they cannot be written as fractions. (Even very small numbers such as 0.0000000001 can be written as the fraction 1 over 10,000,000,000.) There are 'decimals without end' which can be written as fractions, such as 0.333333 ... (1 over 3). Even with decimal numbers that do end, we sometimes want to shorten them to a more convenient form. We do this by 'rounding' the numbers. If we wanted to round 0.31 to the nearest tenth, or in other words to one decimal place, we need to decide which tenth value we are nearest to. Clearly, we are nearest to 0.3 so 0.31 rounded to one decimal place is 0.3. If we had 0.367, this would be rounded up to 0.37 if we wanted to express it to two decimal places, or 0.4 if we wanted to express it to one decimal place. If we have exactly 0.35, and wanted to round to the nearest tenth, the convention when we are exactly in the middle is to always round up. So, 0.35 would become 0.4 to one decimal place.

How can we represent decimals?

Let us consider further the different ways in which we can represent decimals. We have already seen some examples in the previous section, and we can draw out more examples from the research literature. Dickson et al. (1984) highlighted two further representations for decimals, the volume representation and the area representation (see Figure 6.7). These are extensions to the Dienes blocks representations used in Chapter 3 to explicitly represent the place value system, and here we use them for decimal numbers. This time, the block in the volume representation represents a '1', as does the large square in the area representation. As we step down through the decimals, the part of the representation is one tenth of the size of the previous part (i.e. the 0.1 representation is one tenth in size compared to the 1 representation).

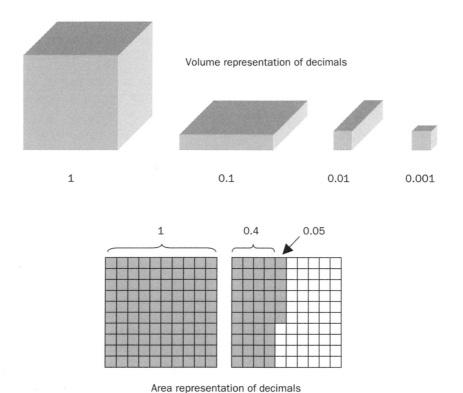

Figure 6.7 The volume and area representations of decimals

The above representations make clear the place value property of decimals. However, we must be aware again that they also have their limitations in displaying the properties of decimals:

A single material may not represent well all features of decimals but rather may capture only particular features. Some materials may represent effectively the discrete side of decimals, whereas others may represent the continuous side. For example, the discrete features of decimals can be represented by base-10 blocks . . . the continuous features of decimals can be represented by a number line.

(Hiebert *et al.*, 1991)

Here, the discrete property is not about discrete objects as we highlighted above. Rather, in representing a decimal with so many tenths, hundredths and so on, we split up the decimal into discrete chunks. Another alternative representation for decimals, to try and represent both their continuous and discrete properties, was put forward by Stacey *et al.* (2001). They advocated the use of 'linear arithmetic blocks'. Essentially,

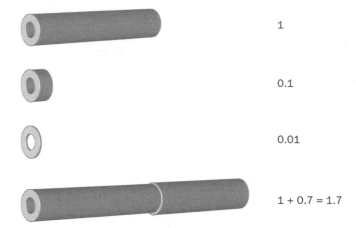

1

0.1

0.01

1 + 0.7 = 1.7

Figure 6.8 Linear arithmetic blocks representations of decimals

these are lengths of tubing, cut to the appropriate size to represent different decimals. Pieces can be cut to give certain decimal representations, for example 0.7 in the bottom picture. By putting them together, they form a linear representation for decimal numbers rather like the number line. Also, like the number line, Stacey and her colleagues felt that these linear arithmetic blocks would be better for illustrating ideas such as number density and rounding. Therefore, whether we choose one representation or different representations, the important thing is that we recognize the different properties of decimals and communicate these in our teaching.

Equivalence to fractions and percentages

> **KEY POINT TO CONSIDER**
>
> All decimals can be symbolically represented as the sum of a set of fractions.

Of course, another representation for decimals would be as other forms of rational number, namely fractions and percentages. This equivalence is useful for when we come to consider how we can carry out operations with decimals. We can move directly from decimals to fractions using the place value property:

$$3.142 = 3 + \frac{1}{10} + \frac{4}{100} + \frac{2}{1000}$$

Using equivalent fractions to add together the fractions:

$$3 + \frac{1}{10} + \frac{4}{100} + \frac{2}{1000} = 3 + \frac{100}{1000} + \frac{40}{1000} + \frac{2}{1000} = 3\frac{142}{1000}$$

Alternatively, we could have recognized that the decimal 0.142 was 142 thousandths using the place value properties. Therefore, because of the base-10 system, when we convert from decimals to fractions, we obtain a fraction with a denominator that is a power of 10. If we wish to do the reverse and convert from fractions to decimals, we need to use equivalent fractions to again obtain a fraction with a denominator that is a power of 10. For example, for $\frac{3}{16}$:

$$\frac{3}{16} = \frac{30}{160} = \frac{15}{80} = \frac{150}{800} = \frac{75}{400} = \frac{750}{4000} = \frac{375}{2000} = \frac{3750}{20000} = \frac{1875}{10000}$$

This is a complicated example, and we have gone through a series of equivalent fractions, multiplying top and bottom by ten, then dividing top and bottom by two in order for the denominator to approach a power of 10. Therefore, $\frac{3}{16}$ in decimals is 0.1875 (we can see that the last decimal starts in the ten thousandth place).

With percentages, things are a little more straightforward because a percentage is easily converted to a fraction with a denominator of 100 (a power of 10 already). Therefore, the decimal 0.175 is $\frac{175}{1000}$ or $\frac{17.5}{100}$ if we divide top and bottom by ten. Therefore, 0.175 is 17.5%. Going the other way from percentages to decimals, 12.5%, for example, is $\frac{12.5}{100}$ or $\frac{125}{1000}$ which is 0.125.

Operating on decimals

Let us now concentrate on how we can carry out operations on decimal numbers. Essentially there are two ways in which we can do this. First, we can regard decimals as a form of fractions, and by converting decimals into fractions, undertake all operations as fractions. This is discussed above and in Chapter 5. The other way of looking at operations with decimals is to see them as extensions of the number system and so we need to see how we

> **KEY POINT TO CONSIDER**
>
> If we view decimals as an extension of the whole number system then we can illustrate all the operations (addition, subtraction, multiplication and division) using the same representations that we used for operating with whole numbers.

can use the same representations that we used for whole numbers with decimals. We will begin by considering addition and subtraction, and then move on to multiplication and division.

Addition and subtraction of decimals

One of the visual representations that we used for adding and subtracting numbers was the number line. The number line in Figure 6.9 has been split into intervals of 0.1 and shows the addition 0.5 + 1.4 = 1.9. Using the number line in its 'empty' format as well, we can also explore the methods used for whole numbers and apply them to decimals. For example,

+0.5 +0.9

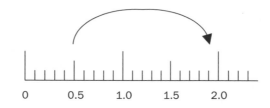

0   0.5   1.0   1.5   2.0

Figure 6.9 $0.5 + 1.4 = 1.9$

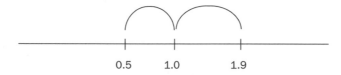

0.5   1.0   1.9

Figure 6.10 Bridging through the nearest unit

Here, we have added up to the nearest unit, then added the rest. Other methods are possible. If we have numbers with units and tenths, for addition we can:

- split both numbers and then add the units, add the tenths and then combine;
- keep one of the numbers unchanged and then add on the other using:
  ○ add tenths and then units;
  ○ add units and then tenths;
  ○ add nearest whole number and compensate.

For subtraction:

- counting back
  ○ units then tenths;
  ○ overjump and compensate;
  ○ to previous unit.
- counting on
  ○ units then tenths;
  ○ overjump and compensate;
  ○ to next unit.

In other words, we can explore all the methods that we worked on with whole numbers but now extend our work into decimals.

We can also draw on other visual representations. For example, we used Dienes blocks to illustrate the addition and subtraction of whole numbers incorporating place value. We can do the same here for decimals. Taking the example of $2.46 - 1.53$, we start with the representation for 2.46 (see Figure 6.11). From this we can take away three hundredths, however, we have to convert a unit into tenths so that we can subtract the required number of tenths. We can therefore represent 2.46 as in Figure 6.12. Now subtracting 1.53 (i.e. 3 hundredths, 5 tenths and 1 unit) leaves 0.93, as shown in Figure 6.13. Therefore, $2.46 - 1.53$ is 0.93 (9 tenths and 3 hundredths).

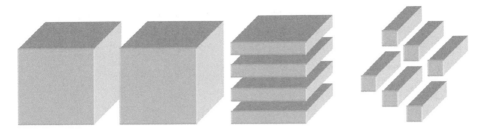

Figure 6.11 2.46 in the volume representation

Figure 6.12 Converting a unit into tenths

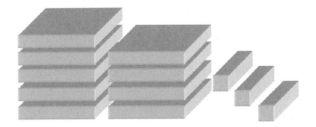

Figure 6.13 0.93 in the volume representation

As with whole numbers, we can represent this in a symbolic form. Using the vertical format for subtraction:

$$
\begin{aligned}
2.46 &= & 2 + 0.4 + 0.06 &= 1 + 1.4 + 0.06 \\
- 1.53 &= & -1 + 0.5 + 0.03 & -1 + 0.5 + 0.03 \\
& & & 0 + 0.9 + 0.03 = 0.93
\end{aligned}
$$

Likewise, a similar addition calculation would be:

$$
\begin{aligned}
3.75 &= & 3 + 0.7 + 0.05 \\
+ 2.6 &= & +2 + 0.6 \\
& & 5 + 1.3 + 0.05 = 6 + 0.3 + 0.05 = 6.35
\end{aligned}
$$

As for whole numbers, this extended number format makes clear the size of the numbers we are dealing with each time, whether units, tenths and so on. We can make this more concise:

$$
\begin{array}{r}
{}^{1}\cancel{2}.{}^{1}46 \\
-\ 1.53 \\
\hline
0.93
\end{array}
\qquad
\begin{array}{r}
3.75 \\
+\ {}_{1}2.6 \\
\hline
6.35
\end{array}
$$

However, in this concise vertical format, we have to make sure that we align the units with the units, the tenths with the tenths and so on. This can be problematic if the numbers in the calculation have different numbers of decimals after the point.

Multiplication and division

With multiplication, we used the array as a visual representation for helping us to understand the operation with whole numbers. With decimals, with the unit parts and the fraction part, this visual method might be more complicated to use. However, a more concise summary for what we did in the array was the grid method. Let us explore this representation.

The grid method allowed us to make explicit the distributive law of splitting up the numbers we were multiplying. Figure 6.14 shows what 25.2×0.35 would become. Now before we multiply each part, what do we mean when we multiply say 0.3 by 20? Well, we are wanting 20 lots of 0.3 or $\frac{3}{10}$ or 3 tenths. Therefore, this would be 60 tenths or 6 units. What, though, is 0.3 times 0.2? In terms of fractions, it is $\frac{3}{10}$ times $\frac{2}{10}$, which is $\frac{6}{100}$. It may be better to refer to our knowledge of fractions to carry out the multiplication (see Figure 6.15). Totalling up the grid, we have 75 tenths (7 units and 5 tenths), 131 hundredths (1 unit, 3 tenths and 1 hundredth) and 10 thousandths (1 hundredth). Therefore, $25.2 \times 0.35 = 8.82$.

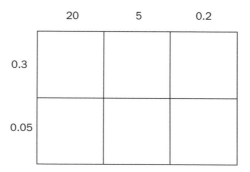

Figure 6.14 Multiplying decimals using the grid method

	20	5	$\frac{2}{10}$
$\frac{3}{10}$	$\frac{60}{10}$	$\frac{15}{10}$	$\frac{6}{100}$
$\frac{5}{100}$	$\frac{100}{100}$	$\frac{25}{100}$	$\frac{10}{1000}$

Figure 6.15 Converting to fractions in the grid method

Although we can see clearly what we are doing, this is a rather convoluted way of doing multiplication. However, we can still use the multiplication of fractions in another way. 25.2 in fractions is $25\frac{2}{10}$ or $\frac{252}{10}$ and 0.35 is $\frac{35}{100}$. Therefore 25.2×0.35 is $\frac{252}{10} \times \frac{35}{100}$. Using the rule that we developed for multiplying fractions, we can now multiply the numerators and denominators separately, which only involves whole numbers. Therefore:

$$\frac{252}{10} \times \frac{35}{100} = \frac{8820}{1000} = 8.820 \text{ or } 8.82$$

This method of multiplying decimals is sometimes summarized as a rule: 'ignore the decimal point, multiply the numbers as whole numbers, then put back the number of decimal points that you ignored'. However, explicitly doing the multiplication as fractions explains why this process works – the 'putting back the decimal places' is equivalent to converting back from the fraction that you end up with.

Likewise, we can use fractions to carry out division with decimals. If we have $57.7 \div 1.28$, as fractions this becomes $\frac{577}{10} \div \frac{128}{100}$. Using the rule that we previously derived for dividing fractions.

$$\frac{577}{10} \div \frac{128}{100} = \frac{5770}{100} \div \frac{128}{100} = \frac{5770}{128}$$

Once again, using fractions, we have ended up with a calculation without decimals (treating the resulting fraction as a quotient or a division). Now we can use the same methods as before for whole numbers (e.g. repeated subtraction) to calculate the answer:

$$
\begin{array}{r|l}
 & 5770 \\
10 & -\ 1280 \\
\hline
 & 4490 \\
10 & -\ 1280 \\
\hline
 & 3210 \\
10 & -\ 1280 \\
\hline
 & 1930 \\
10 & -\ 1280 \\
\hline
 & 650 \\
5 & -\ 640 \\
\hline
 & 10
\end{array}
$$

$57.7 \div 1.28$ is therefore $45\ \dfrac{10}{128}$. We could have done the repeated subtraction with decimals in place, however, not needing to consider the decimals makes the process easier.

Communicating decimals

Decimals, as we have seen, are closely related to fractions as a means of describing a part–whole relationship, therefore children also have to grapple with the language associated with fractions. In addition to this, decimals are also closely related to our knowledge and understanding of place value and therefore the language associated with place value has to be developed accordingly.

Decimals are an extension of place value, with a point indicating the transition from units to tenths. Therefore, it is important for children to recognize the meaning of the point; perhaps 'marker' is a better word to introduce to identify where decimals begin. Earlier we introduced alternative ways of representing the 'decimal point' – perhaps discussion of these methods serves to highlight the use of the point. On top of this, it is crucial that language is related to place value (tenths/hundredths) so that children develop real flexibility in reading and understanding decimals. For example, one problem that children face is that in our number system and place value, large numbers have names but fractional ones do not:

2	spoken as	two
48	spoken as	forty-eight
673	spoken as	six hundred and seventy-three
6.73	spoken as	six point seven three (we would not say six point seven tenths and three thousandths)
8.42	spoken as	eight point four two (we would not say eight point forty-two)

Instead, we depend on children understanding that each digit in the decimal places is ten times larger than the same digit on its right and ten times smaller than the one on its left. The language is not directly associated with place value, although decimals are clearly an extension of the place value system. This 'gap' between language and content needs addressing in lesson design, and sufficient time allocated for children to become confident and fluent when discussing decimals. In particular, children should be provided with plenty of opportunities to demonstrate their sound knowledge and understanding of decimals and place value, since such understanding is crucial before they move on to calculations involving decimals. This, therefore, highlights the importance of using a range of activities which promote children's understanding of decimals. For example, see Activities 6.1 and 6.2.

Activity 6.1 Dice decimals

Throw five dice and make the largest or smallest number:

	Hundreds	Tens	Units	Tenths	Hundredths
Player 1					
Player 2					
Player 3					

Now repeat by throwing a die five times. What strategies might be employed in order to make the highest possible number?

Activity 6.2 Decimal values

Prepare a set of number cards, choose a card at random and discuss the value of each highlighted digit:

42**5**.67   425.**6**7

Moving on to operations with decimals, to some extent addition and subtraction calculations can be relatively straightforward with decimals, with children using the place value structure to help them in vertical calculations. Once again, though, we would advocate the use of other representations such as the number line or extended number notation so that understanding of the structure of decimals is enhanced. Multiplication and division, however, are more complex, and children face the same conceptual difficulties with these operations as they faced for fractions. A problem for many children occurs when dealing with multiplication calculations, when the operation results in a smaller

KEY POINT TO CONSIDER

As with other areas of mathematics, there is a language which the learner needs to understand in order that aspects of decimals can be discussed. Representations are again a key focus for developing this discussion.

product. Children will be very familiar with the concept that when using the × sign numbers get bigger, but when multiplying decimals children are expected to accommodate a new definition that produces a smaller result. In addition, thinking of multiplication as 'repeated addition' does not make sense for a calculation such as 0.4×0.3. Likewise, what does $0.4 \div 0.3$ mean in the context of grouping or sharing? Therefore, with both multiplication and division of decimals, it is important to create problems which both demonstrate and explain these operations, rather than just teaching the rules and merely providing numerous examples to practise these same rules. For example, a series of questions might be as shown in Activity 6.3.

Activity 6.3 Decimal discussion

Show pupils $$6 \div 0.3$$ on a large card?

Ask the pupils what it means to them and compile a set of possible meanings to discuss.

Can we draw a picture of this statement?

Can we write it in a different way using fractions?

How would we work out the answer?

Finally, being able to discuss and work with decimals in this way also implies the ability to work with different formats for rational numbers, for example decimals, fractions and also percentages. It is therefore important to highlight the connections between these and provide a range of activities that make these connections so that children develop fluency and flexibility with these rational numbers. It is also important that neither fractions, nor decimals or percentages are perceived as new systems with new languages, but rather are all part of this concept of rational numbers. For example, the game of 'Snap' provides practice for equivalent fractions, decimals and percentages, or domino games may be played which link decimals and fractions (the same games can be extended to include percentages). See Activity 6.4 for a dominos game.

It is interesting to note that the National Assessment of Educational Progress (NAEP) in America found that most students' knowledge and confidence in this area of mathematics was limited: they could identify decimals and percentages, but not use them effectively in problem solving. As a result, the National Council of Teachers of Mathematics called for students to be provided with many more opportunities to work flexibly with fractions, decimals and percentages, and for teachers to emphasize the connection and importance of teaching the relevant concepts in tandem (Martinez and Martinez, 2007).

Activity 6.4 Rational number dominos

Prepare a set of domino cards as in example below:

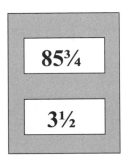

As the pupils play the game note how they decide on equivalence. Note important linguistic aspects of their thinking.

Questions for discussion

1   What are the key representations for decimals? How do these representations help in developing understanding of decimals and operations with decimals? What different concepts do the representations convey?

2   How can the use of different representations for decimals be incorporated into a clear progression for teaching the addition and subtraction of decimals?

3   Adapt the Gelosia method for multiplication (see Chapter 4) for decimals. Explain why this method works for decimals.

4   What real-life situations might involve division by decimals? Can we gain more understanding by considering the meaning of these situations? How does this meaning relate to possible ways of approaching division by fractions? What ways of doing division by fractions can you think of, other than that already given in the chapter?

7

Representing patterns of numbers

Over the preceding chapters, we have progressed step-by-step through the concept of number, the different types of number that there are and different operations that can be carried out on numbers. But we are only just halfway through this book! What is there left to consider with respect to primary or elementary mathematics? Of course, we have not yet examined topics such as shape and space, data handling and measurement, and we will cover these in subsequent chapters. However, these topics seem to be quite different to what we have covered before. Why are seemingly diverse topics such as number and shape included within the subject of mathematics?

The answer lies in what we mean by mathematics. All too often, mathematics is seen solely as the manipulation of number. However, mathematicians have a far broader view of the subject: 'Mathematics is the science of patterns' (Devlin, 1994: 3). Shape and space, or geometry, therefore involve looking for patterns within shapes. We will view data handling and measurement as ways of categorizing and looking for patterns within our physical world. Likewise, we can look at numbers and investigate the patterns that exist within these.

In a sense, then, looking for patterns within numbers is more mathematical than simply applying rules to numbers. There is also a specific benefit to looking at number patterns. Researchers have identified that exploring number patterns can be a way of introducing algebra to pupils:

> There is the notion of an inherent worth in the activity, where the thinking involved in doing repeated patterns leads on in some way to more advanced ideas. It is mostly in the area of algebra (or 'pre-algebra') that repeating pattern work is seen as a conceptual stepping stone, rather than just a teaching opportunity.
>
> (Threlfall, 1999: 21–2)

It is also a way of making algebra more relevant to pupils: 'Involving students in exploratory activities that bring algebra into the "real world" is clearly preferable to staying with more traditional, abstract approaches' (English and Warren, 1998: 170).

Because this book is focused upon primary or elementary mathematics, we will not focus upon algebra *per se*. Rather, we will include algebra as one of the ways in which we can represent number patterns, so we too can make sense of algebra by exploring practical examples.

Misconceptions with patterns

At a fundamental level, the concept of a 'pattern' is a challenging one. Young children think of a design or a picture ('that wallpaper has a nice pattern') without understanding that, in mathematics, it relates to the way items are repeated or the sequence that is produced by the repeating pattern. Radford (2003) describes how a young learner defended the way she continued the picture sequence shown in Figure 7.1. It was clear that she considered the first two terms together. In this case you have $(1 \times 4) + 1$ small squares (five in total) and because, according to her, this rule applies to term 3 (where you have $(2 \times 4) + 1$ or 9 in total), then in the next term you will have $(3 \times 4) + 1$ small squares or 13 in total as shown in the figure, in the following term you will have $(4 \times 4) + 1$ and so on. She provided a logical explanation, but it was based on a misreading of the presentation of the task.

Similarly one of the authors investigated children's explanations of the continuation of following colour pattern with cubes 'red, blue, red ...' as *either* 'red, blue, red, blue, red, blue', etc., *or* as 'red, blue, red, red, blue, red, red, blue, red', etc. Without defining the size of the unit of the pattern, both solutions are possible. One child (playfully) tried 'red, blue, red, white, red, blue, red, white, red, blue, red, white', etc., arguing that the instructions did not say the pattern was complete! The problem again lay in not recognizing what was being repeated in the task. Other kinds of misconceptions with patterns relate to the same kinds of issues that we have seen in other chapters. Learners will overgeneralize their previous knowledge (such as by assuming a number sequence is of a particular kind, for example when encountering geometric sequences with a common ratio rather than arithmetical sequences with a common difference).

With algebra, most students' errors and misconceptions relate to their difficulties

> ### KEY POINT TO CONSIDER
>
> The exact nature of a repeated pattern is important for defining the pattern. It is therefore essential that children examine carefully the way in which the pattern or sequence is produced.

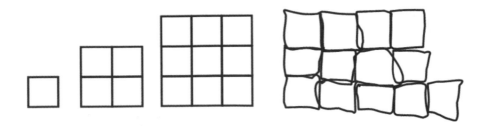

Figure 7.1 An example of a continued sequence given by a child

and misinterpretation of symbolic notations used in the secondary mathematics curriculum (see Kieran, 1989; Leinhardt *et al.*, 1990; and Stacey and MacGregor, 1997). Many of the challenges and problems may be a result of the range of meanings or roles that the same symbol has within algebraic notation. Where a letter such as 'x' is used to denote an unknown, pupils' first experience is usually that it denotes a single quantity (such as the length of the side of a rectangle). Subsequently however, it is often used to denote a variable or a function where its value changes. There is also evidence that some children also believe that letters (p, q, etc.) always stand for the same number, analogous to an alphanumeric code where numbers are substituted for letters.

KEY POINT TO CONSIDER

The equals sign represents equivalence. In order to develop a deeper understanding of algebra, it is important that this concept is clearly emphasized in our teaching.

Some problems clearly relate to pupils' understanding of the '=' symbol (Behr *et al.* 1980; Falkner *et al.*, 1999). The idea that it represents equivalence or a balance between both sides of the equal sign is not usually recognized by older primary or elementary school pupils – it is usually seen as an instruction to perform an operation. This clearly has consequences for understanding algebra with older students.

From looking at the misconceptions, we can say that two issues emerge – we need to ensure that children become familiar with working with patterns, and also that they begin to understand the use of letters in mathematics. We will try and address both issues in the following discussion.

Types of number patterns

Let us look first of all at some of the different types of number patterns that pupils can come across in primary or elementary school. As mentioned in the quote above from Threlfall (1999), the use of repeating patterns can be carried out with younger children in order to develop more advanced ideas (see Figure 7.2). The top example of a pattern of squares is indeed taken from Threlfall (1999). As we can see, this is not a number pattern at all, but of course, repeating patterns can be carried out with

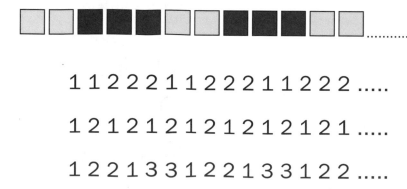

1 1 2 2 1 1 2 2 2 1 1 1 2 2 2 .....

1 2 1 2 1 2 1 2 1 2 1 2 1 2 1 .....

1 2 2 1 3 3 1 2 2 1 3 3 1 2 2 .....

Figure 7.2 Examples of repeating patterns

colours, letters, shapes, sounds and so on, as well as numbers. The repeating patterns can have different levels of complexity: for example, we would expect a pattern with alternating numbers to be easier to recognize as a repeating pattern, compared with a pattern with a larger portion that is being repeated.

Specifically within their work with numbers, primary children are introduced to a range of patterns which we hope as teachers they come to recognize. Frobisher (1999) and Frobisher and Threlfall (1999) provide the patterns in Figure 7.3. These are associated with patterns in multiples of number (with the odd numbers being those that are not multiples of 2). The patterns might be relatively straight forward as in the 10 times table, or more complex as in the 9 times table. We can view these patterns visually using representations such as the hundred square.

There are other visual representations of number that we can draw on. There are 'square' numbers, 'triangular' numbers and 'rectangular' numbers (see Figure 7.4).

1	2	3	4	5	6	7	8	9	10
11	12	13	14	15	16	17	18	19	20
21	22	23	24	25	26	27	28	29	30
31	32	33	34	35	36	37	38	39	40
41	42	43	44	45	46	47	48	49	50
51	52	53	54	55	56	57	58	59	60
61	62	63	64	65	66	67	68	69	70
71	72	73	74	75	76	77	78	79	80
81	82	83	84	85	86	87	88	89	90
91	92	93	94	95	96	97	98	99	100

Even and odd numbers

$1 \times 5 = 5$	$1 \times 10 = 10$	$1 \times 9 = 9$
$2 \times 5 = 10$	$2 \times 10 = 20$	$2 \times 9 = 18$
$3 \times 5 = 15$	$3 \times 10 = 30$	$3 \times 9 = 27$
$4 \times 5 = 20$	$4 \times 10 = 40$	$4 \times 9 = 36$
$5 \times 5 = 25$	$5 \times 10 = 50$	$5 \times 9 = 45$
$6 \times 5 = 30$	$6 \times 10 = 60$	$6 \times 9 = 54$
$7 \times 5 = 35$	$7 \times 10 = 70$	$7 \times 9 = 63$
$8 \times 5 = 40$	$8 \times 10 = 80$	$8 \times 9 = 72$
$9 \times 5 = 45$	$9 \times 10 = 90$	$9 \times 9 = 81$
$10 \times 5 = 50$	$10 \times 10 = 100$	$10 \times 9 = 90$
$11 \times 5 = 55$	$11 \times 10 = 110$	
$12 \times 5 = 60$	$12 \times 10 = 120$	

Patterns in the times tables

Figure 7.3 Repeating patterns in a number square and in times tables

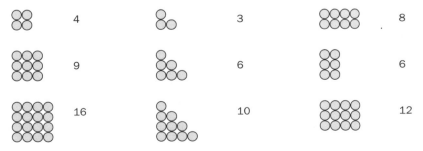

Figure 7.4 Square, triangular and rectangular numbers

The square and triangular numbers are part of a greater range of visual patterns used to represent particular sequences of numbers. See Figure 7.5 for examples from Orton *et al.* (1999). These patterns are visual sequences, often referred to as matchstick sequences, and are examples of the 'real world' patterns referred to by English and Warren (1998) in the introduction to this chapter. If we count the matchsticks, we get the number sequences 4, 8, 12 . . ., 4, 7, 10 . . ., and 3, 5, 7 . . . respectively. These are examples of 'linear sequences' where the same amount is added or taken away each time. We can also have sequences where the amount added or taken away changes in a regular manner. For example, 3, 5, 9, 17, 33 . . . We could carry out other operations on the numbers, or combine previous parts of the sequence in a regular manner. The most famous example of the latter is the Fibonacci sequence:

1, 1, 2, 3, 5, 8, 13, 21, 34, 55, 89, 144 . . .

In this sequence, for each step in the pattern, the two previous numbers are added together.

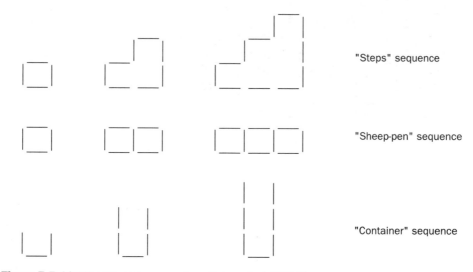

"Steps" sequence

"Sheep-pen" sequence

"Container" sequence

Figure 7.5 Matchstick sequences from Orton *et al.* (1999).

Representing number patterns

Let us now re-examine the above patterns by considering how else we could represent them. Beginning with the first repeating pattern of squares that we gave earlier, we could put the pattern into words. For example:

Two grey squares, followed by three black squares. Then two grey squares, followed by three black squares again. Two grey squares . . .

A more concise description of the pattern would be:

Two grey squares and three black squares; this being repeated over and over.

So what have we developed here? We have not only developed a concise description of the pattern, but we have also put forward a rule or a **generalization** (i.e. the overall property of the pattern). It is this identification of rules and the ability to generalize more abstract properties from the pattern that Threlfall (1999) identifies as conceptual developments that can occur with young children working with repeating patterns. The example is given of different ways to answer 'What colour would the 25th square be?' A basic 'procedural' approach to solving this would be to go through the squares one by one (Two grey squares, followed by three black squares. Then two grey squares . . .) A child with an understanding of the abstract rule or concept behind the pattern would use the repeating block of five, and realize that the twenty-fifth square would be the last of the repeating block of five, i.e. a black square.

Therefore, an important representation of the repeating pattern is a generalized rule, and we can look for the same in the other number patterns. In the multiplication tables, the 5-times table gives an answer which ends in 0 or 5, alternating between them. The answers to the 10-times table always end in 0. In the 9-times table, as we move up through it, the units in the answers go down by 1 each time, but the number in the tens column goes up by 1 each time. This rule only applies up to 9×10. In the number shapes, taking the triangular numbers as a specific example, the pattern of numbers go as 1, 1 + 2, 1 + 2 + 3, etc., so we are successively adding the next largest integer with each step of the sequence.

Likewise, with the matchstick sequences, we can look for the rules that lead us from one step of each sequence to the next:

Steps sequence – add 4 each time
Sheep-pen sequence – start with 4 and add 3 each time
Container sequence – start with 3 and add 2 each time.

Taking the container sequence as an example, the third number in the sequence would be $3 + 2 + 2 = 7$; the seventh number in the sequence would be $3 + 2 + 2 + 2 + 2 + 2 + 2 = 15$. Now, what would be the one hundredth number in the sequence? We could simply use the above rule and start with 3 and keep adding 2 until we get to the one hundredth number. This is what we call a 'recursive' approach, recursive meaning using a procedure that just repeats itself (i.e. the adding of the 2). The above is therefore a 'recursive rule' for solving the problem. Alternatively however, you may have already spotted another pattern to the sequence. This is:

3rd number – start with 3 and add 2 lots of 2
7th number – start with 3 and add 6 lots of 2.

Therefore, the one hundredth number would be 'start with 3 and add 99 lots of 2'. This would be $3 + 99 \times 2 = 201$. We have therefore obtained a more 'general rule' (as it is termed) which allows us to 'jump' straight to the number in the sequence that we want, without going through the recursive process. Therefore, with some number sequences, we can use different levels of generalization in order to represent the number pattern.

KEY POINT TO CONSIDER

Children should be encouraged to see beyond the numbers and the pattern they present and start to look for the general rules. Using letters to represent variables is a powerful tool which allows us to express generalizations. The introduction of letters in algebra needs to be carefully designed to develop children's understanding of the use of letters in algebraic notation.

A further step that we might take is to introduce the idea of a variable through the **investigation** of number patterns. A variable is an unspecified element, and is identified by English and Warren (1998: 166) as 'fundamental to our students' understanding of algebra'. The variable is introduced into our number pattern work by asking the question 'What would be the nth number in the sequence?' The n here represents an unspecified part of the sequence. However, going back to our previous example of the container sequence, whatever step in the sequence n might be, the general rule would be 'start with 3 and add $n - 1$ lots of 2'. More symbolically,

$$n\text{th number} = 3 + (n - 1) \times 2$$

If we wanted to calculate a particular number in the sequence, say the seventy-third number, then we would replace n with 73. Therefore, we have arrived at a general, symbolic representation for this particular number pattern, concisely and usefully summarizing the properties of the number sequence.

Reasoning with number patterns

The ability to find general rules is therefore a development in our mathematical thinking from simply carrying out calculations, and the variable is a powerful tool to enable us to express these general rules. It also enables us to 'prove' properties of number patterns. In this section, we give some examples where reasoning with number patterns enables us to do this.

Let us first of all go back and look at odd and even numbers. We previously expressed these number patterns in the form of a hundred square. However, how else could we show this? For even numbers, the number pattern is 2, 4, 6, 8 . . . A general way of writing this using a variable would be $2n$. This means that when n is 1 (first term in the sequence), then the number in the sequence is 2. When $n = 2$, the number in the sequence is 4, and so on. This way of writing an even number also shows that we can always divide an even number exactly by 2. Now, if we were to add two even numbers together, we could write this generally as $2n + 2m$ (we have used different letters to show that n and m do not have to be the same, i.e. we can add two different even numbers). However, we can also see that:

$$2n + 2m = 2(n + m)$$

Taking the factor of 2 outside the brackets shows clearly that we can also always divide this sum exactly by 2. Therefore, we have shown (or proved) that adding two even numbers together always gives us a number divisible by 2 (i.e. another even number).

What about the odd numbers? If we define odd numbers as being an even number add 1, then a general way of writing an odd number would be $2n + 1$. (This would mean that the number pattern would be 3, 5, 7, 9 . . . Here, 1 is not included. To do so, we would have to extend the possible value of n so that it could be 0. We could even let n be a negative number which would start to include negative odd numbers). Adding two odd numbers would be:

$$2n + 1 + 2m + 1 = 2n + 2m + 2 = 2(n + m + 1)$$

Again, the resulting total is exactly divisible by two. So, when we add two odd numbers together, we can see that we get an even number, not another odd number.

We do not have to use variables for proof. Figures 7.6 and 7.7 are visual ways of proving the above two results, with Figure 7.6 providing a general way of showing an even and odd number visually. Adding two even numbers together or two odd numbers together gives visual proofs as seen in Figure 7.7. Both results can be divided exactly by two and are therefore even numbers.

Another proof is based on the triangular numbers. The triangular numbers we had before were 3, 6, 10 . . . A general way of expressing this pattern is $1 + 2 + 3 + . . . + n$, or adding consecutive numbers up to n. So, for the first step in the sequence, n would be 1, and the sum would just be 1. This is the number in the sequence before the 3. If n is 2, then the number in the sequence would be $1 + 2 = 3$. If n is 3, the number in the sequence is $1 + 2 + 3 = 6$ and so on (see Figure 7.8).

Even number   Odd number

Figure 7.6 Visual representations for even and odd numbers

Even number + Even number   Odd number + Odd number

Figure 7.7 Visual proofs for 'Even number + Even number' and 'Odd number + Odd number'

Figure 7.8 Sequence of triangular numbers

Now, what other general patterns can we discern with this sequence? If we 'play' with the visual sequence, one of the patterns we can find is that shown in Figure 7.9. What we have done here is doubled the triangular number each time. Therefore, for $n = 1$, we have 1×2; for $n = 2$, we have 2×3; for $n = 3$, we have 3×4; for $n = 4$, we have 4×5. You may have now noticed another general rule. When we double triangular numbers, we get $n \times (n + 1)$ for the nth triangular numbers. Taking into account the doubling, we can alternatively say that the nth triangular number is $\frac{1}{2} \times n \times (n + 1)$. As each triangular number is also all the positive integers added up to n, we also have the general rule that:

$$1 + 2 + 3 + \ldots + n = \frac{1}{2} \times n \times (n + 1)$$

Therefore, by looking at the pattern of triangular numbers, we have proved a general rule for quickly adding up the series, starting at one and ending at any given number n.

Flegg (1983) gives other historical examples from 'recreational mathematics' where reasoning with number patterns, or the use of variables, is required. He gives the example of the game 'Nim', where two players take it in turns to remove up to a specified number of matches from a pile. You lose the game if you are left to pick up on the last go. The strategy you adopt depends on the maximum number of matches you can pick up. Let us take the example where the maximum is 3 matches:

- If there is 1 match left for you, you have lost.
- If there are 2, 3 or 4 matches, you can pick up the appropriate number to leave one match for your opponent, therefore you win.
- If there are 5 matches, whatever you do, you will leave 2, 3 or 4 matches, therefore you lose.
- If there are 6, 7 or 8 matches, you can leave your opponent with 5, and therefore you win.
- If there are 9 matches, you have to leave your opponent with 6, 7 or 8, therefore you lose.
- And so on.

Figure 7.9 Doubling the triangular numbers

The pattern is therefore that you lose if there are 1, 5, 9 . . . matches. The general rule for this pattern is $4n + 1$. Now, what happens if you can pick up a maximum of 4 matches?

- If there is 1 match left for you, you have lost.
- If there are 2, 3 4 or 5 matches, you can pick up the appropriate number to leave one match for your opponent, therefore you win.
- If there are 6 matches, whatever you do, you will leave 2, 3 4 or 5 matches, therefore you lose.
- If there are 7, 8, 9 or 10 matches, you can leave your opponent with 6, and therefore you win.
- If there are 11 matches, you have to leave your opponent with 7, 8, 9 or 10 matches, therefore you lose.
- And so on.

This time, the general rule for when you lose is $5n + 1$. It seems that the general 'general' rule for the game of Nim is that you lose if there are $n(m + 1) + 1$ left, where m is the maximum number of matches you can pick up, and n is a whole number starting at zero.

There is another historical example about the Greek mathematician Diophantus, summarizing his life, which requires the use of a variable to solve it:

> God granted him to be a boy for the sixth part of his life, and adding a twelfth part (of his life) to this, He clothed his cheeks with down. He lit the light of wedlock after a seventh part (of his life), and five years after his marriage, he granted him a son. Alas! Late-born wretched child; after attaining a measure of half his father's life (in total), chill fate took him. After consoling his grief by this science of numbers for four years he ended his life.

Let us show how old this person was when they died. Let this age be n. The passage can be interpreted at follows:

1 Was a boy for $\frac{1}{6} n$ years;

2 Started growing whiskers after a further $\frac{1}{12} n$ years;

3 Got married after a further $\frac{1}{7} n$ years;

4 Had a son after a further 5 years;

5 The son died after a further $\frac{1}{2} n$ years;

6 Diophantus died after a further 4 years.

Therefore, the age (n) of Diophantus when he dies was:

$$n = \frac{1}{6}n + \frac{1}{12}n + \frac{1}{7}n + 5 + \frac{1}{2}n + 4$$

Adding the fractions of n and the numbers gives:

$$n = \frac{75}{84}n + 9$$

Subtracting $\frac{75}{84}n$ from both sides gives:

$$\frac{9}{84}n = 9$$

Therefore, n is 84. Diophantus seemingly lived to the age of 84.

Proof and Sudoku

In the previous section on reasoning with number patterns, we made some casual references to the fact that we had 'proved' some mathematical relationships. We will discuss briefly what we mean by proof and suggest a possible way of experiencing some of the methods of proof at primary or elementary school level.

Mason (2001), in trying to define what we mean by proof, also highlights the difficulty of doing so: 'What does "proof" mean in mathematics? A range of positions can be found amongst mathematicians, from formal and formalisable proof in the foundations of mathematics, to reasoning which convinces a community of mathematicians' (pp.13–14).

Nevertheless, in the United States, the NCTM's Principles and Standards for School Mathematics (NCTM, 2000) highlights the place of proof in school mathematics:

> Increasingly over the grades, students should learn to make effective deductive arguments as well, using the mathematical truths they are establishing in class. By the end of secondary school, students should be able to understand and produce some mathematical proofs – logically rigorous deductions of conclusions from hypotheses – and should appreciate the value of such arguments.'
>
> (p.57)

Clearly, we do not wish to cover in detail a topic that students will mainly be covering in secondary school. However, Hanna (2000: 7) has highlighted the general importance of pupils learning about proof:

> Clearly students ought to be taught the nature and standards of deductive reasoning, so that they can tell when a result has or has not been established. But

proof can make its greatest contribution in the classroom only when the teacher is able to use proofs that convey understanding.

The quote also highlights that proof should not simply be covered for the sake of it, but rather that to help build students' understanding in maths.

Given below are a number of methods of proof that are commonly used:

- Deductive proof;
- Proof by exhaustion;
- Proof by counter-example;
- Proof by contradiction.

Now, these methods may look very advanced for the primary or elementary level. However, we can use another example of recreational mathematics that has become very popular, namely Sudoku, to begin to talk about proof with pupils. The rules of Sudoku are simple. We have a 9×9 grid, divided into nine 3×3 grids, in which numbers are inserted into some of the squares. We have to place numbers in the remaining squares so that each row, column and 3×3 grid has the numbers 1 to 9 appearing once and only once in each

> ### KEY POINT TO CONSIDER
>
> Developing deductive reasoning skills is a key element in developing a greater understanding of mathematics. We should therefore try and include a range of experiences in our teaching within which children can start to formulate and develop explanations for conclusions that they have put forward.

case. Let us see how we can use each of the above methods of proof in tackling Sudoku problems.

Deductive proof

A first approach to finding the missing numbers is to use deductive proof. Deductive proof is where we progress from a given starting point through a series of logical steps to reach a particular conclusion. In the context of Sudoku, let us look at the example in Figure 7.10. We can deduce the positions of some more numbers, using the rules of

			1	5			7	
1		6				8	2	
3			8	6			4	
9			4			5	6	7
		4	7		8	3		
7	3	2			6			4
	4			8	1			9
	1	7				2		8
	5			3	7			

Figure 7.10 An example of a Sudoku puzzle

Sudoku and the position of the numbers already on the grid. For example, we see that there is a '1' in column 1 in the top 3×3 grid, and a '1' in column 2 in the bottom 3×3 grid. Because the rules of Sudoku mean that we must have each number once and only once in each column, and we must have each number once and only once in each 3×3 grid, that means that we must have a '1' in column 3 in the middle 3×3 grid. But there is only one available square in this column, in the fourth row from the top. Therefore, we have deduced that a '1' must be in this square (see Figure 7.11).

			1	5			7	
1		6				8	2	
3			8	6			4	
9		1	4			5	6	7
		4	7		8	3		
7	3	2			6			4
	4			8	1			9
	1	7				2		8
	5			3	7			

Figure 7.11 Deductive proof in Sudoku

Likewise, we know that there must be a '2' somewhere in the four available squares in the middle 3×3 grid on the right-hand side. We also know that it cannot be in the bottom row of the 3×3 grid, because there is already another '2' further along to the left in that row. Finally, we can also see that it cannot be the middle column in the 3×3 grid, because there is already '2' further up in that column. The '2' must therefore be in the available square in the left-hand-most column (see Figure 7.12).

			1	5			7	
1		6				8	2	
3			8	6			4	
9		1	4			5	6	7
		4	7		8	3		2
7	3	2			6			4
	4			8	1			9
	1	7				2		8
	5			3	7			

Figure 7.12 Another example of deductive proof in Sudoku

Proof by counter-example

This method of proof, although it may seem trivial, is the one we use all the time in Sudoku. Basically, we know *not* to put a number in a 3×3 grid, column or row because that number is already there. That proves, through that counter-example, that we cannot use that number again in that position. Proof by counter-example is an important part of proof in mathematics. For example, with the statement 'adding three odd numbers always gives a number divisible by three', we can immediately prove with a counter-example that this is not true, for example, $1 + 3 + 7 = 11$.

Proof by exhaustion

Proof by exhaustion involves trying out all the possibilities and checking that a counter-example does not exist. Here is an example of proof by exhaustion with Sudoku. Look at Figure 7.13. We will take the case of the square which is second from the left on the top row. We can see that 1 does not go there because it is in one of the nine squares around it, and the same argument goes for 2, 3 and 4 do not fit because they are on the same row; 5 and 6 do not fit because they are on the column; 7 is on the same row, as is 9. Therefore, by exhaustion, that only leaves 8.

9	?			3	4			7
		1	2			5		
	2						6	
3							7	
4				1				8
	5							9
	6						5	
		7			3	4		
5			8	9				6

Figure 7.13 Proof by exhaustion in Sudoku

Let us look at another example (Figure 7.14). If we look at the square where we have placed an '?', we can try all the possible numbers. It cannot be 1, 2, 3, 7 or 9 because they are all in the same column. It cannot be 6 or 8 because they are in the same row. That only leaves 5. Notice that for both examples, we could not deduce the results directly. Rather, proof by exhaustion has worked where deductive proof would not have.

9		7	2	8	4	6		
2		3	?	6				8
6			1	9		2		
		2				8		9
	3		7		9	1	6	2
		9			2	5		
3	2	8	4	5	6			1
7	9	6	3	2	1	4	8	5
		1	9	7	8	3	2	6

Figure 7.14 Another example of proof by exhaustion in Sudoku

Proof by contradiction

Proof by contradiction uses the principle that if we make an assumption about a situation, and subsequent deductive reasoning leads us to a contradiction, then the original assumption must have been incorrect. The following is an example of the use of proof by contradiction in Sudoku. First look at Figure 7.15. Because of the position of the 9s in rows 1 and 2, we know that a 9 must occur in columns 4, 5 or 6 in row 3. We can discount column 4 because we already have a 9 in that column. That leaves us with the two possibilities shown by the question marks. If we want to use proof by contradiction, we begin by assuming a result, and seeing whether this leads to a contradiction. Therefore, let us assume that the 9 in column 5 is correct. If this is the case, then the 9 in column 6 must be in row 5, as shown in Figure 7.16. Looking horizontally, the positions of the 9s in rows 4 and 5 mean that the 9 in row 6 must occur in columns 7 or 9. However, we already have 9s in columns 7 and 9! We therefore cannot place the 9s in either of these squares according to the rules of Sudoku. Therefore, the original assumption we made about the position of the 9 in column 5 must be incorrect. Therefore, going back, we have proved by contradiction the position of the 9 in column 6 (see Figure 7.17).

7		9	4		3			6
5				8				9
	6	4		9?	9?	2	8	
	9		7		4		1	
		3				6		
	4		3		8		2	
	1	8				9	7	
9				4				1
6			9		1			3

Figure 7.15 A puzzle to solve using proof by contradiction

7		9	4		3			6
5				8				9
	6	4		9		2	8	
	9		7		4		1	
		3			9	6		
	4		3		8		2	
	1	8				9	7	
9				4				1
6			9		1			3

Figure 7.16 Part way through the proof by contradiction

7		9	4		3			6
5				8				9
	6	4			9	2	8	
	9		7		4		1	
		3				6		
	4		3		8		2	
	1	8				9	7	
9				4				1
6				9	1			3

Figure 7.17 The solution from proof by contradiction

Communicating patterns and algebra

Many children and adults have an inherent fear of 'algebra,' perceiving it as a new and especially difficult subject when they encounter it at secondary school. Much of this fearsome reputation – and so barrier to learning – reflects the fact that formal algebra is associated with precise conventions and rules that need to be learned in order to successfully deal with equations. Algebra's non-specific nature and general applicability are its very essence but these virtues can work against mastery of the subject when it is taught in the usual, conventional way. This is because emphasis tends to be put on 'rules' and operations with little or no examples of specific applications. Many beginners find it especially difficult to gain confidence in manipulating the new concepts and language of the subject in an abstract, theoretical way, without the aid of particular applications to demonstrate its use or its power.

However younger children can and should be introduced to the ideas of algebra from their early years, building the essential groundwork of familiarity and confidence which can serve as a base when they later encounter more detailed, formal treatment of the subject. Algebra and algebraic thinking are fundamental for developing mathematical reasoning, and so primary school children can and should be encouraged to formulate

> **KEY POINT TO CONSIDER**
>
> Algebraic thinking is fundamental in developing mathematical reasoning. We should therefore provide opportunities to develop generalizing and reasoning skills from an early stage, rather than merely teach rules and operations.

explanations from an early age through a range of activities related to patterns and relationships. For example, as we have seen with some of the patterns described so far in this chapter, initial work can start orally in the early years with looking at and discussing repeating patterns using a range of familiar objects:

- threading beads;
- figures (teddy bears for colour or size);
- colour patterns in linear sequence – 2 colour then 3 colour;
- shape patterns in linear sequence – 2D and 3D shapes;
- colour and position – focus on patterns in shape and space;

- pegs and pegboard;
- matchsticks;
- multilink cubes.

By simply asking children to describe and explain what they see, you are engaging them in developing language skills and establishing the firm foundations for early algebra (Ryan and Williams, 2007). At this stage, the prompt questions and children's responses will naturally be in the general everyday language using words familiar to them, such as:

next
before
after
first
fifth
repeat
again
continue
guess
check
predict.

Simple questions arising from the children's activities at this stage can provide early opportunities for them to begin generalizing and reasoning:

What colour comes next?
What shape is next?
Which teddy comes next?
What is the next number?

You should expect to hear children explicitly using reasoning language:

if
then
so
because
but.

Activities can then be introduced where the generalizing and reasoning is made more specific by asking children *why* a pattern is as it is:

Input	Output
2	1
5	7
4	?

The number square can also be used as a source of patterns (see Activity 7.1).

Activity 7.1 Number square

1	2	3	4	5	6	7	8	9	10
11	12	13	14	15	16	17	18	19	20
21	22	23	24	25	26	27	28	29	30
31	32	33	34	35	36	37	38	39	40
41	42	43	44	45	46	47	48	49	50
51	52	53	54	55	56	57	58	59	60
61	62	63	64	65	66	67	68	69	70
71	72	73	74	75	76	77	78	79	80
81	82	83	84	85	86	87	88	89	90
91	92	93	94	95	96	97	98	99	100

Choose a 'square' of any four numbers.

- What pattern do you notice about the opposite corners of the square?
- Is this always the case? If so, why?
- Does this work looking at the corner numbers in bigger squares (e.g. 3 × 3 squares, 4 × 4 squares). Why?

Other patterns that might be explored are:

- Vertical lines coloured in – why do the numbers end in the same digit?
- Colour in a number along the top – add 11 and colour in square (repeatedly add 11). Now choose a number down the right hand side of the square and colour in – add 9 and colour in the square (repeatedly add 9). Can you explain the pattern? Where do the patterns meet? What happens if you use different numbers?

As we showed earlier, visual patterns as well as number patterns can be used for this purpose; for example the paving slabs around a garden can be used, and the children can make similar arrangements from multilink (see Activity 7.2). The next step then

Activity 7.2 Paving slabs around a garden

Count the total number of slabs used for each shape and discuss how and why the numbers are increasing from one to the next.

is to develop children's familiarization with the language and notation of algebra. As part of this, it is important to introduce them at an early stage to the use of letters both in shape and number, and this can be achieved with simple, practical activities. For example, they can be asked to describe how to complete a rectangle out of the set of shapes known as a tangram (see Figure 7.18).

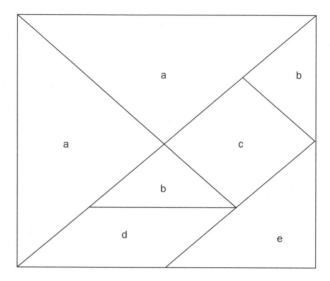

Figure 7.18 A tangram

Another activity for introducing letters is to create 'loop cards' or 'follow me cards' demonstrating box arithmetic – where children can encounter variables when finding missing addends. For an example, see Figure 7.19. This provides the basis for further development and the introduction of letters, laying the foundations for progression to the use of variables in a more difficult context:

$$3 + x = 7$$
$$x + 7 = 11$$

We can then return to previous activities and use the language of algebra in order to communicate our reasoning.

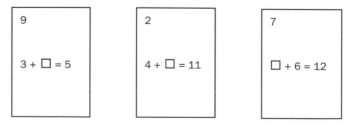

Figure 7.19 Loop cards

Input x	Output 2x − 3
1	−1
2	1
3	?
4	?
5	?
6	?
7	?

However, an additional consideration is that when letters are introduced in algebraic symbolism, we need to ensure that the children do not confuse this use with the use of letters as abbreviations of quantity as in metres (m), centimetres (cm) and litres (l). Therefore, when acquainting children with algebra we also need to introduce them to the idea of variables.

> **KEY POINT TO CONSIDER**
>
> The problems children can encounter with the introduction of algebraic notation have already been highlighted. These can be minimized if the teacher introduces the idea of variables at an early stage and through a range of activities.

Progression in the level of the activities is crucial since it promotes a natural strengthening of skills and deepened understanding. Another example of natural progression in primary algebra is the use of the 'function machine' (Hopkins *et al.*, 1996). In early primary or elementary school, the function machine can be introduced in the form of a large decorated box which the children can walk into and out of, having followed a simple instruction – collect 4 cubes (addition) or leave 3 cubes (subtraction). It can also provide procedures which cover multiplication and division thus highlighting that algebra can be taught alongside number from the beginning. Once again, older primary or elementary children can be encouraged to look for and recognize number patterns, guessing, predicting and progressing to solving simple equations. We therefore hope that by the end of their primary or elementary schooling, children are able to make general statements about familiar number and shapes, possess the ability to explain and generalize about relationships, and progress to expressing these as a formula using letters as symbols.

Questions for discussion

1   Take a number square as above and devise a set of exploratory activities which will help pupils to explore patterns within the square. How would you help pupils to communicate the results they have found?

2   Do you think it would be useful to introduce Sudoku or other such Japanese puzzles into the primary mathematics curriculum? What would you hope to gain from such a move?

3   What are the possible ways in which a child could reason that 'an odd number plus an odd number is an even number'? Which of these are more powerful ways of reasoning this property?

4   What are the different representations for number patterns that we have high-lighted in this chapter? Is there a progression in the difficulty of these representations, and if so, how could you incorporate this progression into a teaching sequence?

8
Understanding shapes

In the last chapter, we began to take a broader look at mathematics, seeing it in terms of identifying patterns. Geometry, although seemingly quite different to arithmetic, is looking for patterns within the properties of shapes, as opposed to looking at patterns within numbers. In this chapter, we describe the mathematics involved in primary or elementary school geometry, or 'understanding shape' as it is referred to in the curriculum in England and Wales. In particular, we highlight the 'patterns' that we can look for, and relate this search for patterns to one of the prominent theories concerning children's learning of geometry. However, before we do so, we will look in more detail at what we mean by shape and space or geometry, so that we have a basis for looking at the mathematics itself.

What is geometry?

There is a variety of terminology used for 'geometry' in different countries' mathematics curricula. In the United States, the topic is indeed called 'geometry'. In the UK, since 2006 the topic has been referred to as 'understanding shape' in England and Wales, as 'shape and space' in Northern Ireland (as it was until recently in England and Wales), and as 'shape, position and movement' in Scotland. Can we be clearer about what the topic entails? Let us examine some definitions for 'geometry' and look at the content of some of these curricula.

The book *The Changing Shape of Geometry* edited by Pritchard (2003) brings together a host of writings on geometry, and in fact begins with two chapters entitled 'What is geometry?'. The first is by the famous English mathematician G. H. Hardy, from which we take the following quote: 'There is one thing at any rate of which a geometry is not a picture, and that that is the so-called real world. About this, I think that almost all modern mathematicians would agree' (p. 16). This might be surprising for those in primary or elementary schools who see geometry as being more directly linked to the 'real world' than say arithmetic. The following quote is from another famous English mathematician, Michael Atiyah:

Broadly speaking I want to suggest that geometry is that part of mathematics in which visual thought is dominant whereas algebra is that part in which sequential thought is dominant. This dichotomy is perhaps better conveyed by the words 'insight' versus 'rigour' and both play an essential role in real mathematical problems.

(Pritchard, 2003: 29)

Therefore, although geometry is not simply the study of the world around us, it does involve 'visual thought'. From an educational perspective, Hershkowitz (1990: 70) identified the spatial and logical aspects of geometry: 'There are two main "classic" aspects of teaching and learning geometry: viewing geometry as the science of space and viewing it as a logical structure, where geometry is the environment in which the learner gets a feeling for mathematical structure'.

KEY POINT TO CONSIDER

Recognizing different shapes and reasoning about their properties are key elements in developing a comprehensive understanding about shapes. It is therefore important to address both issues in planning for progression in mathematical teaching.

Therefore, geometry is a combination of our perception of 'space' and a development of this visual perception to a more logical or sequential conceptualization of 'space'.

We can see how this view of geometry is reflected in some of the mathematics curricula previously mentioned. In England and Wales for example, the Primary framework for literacy and mathematics (DfES, 2006b: 96–7) sets out the following main aims for understanding shape:

- Use language such as 'circle' or 'bigger' to describe the shape and size of solids and flat shapes;
- Use everyday words to describe position;
- Visualize and name common 2-D shapes and 3-D solids and describe their features; use them to make patterns, pictures and models;
- Identify shapes from pictures of them in different positions and orientations; sort, make and describe shapes, referring to their properties;
- Draw and complete shapes with reflective symmetry; draw the reflection of a shape in a mirror line along one side;
- Know that angles are measured in degrees and that one whole turn is 360°; compare and order angles less than 180°;
- Read and plot coordinates in the first quadrant; recognize parallel and perpendicular lines in grids and shapes; use a set-square and ruler to draw shapes with perpendicular or parallel sides;
- Visualize and draw on grids of different types where a shape will be after reflection, after translations, or after rotation through 90° or 180° about its centre or one of its vertices.

In the US, for pre-kindergarten up to grade 5, the following aims are contained in the geometry standards (NCTM, 2000: 96, 164):

- Recognize, name, build, draw, compare, and sort two- and three-dimensional shapes.
- Describe attributes and parts of two- and three-dimensional shapes.
- Investigate and predict the results of putting together and taking apart two- and three-dimensional shapes.
- Identify, compare, and analyze attributes of two- and three-dimensional shapes and develop vocabulary to describe the attributes.
- Classify two- and three-dimensional shapes according to their properties and develop definitions of classes of shapes such as triangles and pyramids.
- Investigate, describe, and reason about the results of subdividing, combining, and transforming shapes.
- Explore congruence and similarity.
- Make and test conjectures about geometric properties and relationships and develop logical arguments to justify conclusions.

In both cases, the curricula move from recognition of shapes to reasoning with the properties of shapes, although this progression is probably clearer in the US standards (the England and Wales curriculum specifies the tools used for analysing properties such as rotation, reflection, etc., but not so much about reasoning with these properties. The US curriculum actually specifies reasoning). Therefore, what we need to consider is how we can move children along this progression.

Representing shapes

One way in which we can consider this progression from recognizing shapes to reasoning with their properties is to think about the different ways in which we can actually represent shapes. Clements and Battista (1992) identified representations of geometric ideas as seen in Figure 8.1.

Concrete manipulatives

Diagrams

Concept images

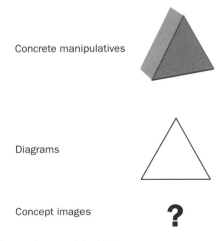

Figure 8.1 Representations of geometrical ideas

In terms of shapes, we of course have our concrete objects that we can handle. Then we can have diagrams. The diagrams may remove details that we feel are unimportant for representing the shape. Then we have our 'concept image' of the shape. This is our mental picture of the shape, which is also linked to other properties associated with the shape (or concept). Essentially, this is the child's understanding of the shape, and may be very different from child to child. For example, our concept image of a triangle may be the equilateral triangle with a horizontal base as we have shown above, and a child may not recognize a shape as a triangle if the base is not horizontal.

What then are the properties that we can associate with shapes? Let us look at the example of the triangle again (see Figure 8.2). The immediate properties that we might perceive are

- Colour
- Size
- Orientation
- Two-dimensional
- Number of sides
- Number of sides which are of the same length
- Number of corners
- Number of corners which have the same angle.

Now, are some properties more important than others? In terms of shape, colour, size and orientation are not important (although children may have developed the misconception that orientation is important). We can have triangles, for example, that vary in all these properties (see Figure 8.3). With two-dimensional shapes, we are more concerned with the outline of the objects than their colour. We will discuss further this issue of important/unimportant properties a little later. We can look at three-dimensional shapes in the same way. For example, take a tetrahedron as in

Figure 8.2 A triangle

Figure 8.3 A variety of triangles

Figure 8.4. The important properties this time are

- Three-dimensional
- Number of sides (or, more properly, edges)
- Number of faces
- Number of corners (or, more properly, vertices)
- The two-dimensional shapes within faces (including number and length of sides, number and angle of corners)
- The angles at which faces meet.

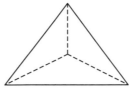

Figure 8.4 A tetrahedron

In addition to the immediate properties that we might perceive, there are other properties we can associate with shapes. These are the **symmetry** properties of the shape. By symmetry, we mean the property of remaining unchanged when the object undergoes certain changes. The symmetries we are usually concerned with are 'reflective symmetry' and 'rotational symmetry'. For example, for reflective symmetry, the equilateral triangle with all three sides of the same length will appear unchanged if its different parts are reflected through a line drawn from the middle of one side, through the opposite corner of the triangle (see Figure 8.5). In fact, for the equilateral triangle, there are three of what we call 'lines of symmetry', one through each of the corners. Three-dimensional objects also have reflective symmetry, but this time they have a 'plane of symmetry' (see Figure 8.6). Similarly, if we rotate the equilateral triangle

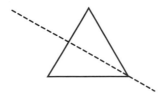

Figure 8.5 Reflective symmetry in an equilateral triangle

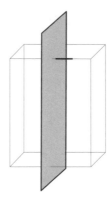

Figure 8.6 A plane of symmetry in a cuboid

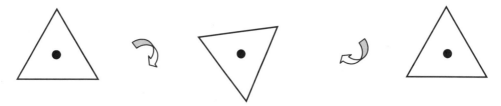

Figure 8.7 Rotational symmetry in an equilateral triangle

through its centre, then as we turn it, there will be times during the turn when it seems as if nothing has changed (see Figure 8.7). In fact, during one whole turn, the triangle will appear unchanged three times (one after a third of a turn, again after another third of a turn, and again after another third, bringing us back to where we were initially). Therefore, the equilateral triangle is said to have a rotational symmetry of order 3. As we can surmise, all shapes have rotational symmetry of at least order 1, because we can always turn it through a whole turn, back on to where it was originally. Three-dimensional objects also have rotational symmetry, except this time they have 'axes of symmetry' (see Figure 8.8).

Figure 8.8 An axis of symmetry in a hexagonal prism

Representing space

In the previous sections, we looked at a number of characteristics of representations of shapes. We will add one more method of representation here. There are two different ways of viewing a shape: we can view the sides of the shape with respect to each other, or we can view the position of the vertices with respect to some fixed point. If we take this second approach, then we need a way of defining the position of each of the vertices. If we drew a shape on a rectangular piece of paper, we might identify the position of each corner with respect to the bottom left-hand corner of the page as in Figure 8.9. To make it easier to define each of the corners of the triangle with respect to, in this case, the bottom left-hand corner of the page, we might say that each corner is a certain distance to the right and a certain distance up. Each corner would therefore be defined by two measures.

What we are essentially doing here is setting up a **coordinate system**. We define a point which is the reference point from which we measure positions – this is the origin of the coordinate system. We also subdivide the space into horizontal and vertical distances (see Figure 8.10).

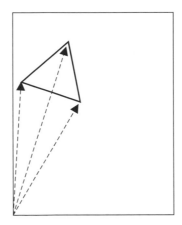

Figure 8.9 Referencing the corners of a shape to the corner of the page

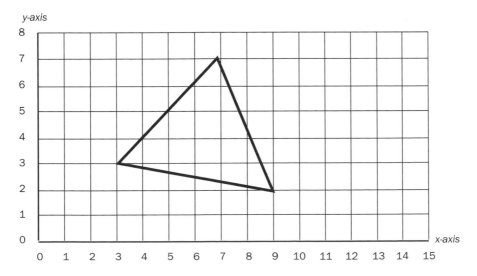

Figure 8.10 A coordinate system to reference the corners of a shape

The coordinate system provides another way of representing the two-dimensional space. The horizontal distances are measured using the x-axis and the vertical distances using the y-axis (it is simply a convention to call them the x- and y-axes). Within this system, the vertices of the triangle are at (3,3), (7,7) and (9,2) (when specifying a point, we give the position on the x-axis first, then the position on the y-axis). So simply specifying the coordinates (i.e. the positions) of the vertices of a shape provides another way of representing a shape. (You may wish to think about how you would specify the position of a shape with no vertices using this system, for example a circle.)

We are not just restricted to having the origin at the bottom left-hand corner – using negative numbers, we can extend the axes to the right and downwards as seen in Figure 8.11. The corners of the rectangle are this time at (−5,3), (−2,3), (−2,1) and (−5,1).

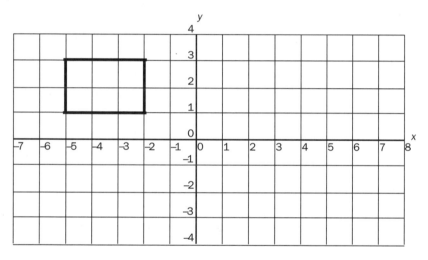

Figure 8.11 Positive and negative axes in a coordinate system

When are two shapes the same?

Using this alternative representation for space, we can not only describe the position of shapes, but also answer the question of when two shapes are the same. This brings us back to the consideration of important/unimportant properties of shapes. We stated that properties such as orientation and size were unimportant for defining a shape. We can show this by making certain changes to a shape, which do not affect the important properties such as number of sides and length of sides, and number and size of corners. These changes are referred to as **transformations** and we give examples of these in Figure 8.12. If we start with the original shape which is the triangle A, we could first of all change its position by moving it. We refer to this as a **translation**. Therefore, A has been translated to B by moving by −4 in the x direction and by +1 in the y direction. Alternatively, shape C is the results of reflecting A through the x axis. Shape D is obtained by rotating A about the point (−1,0) through an angle of 180° (clockwise or anticlockwise). Note that unlike the changes we made

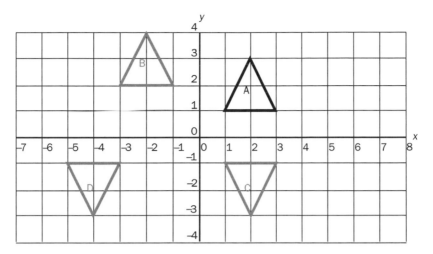

Figure 8.12 Transformations of a shape

when considering symmetry, the line of reflection or the point of rotation do not need to be on the shape. With all these transformations, the important properties of the shape remain unchanged – therefore, we essentially have the same shape.

Another transformation we can carry out is enlargement. In Figure 8.13, triangle A has been enlarged by a factor 2, about the point (−7,−3), to give triangle B. We can see that the distance from the centre of enlargement (−7,−3) to each of the corners of A has been multiplied by a factor of 2 to give the position of each of the corners of B. If we change the position of the centre of enlargement, then the position of the enlarged shape will change. In Figure 8.13, we could alternatively say that shape B had been enlarged by a factor $\frac{1}{2}$ about the centre of enlargement (−7,−3) to give shape A.

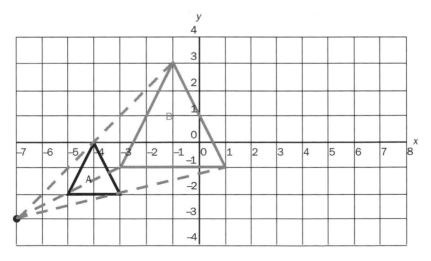

Figure 8.13 Enlargement of a shape

Note that this would be an example of using a fraction as an 'operator', where the number denotes a transformation.

In the case of enlargement, the only important property of the shape that has changed is the length of the sides, although in fact the lengths of sides relative to each other have not changed. Therefore, we might consider this latter property as being more important to the shape than the actual length of each size. With respect to this modified property, the shape remains the same. In fact, when we discuss whether two shapes are the same or not, two important ideas are similarity and congruency. Shapes are said to be similar if they are the same except for their size and orientation. Shapes are congruent if they are the same except for their orientation (i.e. angles *and* sides are the same). We can therefore specify whether shapes are the same in terms of being similar or congruent.

Reasoning between representations of shapes

In order to develop our understanding of shapes, we have discussed the different representations of shapes that we can have. We now look to develop our understanding still further by considering how we can reason between these representations for shapes, not just the shapes themselves. We draw on a particular model of developing understanding in geometry in order to provide this insight.

One of the most influential models for how knowledge about shapes is developed is the van Hiele model. Pierre and Dina van Hiele were Dutch educators who first developed their model for learning geometry in the 1950s. The model consists of a description of the different levels of understanding and reasoning displayed by learners of geometry. Burger and Shaughnessy (1986: 31) provide the following summary for the model:

> KEY POINT TO CONSIDER
>
> The van Hiele model represents the development of knowledge about shape through different levels of understanding and reasoning, from one based on appearance alone to considering shape properties as well as appearance. This is a useful model, the progression through it being dependent on instruction rather than age.

Level 0 (Visualisation): The student reasons about basic geometric concepts, such as simple shapes, primarily by means of visual considerations of the concept as a whole without explicit regard to properties of its components.

Level 1 (Analysis): The student reasons about geometric concepts by means of an informal analysis of component parts and attributes, Necessary properties of the concept are established.

Level 2 (Abstraction): The student logically orders the properties of concepts, forms abstract definitions, and can distinguish between the necessity and sufficiency of a set of properties in determining a concept.

Level 3 (Deduction): The student reasons formally within the context of a mathematical system, complete with undefined terms, *axioms*, an underlying logical system, definitions, and theorems.

Level 4 (Rigour): The student can compare systems based on different axioms and can study geometries in the absence of concrete models.

Burger and Shaughnessy (1986), and also Fuys *et al.* (1988), provide detailed descriptions for each of these levels. Essentially at Level 0, pupils identify shapes by their appearance as a whole, and refer to 'visual prototypes' of shapes (i.e. frequently used examples such as the equilateral triangle). At Level 1, pupils start to identify and compare shapes according to their properties, and this is developed further at Level 2 where the properties are put together as definitions for shapes, recognizing when the properties that you might have are enough to specifically define a shape. At Level 3 we begin to move towards more formal methods of proof, and as this will be outside what we cover at primary or elementary school, we will not consider this further or the subsequent Level 4.

The van Hiele model therefore suggests this development in the way that we reason about shapes, moving from solely considering the visual appearance of the shape to taking into account the properties of the shape as well. Let us look at an example. Figure 8.14 shows a typical example of a rectangle. Children working at Level 0 may recognize it as a rectangle because it is similar to the mental picture we have for a rectangle. (Of course, there will be children working below this level – a pre-Level 0 stage.) But what would happen if we changed the appearance of the rectangle slightly, for example its orientation, or so that it is nearly a square as in Figure 8.15? Children working at Level 0 may not recognize these as rectangles because the shapes do not conform to their 'visual prototype'. We may now need to draw on the properties of a rectangle to in order to confirm that these are indeed rectangles. So, what are the properties of a rectangle? We list these below:

Figure 8.14 A rectangle

Figure 8.15 Rectangles?

- Two-dimensional
- Four straight sides
- Opposite sides parallel
- Opposite sides equal in length
- Four right angles in each corner
- 2 or 4 lines of symmetry
- Rotational symmetry of order 2 or 4.

Notice that there are not just two lines of symmetry or rotational symmetry of order 2 – otherwise, a square would not be classified as a rectangle. Some may argue that this is indeed the case, however, a square is commonly considered to be a special type of rectangle. In any case, a child working at Level 1 can use the properties of rectangles in order to have these discussions, and also use them to classify shapes as rectangles or not. Finally, is there any way that we can refine this list of properties? Are some properties more important than others? Which properties are *sufficient* for clearly defining a rectangle? We can reduce our list to the following:

- Two-dimensional
- Four straight sides
- Four right angles in each corner (in fact, having three right angles would be sufficient as this implies the fourth angle).

Because these properties are sufficient for defining a rectangle, they must imply the properties that we have left out. We can check this by trying to think of a two-dimensional, four-sided shape with four right angles that does not have opposite sides equal and parallel, or two lines of symmetry or rotational symmetry of at least order 2. As we cannot, therefore, these properties are sufficient. We would hope that a pupil working at Level 2 of the van Hiele model would be able to order and refine the properties of a shape in this way.

Therefore, the above description of the van Hiele model, and also our previous discussion on representations of shape, suggests a teaching sequence for understanding shape that we might follow. First of all, we want to provide a variety of representations for shapes that children can work with. This would involve working with concrete objects and also presenting a variety of images of shapes to children. This would develop children's knowledge at Level 0 of the van Hiele model. We then want children to identify the properties of shapes so that they are working at Level 1 of the model. We then want children to work with the properties of the shapes themselves so that they can refine them and move towards definitions for shapes. This would allow children to work at Level 2 of the model, and all the time, we are developing children's understandings or 'concept images' of shapes.

Misconceptions with shapes

Having developed our understanding of shapes, let us now examine some of the misconceptions associated with this area of mathematics. In fact, as we highlighted at the beginning of the chapter, primary age children have always thought of mathematics as almost entirely numerical, and tend not to include shape or geometry in a list of mathematical topics (Kouba and McDonald, 1991). Even after nearly a decade of the National Numeracy Strategy in England and Wales, with explicit teaching of aspects of shape, the authors still found that children in schools in the north-east of England still think of mathematics as being about number and calculation. This suggests a limited understanding about the nature of mathematics and mathematical thinking.

In terms of the understanding of geometrical aspects, we have seen that learners can be thought of as progressing through different stages or levels of thought as outlined earlier in the chapter (van Hiele, 1986; Clements *et al.* 2004). In fact, many of the misconceptions that children develop are directly related to these stages of development, and we can examine some of these here. At the basic level, that of 'visualization', learners identify shapes and figures according to the concrete examples they have seen. For example, a child may say that a shape is a rectangle because it looks like a door, or only recognize a triangle when it looks like an equilateral triangle. These kinds of misconceptions result from over-generalization or over-extension of the visual forms that they recognize. So, for example, young children will not recognize Figure 8.16 as a triangle as it is too different from the picture or prototype that they can visualize.

Some shapes may also be easier to recognize. A study by Clements *et al.* (1999) investigated the knowledge of 4- to 7-year-olds in identifying a collection of two-dimensional shapes, including circles, squares, triangles and rectangles. Circles were commonly identified accurately by 6-year-olds, but without mention or description of any properties. Squares were less easily identified within this age group, though occasionally, some of the properties of squares were mentioned to explain or justify their choice. Triangles and rectangles were much less frequently identified than circles and squares, both in terms of visual recognition and in the use of their properties to help define the shapes. Younger children in the study quite often accepted squares as being 'the same as' rectangles.

> ## KEY POINT TO CONSIDER
>
> *To develop children's understanding of shape, we need to provide opportunities for children to experience particular shapes in a wide variety of forms, so that they can clearly reason why a shape is a given type.*

At the next level of 'analysis', pupils identify shapes according to their properties, and here a learner might think of a square as a figure with four equal sides. The kinds of mistakes that occur at this level are failure to recognize that a square is also a rectangle, a rhombus, a **parallelogram** and a **quadrilateral**, i.e. failing to make connections between different classes of shapes. In turn, at the following level of 'abstraction', learners can identify relationships between classes of figures (e.g. a square is a specific kind of parallelogram) and can begin to discover properties of classes of figures by simple deduction or argumentation. One of the distinguishing aspects of this level is that a learner can identify both necessary and sufficient conditions for defining properties.

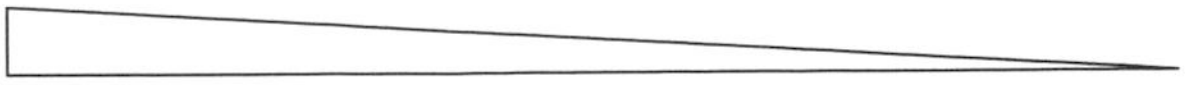

Figure 8.16 A triangle?

Communicating shapes

KEY POINT TO CONSIDER

Appropriate vocabulary is an effective way of describing shapes and for promoting children's discrimination of different shapes. It is therefore important in teaching to provide opportunities for children to use the correct terminology when discussing the properties of shapes.

Although we have presented the van Hiele levels as levels of understanding and reasoning of pupils, in fact, progress from one of the van Hiele levels to the next is more dependent upon instruction than age. Given traditional teaching, most children perform at levels 1 or 2 by the end of primary schooling (Clements and Battista, 1992), though children in the earlier years of primary schooling are also capable of sorting shapes according to their properties and not just their visual features.

However, the teaching of shape can often become an exercise in the learning of names, with assessment correspondingly concerned primarily with the recognition and use of the correct terminology. However, as we have tried to emphasize in this chapter, it is only when children are communicating and reasoning about the special properties of particular shapes that they become really engaged in the mathematics of shapes (Hopkins *et al.*, 1996). Assessment should therefore be more about the ways in which children can articulate notions of shapes via an increasing vocabulary that reflects a growing understanding.

In terms of developing this understanding, pre-school children will have gained knowledge at a very early stage through the practical exploration of concrete objects and the use of informal language to describe shapes in everyday situations – for example, a box of chocolates provides experience of fitting different shapes into given spaces. Educational toys such as jigsaws with large, simple two-dimensional shapes or a box with spaces for selected three-dimensional shapes to be pushed through all provide children with enjoyable activities. Children can be encouraged to develop the relevant vocabulary associated with the shapes through free play and contact with construction kits, bricks, blocks, multilink and a whole range of other resources. Their home environment, the environment of the classroom and the world outside can all provide a further range of experiences relating to shapes. It is therefore valuable to build on these foundations by providing children with a range of practical hands-on activities where they become actively engaged in thinking and communicating about both two-dimensional and three-dimensional shapes, using a variety of resources and materials.

At this early stage, it is important both to help children identify the properties of shapes (regular and irregular) and to encourage them to use the appropriate vocabulary. See, for example, Activity 8.1. Alternatively, with young children, a shape (for example a square) can be passed around the group, each child being asked to state a fact about the shape and then passing it on. When there is nothing more to be said, all the statements can be discussed and the group can arrive at the properties of a square rather than being told and expected to learn that a square has four straight, equal sides and so on. The same activity can be carried out with three-dimensional shapes – by providing cubes, cuboids, cylinders, spheres and cones but also including some unusual shapes such as a triangular-based prism and more unusual shaped boxes (e.g.

a hat box). In these instances, depending on the age range and ability of the children, many properties will arise to do with names, number of sides, number of corners (angles), types of angles, edges and vertices. The children can be challenged further by building models and linking shapes with art (e.g. junk modelling). It is important to introduce children to the terminology early on since it is usually a more efficient way of describing shapes – so it is simpler to say 'triangle' rather than 'a **polygon** with three sides and three corners', or 'quadrilateral' rather than a 'polygon with four straight sides' – and encourage them to use the correct vocabulary throughout such exercises. The lesson design should provide children with the experience necessary to develop a fundamental understanding of the properties of these shapes, parallel with opportunities to learn the appropriate vocabulary to describe them.

Activity 8.1 Odd one out

Present three different shapes and ask the children to identify an odd one out and to give a reason. The set of shapes should be chosen so that there are multiple possible answers that encourage the children to use the appropriate mathematical language to describe the properties of shapes.

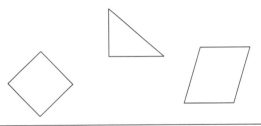

What kind of vocabulary might they need? Children will need to learn that a rectangle is a quadrilateral with four right angles, and that squares are special rect-angles. They will need to know the names for 5-, 6- and 8-sided shapes (pentagons, hexagons and octagons) and also appreciate that their sides need not be equal. Throughout upper primary school, children may be introduced to more complex concepts, such as:

- Parallelogram – a quadrilateral whose opposite sides are equal and parallel – rectangles are special kinds of parallelogram;
- Rhombus – equal sided quadrilateral with opposite sides parallel;
- Kite – quadrilateral with two pairs of adjacent equal sides (this could include a square according to this definition);
- Trapezium – quadrilateral with only one pair of parallel opposite sides.

But as with so much else in maths, it is crucial that children are introduced to these terms alongside a wide variety of practical experience so they come to 'understand' rather than 'learn' by rote.

Imaging and visualizing activities provide excellent experiences for developing children's language relating to shape. They encourage children to give precise descriptions and clear instructions for position, and in doing so help to further develop clear communication skills and clarification of standard vocabulary within the same activity. We can start with simple activities such as 'describe a drawing' (Activity 8.2). Similar activities can be carried out with three-dimensional shapes using multilink or other construction kits, where one child makes an object, and then has to explain cube by cube or piece by piece how to construct the same object. This again can be differentiated as is appropriate to the age and understanding of the children – for example, with older children, a robot figure made with Lego can be constructed by one child and instructions given so that another can make a similar model. Further discussion can be encouraged through comparing and contrasting. A further point to note is that with more sophisticated drawings or models then the language may relate to other areas of maths – for example, from general terms such as on top/beside/in front/right/left to the language of fractions and angles.

Activity 8.2 Describe a drawing

The first child draws a simple diagram or basic picture of house. They have the image in front of them and they then have to describe the shape so that another child (who cannot see diagram) can accurately draw the shape. This is an activity which can be as simple or as sophisticated as is appropriate, and which can incorporate the use of other resources such as tiles or flat shapes.

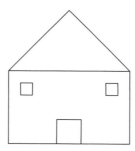

KEY POINT TO CONSIDER

Shape recognition and reasoning about the properties of shapes are essential elements in children's progression to a deeper understanding of shape. A range of practical activities should be included in our teaching which provide the opportunity to develop these aspects.

When it comes to reasoning about shapes, sorting trees or Venn diagrams (see Chapter 10) are effective tools for providing children with the opportunity to articulate about the properties of both regular and irregular shapes. These activities can be as sophisticated or as simple as warranted by the age and ability of the children while also providing opportunities to introduce and practise the range of terminology the children need to become conversant in and confident in using. In other words, such activities can be an effective means of developing and refining general communication skills as well as developing and extending the mathematical vocabulary associated with shape and space as we highlighted above. Other examples of encouraging language development with two-dimensional shapes by providing the opportunity to discuss their properties include those shown in Activities 8.3 and 8.4. Also, in looking at misconceptions with shapes, we identified the problem that children may only recognize some limited types of certain shapes. Therefore, in communicating shapes in the classroom, it is crucial to provide children with the opportunity for recognizing irregular shapes and shapes in different positions and in different contexts. For example, see Activity 8.5 for an activity specifically with irregular shapes. Tangrams also offer the opportunity to create a variety of shapes for discussion and can allow for natural differentiation: some children can start with a two-piece tangram, whilst others can work with a seven-piece tangram and so on (see Figure 8.17). Such activities also encourage and develop the use of language associated with position, such as 'on top, at the side, in front of', etc. Practical activities where the shape can be distorted and alternatives noted and discussed are equally important. For example, the use of Meccano, strips of card with metal fasteners or geoboards can all provide multiple activities with regular and irregular shapes.

Activity 8.3 Folding a piece of paper

Take a piece of A4 paper and make one fold.

- What sort of shape do you get?
- How many sides does it have?
- Has anybody produced a shape with more sides?
- What polygons are possible?
- Are there any symmetrical polygons?
- What quadrilaterals can be made?
- What pentagons/hexagons/octagons, etc. can be made?
- The results for the whole class can be classified and displayed (and added to) with each shape and its correct mathematical name.

Activity 8.4 Make an equilateral triangle

- Show the children how to make an equilateral triangle and discuss its properties.
- Children make their own and with a friend join two together – further discussion of the properties of the new shape.
- What shapes are possible with 3 triangles/4 triangles etc? Progress can then take several directions through polygons/tessellations/symmetry, and further challenges for the children attempted during investigations.

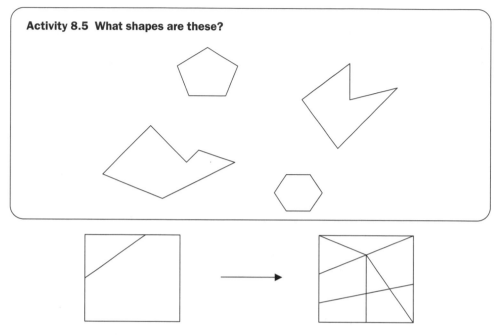

Activity 8.5 What shapes are these?

Figure 8.17 Tangrams

With imaginative teaching, the learning of shape and space can be an exciting and involving experience for all children, whatever their ability, and it can be an effective cross-curricular topic. As stated earlier, it is important that we acknowledge and place the concepts related to shape in a broader context by providing a range and variety of practical activities that allow for 'hands-on' experience so that children can secure their own knowledge. At the same time, lesson design should allow opportunity for the children to adopt a cooperative approach in order to further promote the mathematical reasoning and communication skills essential for progression in mathematical understanding. Many adults feel insecure in their knowledge of shapes, particularly three-dimensional shapes, since they have never been encouraged to look at examples in the real world and to explore shapes from different angles (Lewis, 1994), so it is crucial that children are given opportunities to do just that. These can best be provided through a broad scheme of work on shapes designed with an underlying emphasis on doing, describing and explaining.

Questions for discussion

1 Shape is often considered as a very practical topic within mathematics. Do you agree that it also lends itself to appropriate work on reasoning as discussed above?

2 Using some of the practical activities you already use in the classroom, could they actually be easily adapted so that they also have a 'reasoning' focus?

3 How does the teaching progression set out in the curriculum that you work with fit in with the van Hiele model for developing understanding in geometry?

9

Measurement

In the previous chapter, we outlined some of the properties of shapes that we can identify and reason with. Some of these properties involved the process of counting, for example the number of sides, the number of lines of symmetry or the order of rotational symmetry. Other properties would require us to carry out the process of measurement, for example to measure the length of sides to see if they are the same length, or the measurement of angles within the shape for equal angles or parallel sides. Therefore, the notion of 'measurement' is an integral part of our notion of understanding shapes, and also of our understanding of the world around us.

Researchers however have found that there is a lack of understanding about measurement which is displayed both by primary or elementary school pupils, and also by secondary school students. For example, Ryan and Williams (2007) identified that children's thinking about measurement remained typically 'tied' to specific measures, rather than having a broader understanding of the concept. 'There is a lack of transcendence in thinking about what is involved in the act of measurement as such; to go beyond this stage might involve some means of gaining access to the way in which measurements are constructed' (p. 102).

Dickson et al. (1984) also highlighted the problem that because children are brought up in today's society to use sophisticated measurement instruments, they do not have a broader appreciation of the process.

> They have missed out on the historical development of measurement which means that they do not appreciate the need for measurement in the first place and how this emerged from a 'socially agreed notion of equality' when comparing size, worth, value etc. in trading situations.
>
> (pp. 79–80)

Therefore, in this chapter, we will begin by taking a broader look at exactly what we mean by 'measurement', and also at what the general process of measurement entails, before we examine particular attributes and their specific measures.

What is measurement?

The concept of measurement is broader than we might imagine. For example, not only can we measure physical properties such as length, weight and so on, but we might also seek to measure properties such as attitude towards mathematics or maths anxiety. In fact, the literature on measurement in general (we refer here to Hand, 2004) makes the distinction between 'representational' and 'pragmatic' aspects of measurement. The measurement of physical properties is identified with the representational view of measurement, and since we concentrate on these properties in the school mathematics curriculum, so we will restrict our discussion to this aspect.

The representational aspect of measurement is defined by Hand (2004: 15) as follows:

A representational approach seeks to construct a numerical system in which the relationships between the numbers match the relationships between the objects arising from some attribute (or, more generally, attributes). It is thus an idealized mathematical construct, a representation, which provides a reasonable approximation to the behaviour of natural objects.

KEY POINT TO CONSIDER

Measurement is a means of assigning numbers to concisely describe differing properties of objects. It is therefore important to clearly demonstrate the relationship between the system of units and the particular property in all aspects of teaching measurement.

The process of measurement therefore attempts to represent an attribute of an object with a number. In doing so, it provides a way of describing that attribute, otherwise how would we communicate the idea, say, of the length of a piece of wood, other than showing an object with the same length? Using numbers provides a concise way of describing properties. Also stated in the definition above is the fact that the relationships between the numbers represent the relationships between the objects in terms of the given property. If the length of a piece of wood is twice that of another, then this is therefore reflected in the numbers assigned to these lengths. This therefore implies the use of units of properties.

We can count stones, sheep and people, but we cannot count length, weight, or time. In order to apply arithmetic to continua such as these we have to discretize them: divide them into chunks which can then be counted. Attributes such as length, weight, and time are quantifiable simply because they can be divided in quanta, which can then be counted.

(Hand, 2004: 12)

Hand also identifies two processes implicit in the process of 'discretization'; that of comparing objects (so that we can see when a number of shorter pieces of wood, if that is our unit or **quanta**, is longer than a larger piece of wood) and that we can 'concatenate' the units properly (it is no good laying the shorter pieces of wood in parallel rather than end to end).

Therefore, in defining what we mean by measurement (assigning numbers to properties), we have started to identify fundamental ideas and processes involved (quanta or units, comparing, concatenating). We can develop this further by looking at some of the educational and psychological literature on measurement. Dickson *et al.* (1984) highlight Piaget's work on measurement, and his identification of two fundamental operations on which the measurement process is based: **conservation** and **transivity**. Conservation can be described as 'the shaping of the concept in such a way that irrelevant distracters begin to be ignored' (Ryan and Williams, 2007: 90). For example, when measuring the number of objects in a group (i.e. counting them), we need to realize that irrelevant properties such as the arrangement of the objects have no bearing on the number. Another example is for height and realizing that the direction we measure a person's height (from the bottom up or from the top down) has no bearing on the measure. Also using different units for height (centimetre or feet/inches) has no bearing on the underlying property, although the numbers we ascribe to the property might end up being different. Transitivity on the other hand is the idea that if we measure a property of one object using some instrument, then we use the same instrument to measure the same property in another object, then we can deduce the relationship of the property between the first and second object. Figure 9.1 illustrates this concept. The property of transitivity allows the use of a measuring instrument as a comparison tool.

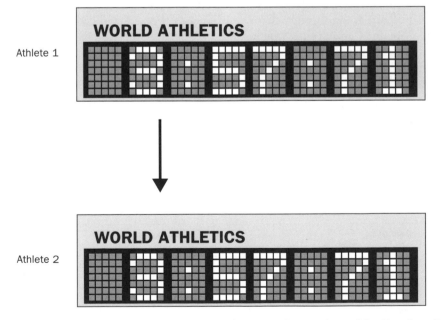

Figure 9.1 If the time for athlete 1 is so many minutes and seconds, and the time for athlete 2 is the same amount of minute and seconds, then we can say that the time for athlete 1 is the same as for athlete 2

KEY POINT TO CONSIDER

The process of discretization is important for understanding not only the use of appropriate units for particular properties, but also why measurement is an approximate process.

Dickson *et al.* (1984) also highlighted the notion that measurement is an approximate process. This was also implied in the first quote from Hand, that measurement 'provides a reasonable approximation to the behaviour of natural objects'. Why is measurement necessarily approximate? Over and above the issue of accurately manufacturing instruments, the process is constrained by the quanta or units that we use. Because we are '**discretizing continua**', some information is lost when we do this because we are measuring to the nearest unit. We could use smaller units, but because we are dealing with continuous properties, we can never have sufficiently small units. In the diagram above then, we might recognize that we have made a mistake. The times for the two athletes will not be the same. It is just the numbers that we ascribe to their times, constrained by the size of the unit on the stopwatch, that happen to be the same. Therefore, when we measure a property, we need to also consider how approximate the measure we obtain is.

Ainley (1991), in looking at measurement in school mathematics classes, highlighted four separate processes that seemed to be present; estimation, using measurement instruments, the structure of the system of units, and approximation and appropriate accuracy. We have already, to some degree, touched on the last of these. We will also cover the second and third processes, the use of measuring instruments, and the units that we use and the relationships between them. The first process, that of estimation, is seen as important as it allows us to obtain very approximate measures without perhaps going through the measurement process, or to check measures that we have obtained and seeing whether they are reasonable (for example, we might expect a height measure of 175 metres for a person to be very likely wrong). It also allows us to convert between units and to check this conversion.

KEY POINT TO CONSIDER

Identifying the processes involved in measurement provides insight into what we need to teach in the topic. For example, recognizing the process of concatenating is particularly important when teaching area and volume.

Therefore, we summarize the concepts and processes that seem to be part of 'measurement' in Figure 9.2.

In the ideas raised by previous research, we have identified the processes involved in measurement, in other words the things we do when we measure. We have included the

Concepts	**Processes**
Discretization	Comparing objects
Conservation	Concatenation of units
Transitivity	Assigning numbers to properties
Approximate nature of measurement	Structure of the system of units
	Use of measuring instruments
	Estimation

Figure 9.2 The concepts and processes involved in measurement

structure of units here because working with units and moving between different units is something we see as what we 'do' in measurement. We have also identified the more abstract concepts that lie behind measurement. We would not imagine that teachers start with the abstract properties but rather with the processes of measurement. The concepts would develop as children reflect on the measurement process. In this, we are in agreement with what Dickson *et al.* (1984) called the 'Russian approach' to teaching measurement, developed by Russian educationalists. Their approach involved moving from comparing objects and identifying appropriate units (informal units such as 'spoonfuls of' or matchsticks) to assigning numbers to properties, and then to looking at the relationships between different units (what happens if length is measured in straws rather than matchsticks?) We can see the parallels between these activities and the processes we have identified above.

Measuring different properties

In examining what we generally mean by measurement, we have still to go into some detail on two of the processes, namely the structure of the system of units and the use of measuring instruments. As both of these processes differ according to the property that we are looking at, we will consider them in this section, which considers some of the different properties we can measure. Dickson *et al.* (1984) made the distinction between the measurement of physical space which is more easily perceived, namely the properties of length, area, volume and angle, and that of less easily perceived properties such as mass, weight, time, temperature and money. We begin with perhaps the most easily perceived property, that of length.

Length

Length is defined as 'the distance (shortest connecting line) between two points in space' (Benenson *et al.*, 2000: 9). Relating this more directly to objects, length is the extension of a physical object in space in one direction. As such, it is most easily measured in comparison with other objects that have length. Roche (1998), in a historical review of measures, highlighted that many ancient units of length that were on a human scale were based on parts of the body. 'The finger, palm, span, foot, cubit (the length of the forearm to the tip of the middle finger), step and fathom (separation of outstretched arms) each became an autonomous and largely incommensurable natural unit, and the basis of higher multiples' (p. 23).

There are two problems here. First, the units of length will differ from person to person because their bodies will vary. Second, as highlighted in the quote, the measures can be 'incommensurable' (i.e. impossible to compare with one another). Therefore, the development of the measurement of length occurred with the standardization of units and relating them to one another. Roche provides another quote from a statute for measuring land, believed to date from the early fourteenth century: 'Be it Remembered, That the Iron Yard of our Lord the King, containeth three Feet and no more. And a Foot ought to contain Twelve Inches ... It is ordained that three grains of Barley dry and round do make an inch; Twelve inches make a foot; Three feet make a Yard' (p. 25). This quote highlights another source for units of length, namely those based on agricultural practices. We have the inch based on grains of barley, and elsewhere we have the furlong defined as 'the length of a furrow that an ox-team would plough in a common field before stopping for a brief rest' (Chapman, 1995: 20). The furlong was later defined as one-eighth of a mile.

The notion of the 'iron yard' leads us to a more modern definition for the unit of length. The metre was defined as the 40-millionth fraction of the earth's circumference, and a standard metre bar made of platinum-iridium was developed in the nineteenth century and kept in the International Bureau of Weights and Measures in Paris. In 1983, this definition was changed to 'the distance travelled by light in vacuum during 1/299792458 of a second' (Benenson et al., 2000: 9), because the speed of light can be measured so accurately.

KEY POINT TO CONSIDER

The accurate use of a relevant instrument is crucial for all aspects of measurement. Therefore, it is important to build in plenty of time for practice in our lesson planning.

The metre (abbreviated to 'm') is therefore the basis for the metric system of measuring length (although we can have other systems such as the imperial system with inches, feet and yards). The measuring instruments we commonly use for lengths are therefore based on this unit, and fractions or multiples of this unit. An example is given in Figure 9.3 of a 10 centimetre ruler (a centimetre or cm being 1/100th of a metre), which is further subdivided into millimetres (a millimetre or mm being 1/1000th of a metre). How would we use this ruler? We could try and line one end of the crayon exactly with a zero mark on the ruler. Note that this is not usually at the end of the ruler but the scale is printed on the ruler with spaces at the ends. Alternatively, we could see where the start of the crayon is (0.8cm) and where the end of the crayon is (5.4cm) and find the difference (5.4cm − 0.8cm = 4.6cm). This avoids the problem of exactly lining up a particular mark on the ruler with one end of the object being measured.

For larger distances, we can use tape measures which work in the same way as rulers, or trundle wheels (see Figure 9.4). The wheel of this device has a circumference of 1m and as you push it forward, you count the number of revolutions the wheel makes. This is essentially how a car measures distance as well (with perhaps different circumferences) although it would measure distance in kilometres (if in metric units – a kilometre or km is 1000m). Again however, we would need to note the start and end points in order to calculate the distance moved through.

Figure 9.3 A diagram of a 10cm ruler measuring a crayon

Figure 9.4 Diagram of a trundle wheel

Area and volume

Moving on to area and volume, both of these are properties which can be thought of as 'extensions' of length into two or three dimensions respectively. Area is therefore a measure of the amount of 'surface' covered by an object, and volume is a measure of the amount of 'space' occupied by an object. If we think of the measurement of length as the 'discretizing' into smaller lengths, then the measurement of area can be thought of as the discretizing into smaller areas (see Figure 9.5). Of course, the smaller areas need not be squares but could be any shape that completely covers a surface. By convention though, the modern units of area are squares based on the metre. So we have the square metre (or m^2) with each side of the square being 1m, and likewise we have square centimetres (cm^2) with each side 1cm, square millimetres (mm^2) or square kilometres (km^2). In the past however, areas were again based on agricultural practices, with an example being the acre which can be defined as 'the area that a team of oxen can plough in a morning' (Chapman, 1995: 26).

Logically then, the measurement of volume is the discretizing into smaller volumes, and by convention we use cubes based on the metre – cubic metre (or m^3) which is a cube with each side being 1m, cubic centimetre (cm^3) and cubic millimetre

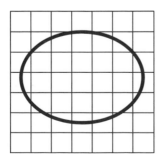
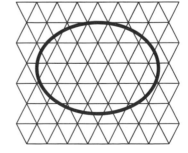

Figure 9.5 Discretizing area

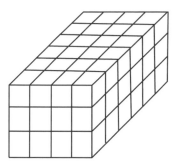

Figure 9.6 Discretizing volume

(mm³) (see Figure 9.6). In the past, measures of volume could be based on non-metric units (e.g. cubic foot). We also have slightly different units for measuring the volume of liquids. In the past, we had measures such as the barrel and we also have imperial measures such as gallons and pints. In metric units, we have the litre (with symbol 'l') which is equal to 1000 cubic centimetre (for liquids this is sometimes written as 1000cc rather than 1000cm³). These units for volumes can also measure the **capacity** of an object, defined as how much volume it can hold (e.g. the capacity of a bottle). We can also have fractions of litres (centilitres or cl, millilitres or ml).

When we measure area and volume in schools, rather than using specific instruments, we may use the dimensions of the area or the volume (if it is a regular 2D or 3D shape) for calculation. So a rectangular area is length of base × length of height. As area requires two lengths to be multiplied together, hence the square units measure. The volume of a cuboid shape is length of base × length of width × length of height. As volume requires three lengths to be multiplied together, hence the cubic units measure. We may alternatively, especially with area, estimate the measure using squared paper as in Figure 9.5. However, there are instruments to measure both area and volume. For area we have an instrument called a planimeter, and for volume we have any graduated (i.e. with a measuring scale) container (see Figure 9.7). The planimeter works by moving one of the arms of the instrument round the outside of a given 2D shape, regular or irregular. The container obviously measures the volume of liquids, but if we have an irregular 3D object, and if that object will not soak up any of

Figure 9.7 Measuring instruments for area and volume

the liquid, then we can simply drop the object into some liquid in such a container, and find the increase in the liquid level. This increase is the volume of the object.

Angle

An angle can be defined as 'the measure of divergence between two straight lines in a plane' (Benenson *et al.*, 2000: 11; see Figure 9.8). However, this definition is not sufficient as it is also important to have a concept of angle as a measure of turn (see the misconceptions section). For example, how would we view angles greater than 180°, or even greater than 360°, using the above definition? So we need to view angles as a measure of both static and dynamic situations. In the past, Babylonian astronomers used a measure of angle based on the circle divided into twelve intervals, each of 30 degrees. This is what our unit of degrees is based on, 360 of which result in a line being turned through a full circle. However, the official scientific measure of angle is the 'radian', which is defined as the angle formed at the centre of a circle when the length of the arc is equal to the radius – as shown in Figure 9.9. A full circle, perhaps rather confusingly for inexperienced users of the unit, has 2π radians.

The measuring instrument we most commonly associate with the angle is the protractor (see Figure 9.10). To measure the angle, we place the centre of the baseline of the protractor on the point of the angle. We can then either align one of the sides of the angle with one of the zero-points of the protractor, or we can read off the position of each of the sides on the scale. In the above case, one of the sides is at 10° (° is the symbol for degrees) and the other is at 46°. The angle is therefore $46 - 10 = 36°$.

Returning to the idea of the use of angles in astronomy, we also have another instrument, the quadrant, so called because it is a quarter of a circle. Figure 9.11 shows its use in determining the angle of any object above the horizontal. As we tilt the

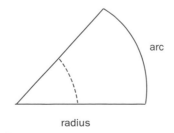

Figure 9.8 An angle

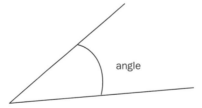

radius

Figure 9.9 An angle of 1 radian where the radius equals the length of the arc

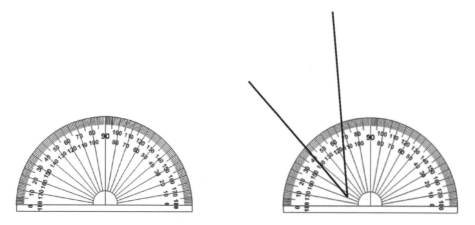

Figure 9.10 The protractor and its use

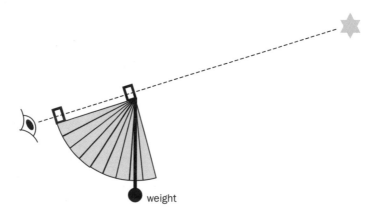

Figure 9.11 Using the quadrant

instrument back to look at objects at greater angles, the hanging weight attached by a string moves round the scale on the quadrant and we can read off the angle we are looking up at.

Mass and weight

Having looked at what might be regarded as the more easily perceived properties, we now move on to a much more difficult property to perceive, that of mass. What is mass? Objects 'just have' mass and Benenson *et al.* (2000) simply define it as an 'elementary property ascribed to a body'. It turns out that the concept of mass is very difficult to define. The way we usually perceive mass is indirectly through the property of weight. Weight is the force due to gravity that acts on objects with mass. The greater the mass of an object, the bigger the force pulling it downwards. This is the basis for older measuring instruments for mass such as the balance (see Figure 9.12).

Figure 9.12 A balance

If we place the object that we want to measure on one side of the balance, the force of gravity pulling down on the object will tip the balance over to that side. If we then place other objects, for which we know their mass, on the other side of the balance so that the instrument balances again, then we have found the mass of the initial object. In fact, by definition, we have also balanced out the weights as well, so we can also say that the objects on the two sides of the balance have the same weight. Therefore, although mass and weight are different properties, we can see that they are very much related.

This measurement of mass and weight requires standard 'masses' or 'weights' to use in the balancing process. Early measurements were in fact based on the use of seeds for small masses or weights (Roche, 1998); for example the carob seed from which we derive carat weight for gold, and an old English measure called the Troy grain was based on the barleycorn. Twenty-four Troy grains weighed the same as one old penny (denomination of money) in England, so there was also the Troy pennyweight (24 grains), the Troy ounce (20 pennyweights), the Troy pound (12 ounces) and the Troy hundredweight (100 pounds) (Chapman, 1995). The modern metric system of measuring mass is based on the kilogram (kg) and its fractional values – a gram (g) which is 1/1000th of a kilogram, and the milligram (mg) which is 1/1000th of a gram. The definitive kilogram is a platinum-iridium cylinder kept in the International Bureau of Weights and Measures in Paris.

For weight, because it is actually the force acting on mass, we measure it in the units of force which is Newtons (N). On Earth, a force of 9.8N acts on a 1kg mass, although this force will be different if the strength of gravity is different (say, as we

> ### KEY POINT TO CONSIDER
>
> The concepts of weight and mass are difficult to grasp and often confused. It is therefore important to distinguish between the two concepts and use the correct terminology from the earliest stages of our teaching.

leave the planet Earth). We use this relationship between force and mass to measure masses as well, for example using a force meter (see Figure 9.13). The meter has been calibrated so that as the force increases on the bottom of the instrument, an arrow moves along the scale. Once we have obtained the measure in Newtons, we can convert to kilograms by dividing by 9.8. This is similar to how modern weighing machines work, with mass calibrated against a measurement of weight.

Figure 9.13 A force meter

Temperature

Another property that we measure indirectly is temperature. Benenson *et al.* (2000) define temperature as being related to the energy of individual particles in a substance. When we touch a hot or cold object, we actually 'feel' the transfer of energy to or from our fingers. To measure temperature, we actually measure the impact that this energy has on the properties of other objects. For example, we commonly use a 'liquid thermometer' (see Figure 9.14). This type of thermometer contains a liquid (mercury or alcohol are commonly used) encased in glass. Putting the thermometer in 'hotter' or 'colder' environments results in the liquid expanding or contracting. The end of the liquid can be read off on a scale, indicating the temperature. Like other measures, the temperature scale needs to be referenced against some standard. This was done in the Celsius scale of temperature where the point at which water boils at normal atmospheric pressure (because this can affect things) was defined as 100 degrees Celsius or 100°C. The point at which water freezes at normal atmospheric pressure was defined as 0°C. Having defined these 'calibration points', we could divide any scale based on this into smaller units. We also have other scales of temperature – for example the Fahrenheit scale which has different calibration points, and the Kelvin

Figure 9.14 A thermometer

scale which is the standard scale in science. At zero Kelvin, which is equal to −273.15°C, all motion of atoms and molecules is said to cease, i.e. they have no energy.

Time

Perhaps the least easily perceived property that we measure is time, and like other properties such as mass and temperature, we measure time in terms of other things happening. An obvious occurrence that we can associate with time is the day going to night going to day. Roche (1998) suggests that the 24-hour day was invented by Egyptian

priests, although initially the concept of an hour changed with the seasons. The Greeks then decided to use equal hours at the expense of changing lengths of day time and night time. Finally, from the middle ages, the concept of the hour was further divided into minutes and seconds. The second, which is the basic unit of time, was originally defined as 1/86400th of an average day, based on 24 hours, each with 60 minutes, and each minute with 60 seconds. Today, the second is defined more precisely than with reference to the 'average day'; it is defined rather complicatedly as '9,192,631,770 periods of the radiation of the electromagnetic radiation from the transition between the hyperfine structure levels of the ground state of Cesium 133' (Benenson *et al.*, 2000: 8). Once again, like length, we can measure light or radiation more accurately than anything else, and therefore the unit of time is based on this.

With time being based on the progression of the day, the earliest instrument for measuring time was based on the movement of the sun, i.e. the sun dial (see Figure 9.15). Depending on the position of the sun, it would cast a shadow which would

Figure 9.15 A sundial

indicate an approximate time on the scale of the sundial. Later, more accurate measurements of time were achieved with mechanical instruments, typified by the clock with which we associate the measurement of time today (see Figure 9.16). On the clock face, we have the traditionally shorter hour hand. Like the sundial shadow, this slowly moves round the numbers on the clock face, indicating roughly the hour of the day according to the number it is pointing at. Of course it does not indicate whether the hour is 'am' (from the Latin *ante meridiem* meaning before midday) or 'pm' (*post meridiem* – after midday); we have to work that out for ourselves. We could just have the hour hand on the clock, and roughly judge the time from that. However, for greater accuracy, we have a minute hand, which turns around the full dial, starting at the top, in 60 minutes. We can see the division of a scale into 60 parts around the outside of clock face. We can read off the number of minutes using the minute hand. Therefore, Figure 9.16 shows 11 hours and 0 minutes, or 11.00 (am or pm). For even greater accuracy, the clock could have a second hand that makes a full turn once a minute, therefore showing on the outside scale the number of seconds.

Confusingly, we sometimes refer to the time without specific reference to hours and minutes. So we might refer to 'quarter past 11', meaning a quarter of an hour past 11 o'clock, or 'ten to 12', meaning ten minutes to 12 o'clock. We also have the digital way of displaying time, shown in Figure 9.17. The first two digits on a display show the hours and the second two digits display the minutes. Some digital clocks show the time in 24-hour format, meaning that the hours change not from 1 to 12, but from 0 to 23. This means that we now know whether it is am or pm. So, 00:12

Figure 9.16 A clock face

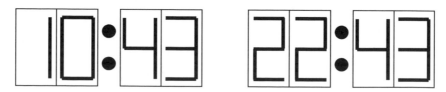

Figure 9.17 Digital time

is twelve minutes past 12 in the morning, 12:12 is twelve minutes past 12 in the afternoon.

Dickson *et al.* (1984) highlighted the fact that there is a difference between 'telling the time' and the concept of time. In fact, our discussion so far has largely concentrated on telling the time, because it is about saying what time of day it is. We can also of course measure time intervals which are not connected with the day (how long a journey is, the time to run 100m, etc.). The process of measurement is more concerned with the second notion of time, and as we said previously, the second is used as the scientific unit for measuring time periods. We can still have multiples of seconds, in this case minutes or hours, or we can have fractions of seconds such as milliseconds. We might use a measuring instrument that only measures some duration rather than telling the time, such as the stopwatch (see Figure 9.18).

In fact, the act of telling the time may not seem like measurement because we are simply labelling moments of the day, rather than measuring a time period. One way of linking telling the time with measurement is to keep in mind that telling the time is measuring the time period since midnight or midday (am or pm). When we give the time as 11.00am, what we are saying is that it is 11 hours and 0 minutes since midnight. Again, Dickson *et al.* (1984) point out that if we simply concentrate on telling the time by asking children to just recognize different examples of the clock face, then their concept of time will be divorced from any concept of measurement.

Figure 9.18 A stopwatch

Money

The final property we will look at is money. Although money is commonly included as a form of measurement, Dickson *et al.* (1984) suggest some particular differences between money and measurement:

- There is no absolute scale for monetary value that we can refer to – the cost of an object is determined by people.

- Money is discrete because we can only go down to the lowest denomination of money (for example a 1 pence coin in the UK). This is the limit to the accuracy of money.

- Money is represented by the exchange of physical tokens which are agreed to have particular values. In the measurement of other properties, we do not represent the property by tokens.

In fact we would both agree and disagree with these suggested differences. One source of confusion we feel is the definition of the property that we are measuring. We are actually measuring monetary or economic value of an object. And indeed, there is no absolute scale of monetary value we can refer to. However, monetary value can be expressed as accurately as we wish. For example, one US dollar can be worth 1.9865 UK pounds. Therefore, the value of an object, like other properties, is a continuous property which we discretize by labelling it with a number. The scale that we use is the particular currency that we might be working with. Finally, we do have the physical tokens of money but we see these as being separate from a process of measurement. The use of money is more associated with the exchange of goods. Therefore, in the context of measurement, it is important that we recognize that monetary values can be ascribed to objects, although unlike other properties, there is no agreed scale and also no instrument with which we can measure this property. Outside of the context of measurement, we have the use of money where we learn its use in the exchange of goods, and that we need to recognize different coins and notes, and their different relative values.

Misconceptions in measures

Having examined the various 'measures' that we consider in primary or elementary mathematics, let us consider some of the problems that children have within the various areas. First of all, with length and area, we see common errors and misconceptions occurring. Children especially need the opportunity to build key ideas about measurement of length and area (Hiebert, 1984; Zacharos, 2007), in particular the following key principles (Clements, 1999):

1   Appropriate units: units for measuring area are not the same as those for measuring length and millimetres are not appropriate for measuring driving distances. A common error is to measure the perimeter of a shape when the area is required.

2   Standard units: we use square centimetres for area because these are standard or identical measures. Young children do not see the need for the measures that they use (such as hand-spans) to be the same.

3   Accuracy of cover: units need to be placed so as to cover a length or area completely and then counted precisely. A number of errors with using equipment relate to this principle.

As we can see, a number of common errors occur when pupils use both non-standard measures and measuring devices such as rulers or protractors. One of the more common errors related to accuracy of cover is to start from the edge of the ruler rather than the zero mark – this indicates some understanding of the concept (edge to edge) but not an understanding of some of the common conventions with measuring devices (that zero is not at the end). Similarly, with protractors for measuring angles, children find it hard to use them to measure an angle which is not horizontal to the page and to read the scale in the appropriate direction (Hansen, 2005).

Within this area of measuring angles, there is considerable evidence that angle and its measurement are difficult concepts. Many pupils believe that the size of an angle depends on the length of the arms or the radius of the arc marking the angle, or that one arm must be horizontal and the direction of the angle anti-clockwise. Students have difficulty recognizing right angles in different orientations and learning to use the standard protractor. Primary school children's understanding of angles was explored by Mitchelmore and White (1998). They explored how children understand angles in a range of fixed and movable situations with everyday objects. Children initially think of an angle as a static image, rather than as dynamic turning. Mitchelmore and White (1996, 1998) suggested that this is because of their experience of particular contexts. They showed that primary school pupils encountered angles in a range of contexts, some of which were dynamic, such as the use of scissors or opening and closing doors, while others were static, such as an angle on a shape. They found the following development in children's ability to recognize similar angles:

- The context of walls, road junctions and tiles
- Scissors
- Fans and sloping signposts
- Door opening and hill slopes
- Turning wheels.

The scissors, fan and door were all openings, the hill slope and slanting signpost were similar visually, while the turning wheel was the most difficult because no 'arms' of the angle were visible. Mitchelmore and White (2000) suggest three stages in the development of angle concepts for primary school pupils:

- Situated: 'limited to situations which look alike, involve similar actions, and are experienced in similar social circumstance' (p. 214);
- Contextual: 'most children have formed clear and distinct contextual angle concepts of slope, turn, intersection and corner by the age of 9 years but that their concept of bend [as a turn] is still vague' (p. 215);
- Abstract: 'recognition of similarities between different angle contexts is . . . a constructive process requiring reflective abstraction' (p. 216).

Gates and Griffin (1988: 12) suggest that 'describing an angle as a measure of pointedness is fine when an angle is acute, but if pupils are asked to consider an obtuse (between 90° and 180°) or reflex (between 180° and 360°) angle such representation may lead to errors'. The fixed or static

KEY POINT TO CONSIDER

Angles need to be represented as both static images of 'pointedness' and as dynamic examples of 'turns' in order to develop understanding of the topic.

descriptions become unhelpful as the angles become more unusual. For example, describing a reflex angle of 300° as a 'corner' or a 'point' is misleading and as Gates and Griffin (1988: 14) point out 'in the case of angle it seems common for pupils of all ages to confuse "angle" with "arc" and "vertex" '. The implication therefore is that the teaching for two-dimensional angle should include not only various static situations, such as corners of tiles, road junctions and so on, but also experiences of more dynamic contexts, such as scissors and fans, where the moving 'arms' can be visualized, progressing to other rotations such as on a wheel. It is likely that dynamic software such as Logo, and the use of Roamer or other programmable toys which all emphasize the difference between movement in a straight line and turning, and the measurement of both, will help children's understanding (Clements and Sarama-Meredith, 1993).

Magina and Hoyles (1997) also investigated how children interpret angles on an analogue clock or watch face. They discuss the findings of previous research into children's misconceptions on angles (such as APU, 1980; Hershkowitz, 1990). They report, for example, children's confusion between the length of the 'arms' and the angle represented between them, and also the difficulty with recognizing the difference between acute, obtuse and right angles when presented with them other than in the standard vertical or horizontal configurations. This is analogous to the idea of concept image mentioned in the chapter on shapes. With measurement of time more broadly, a number of challenges arise (Long and Kamii, 2001). Some of these are directly related to angles in an analogue clock face with its conventions of quarters and halves, and some to digital clocks where children often make mistakes by applying their decimal number knowledge. So, for example, with the following question, 'If a cake goes in the oven at 9.20 and takes 50 minutes to cook, when will it be ready?', a common error for 8-year-olds is to give the answer 9.70 rather than 10.10 (Ryan and Williams, 2007).

Other misconceptions have been documented in the area of science teaching (Hapkiewiz, 1992) but which relate directly to children's experience of measures in mathematics:

- Measurement is only linear.
- Any quantity can be measured as accurately as you want.
- The metric system is more accurate than other measurement systems (such as Imperial measures).
- You can only measure to the smallest unit shown on the measuring device.
- Only the area of rectangular shapes can be measured in square units.
- You cannot measure the volume of some objects because they do not have 'regular' lengths, widths, or heights.

Other kinds of measures, such as weight, capacity and temperature have similar problems, some of which relate to difficulties with measuring devices such as reading the scale, and others to understanding of numbers and number operations such as multiplication and division and the use of fractions and decimals when these are involved.

Communicating measures

Measuring is a vital part of everyday life and involves a wide range of contexts, with each context often having a particular vocabulary. The language of measurement is so much a part of everyday speech that children will have become very familiar with the terminology from a very early age:

> you're too heavy;
> it's too small;
> the bottle is full;
> the bath is empty;
> in two minutes;

and so on.

The measurement of time alone provides a vast vocabulary as identified by Cockburn (1999): second/minute/hour/meantime/sometimes/days of the week/ months of the year/soon/not long/last year/next year, are but a few of the possible examples. It is accordingly important when teaching any aspect of measurement that this prior experience is utilized, and in particular that the language children are famil-iar with forms the foundation upon which to introduce the more precise mathematical language associated with measurement.

Children's early measurement begins with their use of non-standard measuring, but they need lots of practical activities with a range of resources to develop a sound understanding of the purpose of measurement. See, for instance Activity 9.1. The relevance of the measurement of weight emerges from the activity, rather than the children merely practising for practice's sake, although practice is necessary for reinforcing understanding and for developing accuracy. This kind of activity can be adapted for older children by, for example, comparing fresh fruit and vegetables with tinned and/or dried fruit and vegetables, and also comparing dried with soaked, to discover which is the most economical.

Activity 9.1 Vegetables and fruit

When introducing the concepts of 'heavy' and 'light', a variety of vegetables or fruit can be brought into the classroom for comparison. The potatoes or carrots can be com-pared, predictions made as to which is heavier and which is lighter, and the predictions then tested using balance scales, and cubes or counters. Or from the contents of a bag of apples: 'Which is the largest/fattest and who can guess its weight?' The children can be encouraged to discuss why it may be important to know the weight of the apples or potatoes.

Children need to appreciate the importance of accuracy, even with non-standard measures. In fact using hand spans to measure the length of a table is a good introduc-tion to the relevance of having standards measures. The children can be asked to measure their table in the classroom and the results recorded – assuming the tables are all the same size the results should be the same. However, much depends on the hand span of the individual children and the accuracy of their measuring. All children can then compare their hand spans and at this point rulers can be introduced as an example of a standard measuring device.

KEY POINT TO CONSIDER

Measurement is a skill we need to develop in mathematics. It is important to ensure all relevant topics and processes are fully covered in our teaching, and that the activities chosen relate to real-life experiences so that children can practise their skills.

The sheer scope of measurement as a topic, encompassing as it does such a range of facts and basic skills to be taught, learnt, practised and understood, poses particular challenges for its effective coverage in the curriculum. It is therefore crucial that children are given time and opportunities to practise these important life skills with activities that are both interesting and which demonstrate the real-life relevance of each aspect of measurement. While practising their skills, they should also be encouraged to use and develop their use of the more precise vocabulary that is appropriate to the given topic of measurement.

As we highlighted earlier, linear measure is conceptually the simplest area to begin with, although not all children find using rulers accurately an easy task, and some very young ones may not have fully developed the motor and coordination skills necessary for handling rulers. So that such developmental issues are not a constraint and that the children possess the relevant skills, their proficiency at using a ruler, metre stick or trundle wheel for measuring length will depend on the opportunities they have had to repeatedly use these tools in relevant and engaging tasks. And it is in completing these that they will also begin to develop an understanding of the relevance of scale. See, for example Activity 9.2.

Activity 9.2 Myself

A topic on 'Myself' provides many measuring activities, including some not solely concerned with measuring straight lines:

Who is the tallest/shortest?
Who has the largest head?
Who has the longest/shortest arm?
Who has the biggest/smallest feet?

Another simple activity involving the use of a metre stick or trundle wheel can be for the children to estimate the length of a line if they all stood side by side (or holding hands) – the estimations can then be checked with the appropriate tool. For an experience of measuring larger areas that allows for discussion about the appropriateness of the measuring tool, and which can also introduce the language of area and perimeter, the children can be involved in measuring a carpet (real or prospective/imaginary for the reading corner). A more challenging task, suitable for older children, can be for them to design a garden for the school, or for older children in the school to design a play corner for the nursery. These activities give rise naturally to much discussion during which the children can be encouraged to develop their proficiency in the language associated with measuring in a meaningful and relevant context.

For the introduction of weight and children's experience of measuring grams and kilograms, cooking provides the most obvious source of activities. And for the children, these can be particularly meaningful if there is something good to eat at the end of the task! Cooking activities can provide both practice at exact measuring and at reading scales, but also can highlight the relevance of exact measuring. A recipe for a sponge cake can be followed using quantities of the ingredients as specified, and at the same time another sponge cake made with, perhaps, twice as much and a teaspoon of sugar. The relevance of exact measurements will be apparent from tasting the result, but the activity also provides the opportunity for much discussion.

A comparable activity can be used when covering the topic of capacity. In their early years, children spend much time at the sand and water trays, measuring with cups and various other utensils. But when standard measures are introduced, they need lots of experience with measuring jugs and in particular in reading scales accurately. As with the cooking activity, they can, for example, make a jelly using the exact amount of water specified, while another jelly is made using too much water and another made with too little water. The results provide opportunity for discussion. A similar activity uses concentrated fruit juice which is diluted with varied quantities of water and the results discussed. A more challenging task is to work out how many bottles of lemonade or cola might be required for the teddy bears' picnic or school disco respectively.

Children can become confused with volume and capacity, and so it is important that activities clearly demonstrate the difference. Activities related to volume should, in their simplest form, relate to filling a space. In the early years, children can experiment to discover how many cubes are needed to fill a particular box, but here it is important to provide a range of boxes of both different sizes and shapes to encourage discussion. Multilink cubes, and plasticine because of its malleability, are excellent for providing children with the opportunity to create and discuss different shapes of the same volume. Further challenges for older children can be to find the optimal combination of different shaped food items to fit into a lunch box, or the best use of available space when packing a shopping bag or suitcase – again real life situations that bring home the relevance of the concepts to the children.

Time is so much a part of our everyday life and our culture that neither children nor adults see it as a mathematical topic (Cockburn, 1999), and yet it is a difficult topic to teach effectively. As noted earlier, the range of language associated with time is vast and in order to cover this range it is important to provide activities that engage the children and make sense in terms of the everyday language they are familiar with.

Most pre-school children will have experience of the language and units of time associated with the days of the week and months of the year. This prior knowledge can be built on in the early years by looking at the passage of time during the school day – starting with the basics of play time/dinner time/home time and then building in the length of lessons and assembly, etc., which can all be checked against the clock. Time can also be covered in other areas of the curriculum – a stopwatch can be used in PE to record how many hops/how many jumps/how many skips can be achieved in one minute. In science, a growth graph for an amaryllis can be recorded over a given period, or in history the construction of time lines can be introduced to represent intervals within a longer, historically defined period such as the reign of Queen Victoria. For older children, timetables provide a resource for a number of activities – not just reading for practice, but planning journeys in a given time, or times of journeys using different means of transport – whether local or global. Examples that derive naturally from the children's experience of summer holidays are an obvious source of activities here.

In summary, children need a wide range of experiences in order to cover all aspects of measurement in the curriculum. The important role of the teacher is to encourage the use of appropriate language for the task, as well as to introduce the more precise vocabulary associated with measurement. This is so that the children become competent and confident at measuring within a range of contexts; are equipped with a range of tools to do so; and fully understand the relevance of how and why we measure – so providing them with the fundamentals of an essential life skill. Practice is a crucial aspect of this, and so sufficient time for adequate practice needs to be built into lesson design and planning at all stages. However, failure to do so in the early stages is particularly detrimental, since children are doubly disadvantaged later on. They will, for example, have continuing difficulty in secondary school geometry when attempting to use a protractor or compass effectively if time has not been allowed to master these skills at an earlier stage.

Questions for discussion

1   How would you incorporate the important aspects of measurement into a teaching sequence – perhaps taking a particular property such as length as an example?

2   How can a historical perspective on measurement help to develop children's understanding of the concept? Again, how can this be incorporated into your teaching?

3   This chapter highlighted the difference between 'telling the time' and the concept of measuring time. What is the focus within the curriculum that you work with? Is more of a 'measurement perspective' required and how could this be incorporated into your teaching?

4   Should money be included with measurement? If not, where should we include it?

10
Data handling

Throughout this book, we have tried to define carefully the concepts that we have been looking at, in order to gain insight and to clarify the mathematical issues involved. In this chapter, we begin by doing the same thing for data handling. However, we will take a further step back and ask what we mean by 'data', before we consider how we handle this concept. The *Collins English Dictionary* (2004) defines data as 'a series of observations, measurements, or facts; information'. Technically, 'data' is the plural for 'datum', a single observation, measurement or fact, but 'data' is commonly used in a singular sense as well. We can see that data can be the result of our topic in the last chapter, that of measurement. Data can also be observations, both in the sense of observing 'how many', i.e. counting something, and also in a broader sense of observing an occurrence or situation. We can have quantitative data based on numbers (i.e. counts or measurements) or we can have qualitative data (e.g. the data obtained from interviewing someone). Therefore, 'data' has a broad meaning. In the context of primary or elementary school mathematics, we take a quantitative view of data, looking at counts and measurements. We will therefore describe the various ways in which we can 'handle' this type of data.

What is data handling?

Within their 'data handling and **probability**' standard for teaching mathematics, the National Council of Teachers of Mathematics (NCTM) in the US recommends that 'students formulate questions that can be answered using data and addresses what is involved in gathering and using this data wisely' (NCTM, 2000: 48). If we break down this statement, we can identify some of the components of data handling:

- Formulating questions
- Gathering data
- Using the data.

This is similar to the four-step process that Graham (1991) highlighted for data handling:

- Pose the question
- Collect the data (collecting and recording)
- Analyse the data (processing and representing)
- Interpret the results.

Shaughnessy *et al.* (1996) stated that 'data analysis emphasizes organising, describing, representing and analysing data' (p. 205), and Watson and Moritz (2001) highlighted the representing, interpretation and prediction aspects of data handling. Shaughnessy *et al.* (1996) also referred to and extended previous work by Curcio to put forward four aspects of data handling:

- Look at the data (analysis)
- Look between the data (comparison)
- Look beyond the data (inference)
- Look behind the data (look at the beliefs and attitudes lying behind data).

KEY POINT TO CONSIDER

There are several components of data handling. To develop understanding, they need to be clearly distinguished, so that children can be clear about what they are doing in data handling.

Therefore, we can see that data handling covers a number of different aspects and processes, with different researchers and sources emphasizing different areas. Now, in our discussion of understanding mathematics, we have drawn upon the ideas of 'representing' and 'reasoning', and we use these ideas here to bring together the views of data handling into a whole that we can explore further. We therefore suggest the components to data handling as shown in Table 10.1. In formulating data handling in this way, we hope that we have answered another question, namely why do we do data handling? Data handling provides us with the opportunity of representing an observation, a measure or a fact in a different way, so that we can more easily explore, reason and draw conclusions about them. Without this process of 're-presenting' or reorganizing the information, it is difficult for us to make sense of it.

Table 10.1 Components of data handling

Component	Activities involved
What shall we represent?	Formulating the question
Representing the data	Collecting, recording and organizing the data Processing and analysing the data
Reasoning with the data	Interpreting the data Comparing data Predicting and inferring with the data
Reasoning about the data	Looking behind the data at its collection

Having formulated our conception of data handling, let us move on to examine each of the above components.

What shall we represent?

Graham (1991) points out that deciding on what question to answer in a data handling exercise has repercussions for all the other stages. For example, we might have two similar questions: 'Which class has the fastest runner?' and 'Which class is better at running?' The data that we collect will be determined by what we mean by 'fastest runner' or 'better at running'. Should we have a race (deciding on the distance to be run) and then record the finishing positions of everyone in

> **KEY POINT TO CONSIDER**
>
> Data can provide information to answer a range of questions, and can be represented in a variety of ways. Understanding the nature of the question being asked is therefore important in order to decide on the most appropriate method of representation.

the race? Should we alternatively have everyone run a certain distance individually and record their time? The answers to these questions determine what kind of data we will collect. Also, if we decide on the question 'which class is better at running', how will we compare different classes? What would be the best way of presenting this data to help with this comparison? We therefore have to consider the way in which we will represent the data in light of the kind of question we want to ask. Therefore, we simply have to be aware of this relationship between the question we wish to ask and the way we will handle the data; to put it another way, between what we will represent and how we will represent it. It is all too easy to rush into the data collection and realize that it does not in fact help with the question that you asked!

Representing the data

Let us now explore the variety of ways in which we can represent data. Orton and Frobisher (1996) highlight different ways of presenting data, with a range of graphical representations but also tables of data as well. The examples that they give for the tables use tallying methods for recording data onto paper. In the example given in Figure 10.1, when the question of 'How do you usually get

> **KEY POINT TO CONSIDER**
>
> There are several ways of graphically representing data. All of these should be covered in our teaching so that the most appropriate graph can be selected to represent the relevant data.

to school?' was asked of the children in the class, a tally mark was made against each mode of transport according to the responses of the children. Representing the responses of children in this way allows us easily to count the number of times children gave each response (or what we call the **frequency** of each response). We can then use graphical methods to further represent the data (see Figures 10.2, 10.3 and 10.4). The **pictograph** in Figure 10.2 is clearly related to the tally marks, with a one-to-one correspondence between the pictures and the counts. We can make this simpler but more abstract with the block graph and even more so with the bar chart

How people in my class get to school	Tally	Count or frequency
Walking	1111	5
By car	1111 1111 11	12
By bus	1111 1111	9
By bicycle	11	2

Figure 10.1 An example of tabulated data

How children in my class get to school

Walking	Walk	Walk	Walk	Walk	Walk						
By car	Car	Car	Car	Car	Car	Car	Car	Car	Car	Car	Car	Car
By bus	Bus	Bus	Bus	Bus	Bus	Bus	Bus	Bus	Bus			
By bicycle	Bike	Bike										

Figure 10.2 A pictograph

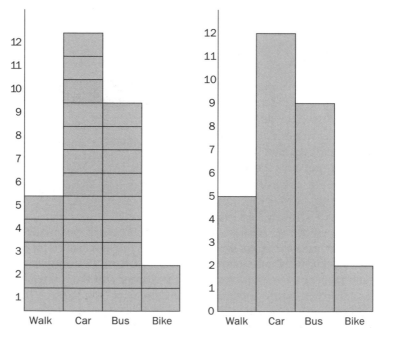

Figure 10.3 A block graph and a bar chart

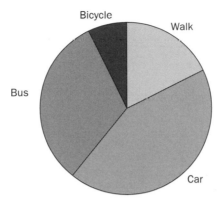

Figure 10.4 A pie chart

(see Figure 10.3). In each of these graphs, the length of the portion of the graph signifies the number or the frequency of the particular category. The pie chart (see Figure 10.4), however, represents the data quite differently. The size of each part of the pie chart represents the number of data in a particular category as a proportion of all the recorded data. For example, for those stating that they used a car to get to school, 12 children out of a total of 28 gave this response. Therefore, almost a half of the pie chart represents the car category. More exactly, the angle at the middle of the circle for this 'piece of pie' would be $\frac{12}{28} \times 360°$ (i.e. the fraction of the total angle of the circle which we should give over to the car response) which is about 154°. The bicycle response, with only 2 out of 28 responses, would cover only about 26° of the circle.

Two other graphs are shown in Figures 10.5 and 10.6 – a line graph and a scatter graph. Whereas the previous graphs have concentrated on measures (specifically counts) related to categories, these two graphs show two measures in relation to each other. We see how one measure is 'dependent' on the other, i.e. how the temperature in Tokyo is dependent on the time of year, or how a child's Year 4 mark is dependent on their mark from the previous year. The measure that we look at to see how it changes is usually referred to as the **dependent variable** and is conventionally plotted on the vertical axis of the graph. The other measure that we look at to see how it affects the dependent measure is referred to as the **independent variable**. For each value of the independent variable and the related dependent variable, we place a point at the corresponding position on the graph. With a line graph, the points are joined together with a line. With a scatter plot, they are left as they are.

We will now look at two more graphs. Unlike the tables or graphs in Figures 10.1 to 10.6 that summarize data, in Caroll and Venn diagrams, we can actually place objects within the graphical representations (see Figures 10.7 and 10.8). Depending on the properties of the objects, they are placed in different parts of the diagrams. For example, '2' is placed in both the even numbers and prime numbers parts of the Venn diagram, and '9' is placed outside both. Strictly speaking, these two types of graphs are not used to 'handle data', however they are used for reasoning, which we will describe in more detail below. We therefore include them here.

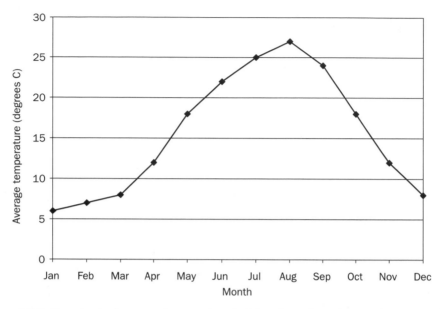

Figure 10.5 Line graph of average temperature in Tokyo throughout the year (measured in the middle of each month)

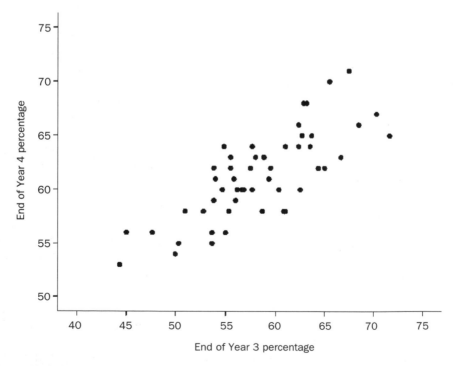

Figure 10.6 Scatter graph of Year 4 marks against Year 3 marks

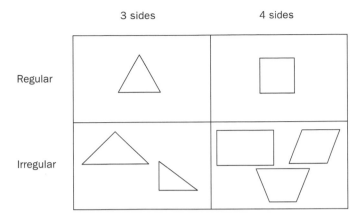

Figure 10.7 Caroll diagram categorizing 3- and 4-sided shapes

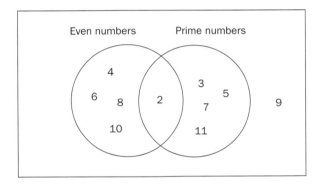

Figure 10.8 Venn diagram categorizing numbers

Reasoning with the data

Having represented the data graphically, this then helps us to reason with the data, specifically to make interpretations, comparisons and predictions. How can we interpret some of the graphs discussed? With the pictograph, the block graph and the bar chart, we can see which are the most popular or least popular ways of getting to school. Likewise with the pie chart. With the line graph, we can get a feel for how the temperature in Tokyo varies

over the year – when it is hottest there and when it is coldest. With the scatter graph, we can see that there seems to be quite a close relationship between the mark that children get in Year 3 and in Year 4 – the higher the mark in Year 3, the higher the mark will most likely be in Year 4. Finally, in the Caroll and the Venn diagrams, we can start to interpret the properties of the objects. For example, does the Caroll diagram tell us more what we mean by a 'regular shape'? Well, from the objects that are included in this category, we can interpret the category as being shapes which have all sides of the same length. However, we can see that there is a rhombus (a parallelogram with four equal sides) included in the 'irregular shapes' category. So a regular shape is more than just equal sides, it must have all angles equal as well. Likewise, we can deduce some properties of prime numbers as well. For example, they are always odd numbers apart from '2', but they do not include all odd numbers.

We can make comparisons with the graphs as well. For example, we can say how many more people come in a car compared to the bus, based on the pictograph, the block graph and the bar chart. In the line graph, we can compare the differences in temperature between different months. Alternatively, we could plot another set of data on the graph such as the temperatures for another city. In Figure 10.9 we can see, for example, the difference in when we have the hottest months in a northern hemisphere city and a southern hemisphere city.

Finally, let us make some predictions from our graphs. We could say from our data collection on modes of transport that if we look at another class in the school, we would predict that most children would come by car to school. As we will see, whether this prediction is true or not will depend on a variety of other factors. The scatter graph is also particularly useful for making predictions. If we have identified a possible relationship between two properties, we can put in a 'middle line' (more technically known as the 'line of best fit') to show this relationship. The line does not necessarily need to be straight, however this is the easiest type of line to put in. From this line, we can make quite specific predictions. Looking at Figure 10.10, if, for example, a child gets 65% in the end of Year 3, then reading off from the line, we would expect them to also get about 65% in the end of Year 4 test.

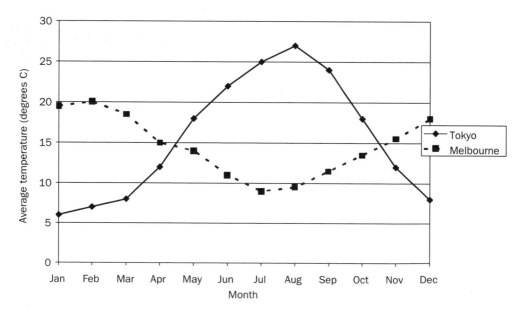

Figure 10.9 Comparing the temperatures in Tokyo and Melbourne

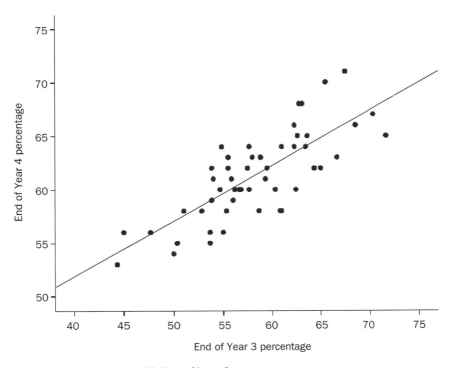

Figure 10.10 Scatter graph with line of best fit

Reasoning about the data

In light of our discussion above, there are a number of issues we could think about with regards to the data more generally. For example, we could think about how accurate the data might be. With the temperature data, how much variation do we see from year to year? In the test data in the scatter graph, are there children that achieved unusually high or low scores? In both cases, we could consider how we could make the data more accurate. Related to this is how accurate our predictions might be. Let us assume that the data

> ### KEY POINT TO CONSIDER
>
> Reasoning about the properties of the data is an important aspect of the topic on data handling. Questioning the validity of data and considering the nature of the data representation should be a feature in our teaching in order to promote children's more sophisticated reasoning with data.

for our block chart was from a Year 3 class, and we decide to get data from a Year 6 class as well. In Figure 10.11 we can see that our initial prediction that children in other classes would most likely travel by car was wrong. We need to reason about the data to explain why that might be. It might be because the Year 6 children are different from those in Year 3 in terms of age; they are more able to travel by foot, bus or bike, and this is therefore reflected in the differences between the graphs. So the **sample** of children that we looked at in each case is quite different.

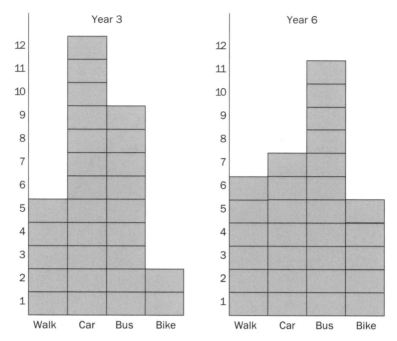

Figure 10.11 Comparing data from Year 3 and Year 6

One last issue that we can consider about the data is the method we choose to represent the data. Why do we end up choosing a bar chart or alternatively a line graph? Does the choice matter? Well, we have already seen that it does matter in terms of the question we are trying to answer. The pie chart is more useful if we wish to talk about the proportions of children choosing different modes of transport, but block graphs or bar charts might be more useful for reading off actual numbers of children. However, could we not have chosen something like a line graph to show the data (see Figure 10.12)? If we do plot a line graph for the modes of transport data for Year 3 children, let us look at what we have. We still have the peak for travel by car. However, do the lines joining the points have any meaning? In the temperature graph, the line did have meaning because it gave us an indication of the temperatures between the middle of the months. This is because the property that we were plotting, the time of year, was a 'continuous' property, and we had just taken data at specific points along the continuum. However, for the modes of transport, we have 'discrete' categories, so any point between the categories has no meaning (we are not implying a mix of walking and using the car by using the line between the points). Therefore, the line graph for a discrete property is not meaningful. When we represent the data, we need to reason more broadly about the properties we are looking at so we can present the data in meaningful ways. This is not to say that we cannot use something like a bar chart for continuous properties. However, when we do so, we have to collapse the data into discrete categories. For example then, in Figure 10.13, the frequencies are for the number of children achieving marks within the given ranges – from 50 up to (but not including) 55, from 55 up to 60 and so on.

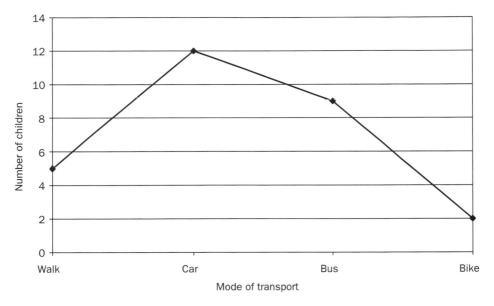

Figure 10.12 A line graph of categorical data?

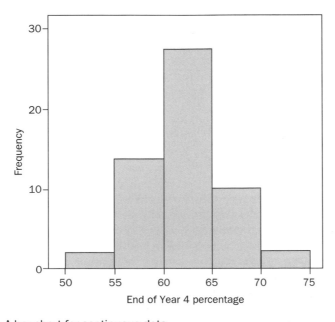

Figure 10.13 A bar chart for continuous data

Representing the data using average and spread values

In addition to the more visual ways of representing data that we have so far discussed, we can try and summarize data in a concise, numerical format. Doing so, we draw on the notion of 'average' values. Turning to the *Collins English Dictionary* (2004) once again, 'average' is defined as 'the typical or normal amount, quality, degree, etc.' Mokros and Russell (1995) highlight that 'young children use this word in an informal way to refer to typical, usual or middle. Older children also use the word to indicate the mean, median, or mode – terms they have learnt in school' (p. 20). There is therefore an intuitive way of thinking about averages, and also a more school-based mathematical way. What we need to do is to make connections between these two views.

If we were to look at Figure 10.11, what would we say were the typical modes of transport for Year 3 and Year 6 children? The one property that we can easily identify from the graph is the category with the largest count or frequency. Therefore, we could say that the car is the typical mode of transport for Year 3s, and the bus for Year 6s. Looking for the most frequent category is one type of average we can use, and we call this the 'mode' or the 'modal' category. Likewise, in Figure 10.13, we can see that marks in the range 60% to 65% is the modal category. We can see that this agrees with our intuitive view of average, and we could use the mode to describe the data that we have collected.

The problem with using the mode is that in summarizing the data, we lose all the information about the non-modal categories. For example, the graph shown in Figure 10.14 can be summarized by the same mode as for Figure 10.13, however, we can see that the data is very different. Therefore, just using the mode can misrepresent the data.

One way of taking into account more of the data is by taking the middle value of the data. We can list all of the marks used in Figure 10.14:

60, 60, 60, 60, 60, 60, 60, 61, 61, 61, 62, 62, 62, 62, 62, 62, 63, 63, 63, 63, 63, 64, 64, 64, 64, 64, 68, 69, 70, 70, 71, 71, 71, 71, 73, 73, 73, 73, 73, 73, 74, 74, 80, 80, 80, 81, 81, 82, 83, 83, 85, 86

There are 52 data values, therefore the middle value would lie between the 26th value (in this case 64) and the 27th value (68). We therefore say that the middle value of the data set is halfway between these two, i.e. a mark of 66%. If we had an odd number of data values, then we would just choose the middle value, rather than finding the halfway point between two values.

We refer to the middle value as the 'median' and we can again see that it is intuitively fairly easy to understand the use of this kind of average value to describe the data. Also, if the data changes, the median can change as well. For example, in comparison, the median from the data in Figure 10.13 is 61.5%, much lower than in

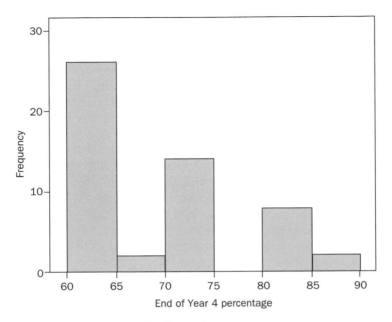

Figure 10.14 Another bar chart for the Year 4 data

Figure 10.14. Representing the data in this way also allows us to reason with the data. Comparing the median values of 61.5 and 66 allows us to reason that the marks in the second set of data were generally much higher. We can reason this without actually looking at the individual data values. Using the median value also has its drawbacks though. For example, if the lowest score listed above was 40 instead of 60, or the highest score was 100 instead of 86, the median would still remain the same. Therefore, we still lose a lot of information about the extreme data values.

Yet another way of showing the average of a set of data is by using the 'mean'. The mean can be thought of in terms of the value we would have if we had a 'fair share' or a 'balance' or a 'levelling out' of what we are measuring over all the instances we are measuring (Mokros and Russell, 1995). For example, if we shared out all the marks listed above in a balanced way over the 52 children that sat the test, what mark would each child get? Well, the total percentage that everyone had was 3578 (adding all the percentage marks together). Therefore, sharing this out equally would give 3578 ÷ 52 = 68.8. The mean mark then is 68.8%. In contrast, the mean mark for the data in Figure 10.13 is 61.3%. We can see that if one of the marks listed was changed, then this would change the overall average using the mean. The mean value is therefore sensitive to these changes.

The drawback to the mean is that it is not intuitive as an 'average' value and more complicated to calculate. In addition, there are times when we cannot use the mean, or in fact the median, in a meaningful way. For example, going back to our categorical data with our modes of transport, there is no meaningful way to order the data in order to choose the median. We need data with an inherent order to be able to work out this average. Likewise, we cannot add together the measures (i.e. the modes of transport) in order to spread them out evenly. We need continuous numerical data to do this rather than categorical data.

Average values are not the only way in which we can concisely represent sets of data. We can also indicate the 'spread' of data. Figure 10.15 shows two sets of data, one (on the right hand side) with a far greater spread, even though they have the same median and mean values. There are a number of ways in which we can represent the spread of data. One way is to use the **range** of the data, i.e. the highest value take away the lowest value. Therefore, in the data listed previously, the range is 86 − 60 = 26. Alternatively, we can calculate the **inter-quartile range**. Like finding the median value, we can find the quartile values which are the values at the quarter point and the three quarter point. So, out of a data set of 52 values, dividing the data set into quarters (i.e. sets of 13 data), the first quarter value will be between the 13th and 14th data (i.e. 62) and the three quarter point will be between the 39th and 40th data (i.e. 73). The inter-quartile range is the difference in these values; 73 − 62 = 11. The inter-quartile range is preferable to the overall range in that it is not affected by the odd very high or very low value.

These measures of the spread of data can of course only be used with data with some inherent order, as in the case of using the median. However, we can again reason with these values. For the two sets of data given above in the graphs, the data on the left has an inter-quartile range of 6, but the data on the right has an inter-quartile range of 12. We can therefore reason that the marks for the second set are much more spread out than the first.

In addition to using the inter-quartile range, another indicator of the spread of data is the 'standard deviation' of the data. We use this when we can calculate a mean average for the data. We can then work out the extent to which each measure in the data set is separated from this mean. This gives the standard deviation value. In the

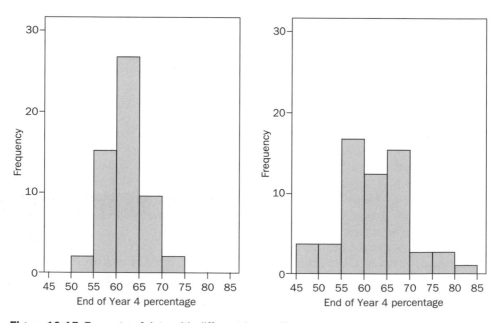

Figure 10.15 Two sets of data with different 'spread'

above graphs, the standard deviation values for the left- and right-hand data sets are 4.0 and 8.1. Like the inter-quartile range therefore, we can represent the spread of the data with this numerical value. The standard deviation can be thought of as being more accurate than the inter-quartile range because it takes into account all of the data points, rather than the middle 50%. However, it is more complicated to calculate.

There is in fact a diagrammatic way of summarizing the information on the spread of data, specifically that of the inter-quartile range. Figure 10.16 shows 'box and whisker' plots that do just this. This graph summarizes the same two sets of data in Figure 10.15. The box and whisker plot has five important parts: in the centre of each plot, the line represents the median of the data. The top and bottom of the box represents the third quarter value and the first quarter value of the data respectively. Therefore, the length of the box represents the inter-quartile range. Finally, the ends of the top and bottom 'whisker' represent the maximum and minimum values of the data respectively. In Figure 10.16, we can see that both data sets have the same median values. However, the second data set has a larger spread of data both in terms of the inter-quartile and the overall range.

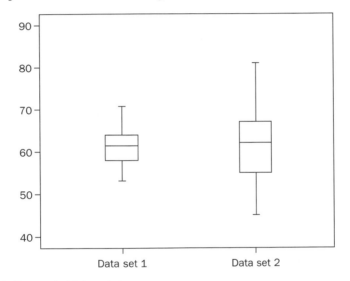

Figure 10.16 Box and whisker plots

Probability

Returning once again to our view of data handling, we will say a little more about 'predicting' within the 'reasoning with data' component. Previously, the predictions that we made with our data were very simple – we would predict that most children would travel by this mode of transport, and so on. We can make our predictions a little more sophisticated using the idea of probability.

KEY POINT TO CONSIDER

Prediction is a component of reasoning with data. It is important for children to understand that probability is a more sophisticated way of making predictions and to highlight this connection in our teaching.

Probability is the measure of how likely an event will happen. Let us return to our Year 3 data for how they get to school (Figure 10.17) and decide how likely it is that a child will come by a certain mode of transport. As we did before, we could say that a Year 3 child is most likely to come by car, and least likely to come by bike. We can be more precise and say 12 out of 28 children came by car. Therefore, if we were to look at another Year 3 class, we might expect a similar proportion to come by car as well. The proportion in this case is

$$\frac{\text{Number who came by car}}{\text{Total number of children}} = \frac{12}{28} = \frac{3}{7} = 0.43$$

If we were to look at another Year 3 class therefore, we can predict that $\frac{3}{7}$ of the class, or 0.43 or 43% of the class, would come by car. In fact, what we have calculated here is the probability of a child coming by car. In general, we calculate probability by finding the number of times a particular event happens out of the number of times any event can happen. This probability is expressed as a proportion (see Chapter 5), i.e. in this case as 3 out of 7 or as a fraction, percentage, etc.

Let us look at another example, that of rolling a single die. We could roll the die a certain number of times, record the number of times that each number shows (perhaps in a tally chart) and then present the information in a graph (maybe a bar chart). Figure 10.18 shows the results after rolling a die 20 times and then after 1000 times. What is the probability of rolling a '2' say? After 20 times, our calculated probability is

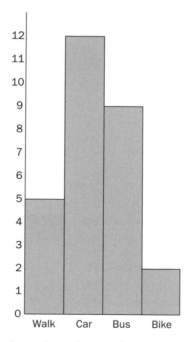

Figure 10.17 How likely is it that a child will travel by a given mode of transport?

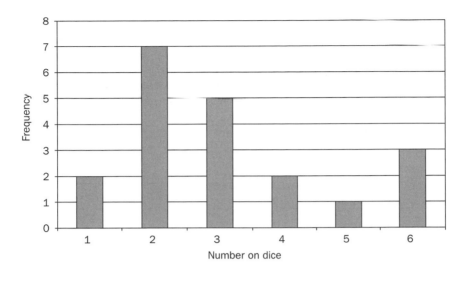

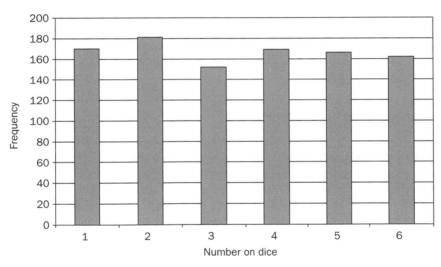

Figure 10.18 Rolling a die 20 times (top) and 1000 times (bottom)

7 out of 20 or $\dfrac{7}{20} = 0.35$. After 1000 times, though, the probability is 181 out of 1000

or $\dfrac{181}{1000} = 0.18$. Why has our probability changed? Well, we have to decide whether, when comparing two sets of data, predictions such as probability are different because there are important differences between the situations that we are collecting data from (for example, in the case of Year 3 and Year 6 children's modes of transport), or the differences are just due to random chance. In this case, we are using the same die so nothing has changed except the number of times we rolled the die. Therefore, the differences are likely to be due to random chance. In fact, when we look at only a small number of data, then predictions are more likely to be affected by chance. It is better to look at a large number of data so that we can make predictions that are less likely to be affected by random events. The size of the sample is therefore important for making predictions.

What we have done in the above examples is calculated 'experimental probability'. However, we could calculate the probability *theoretically* as well. Because there are six faces on the die, and since each face is equally likely to land face up, then we would expect each face would have a likelihood of coming up once out of every six times. Theoretical probability is therefore calculated as:

$$\frac{\text{Number of ways a given event could happen}}{\text{Total number of ways that any event could happen}}$$

The theoretical probability of getting a '2' is therefore $\frac{1}{6}$ or 0.17. We can see that this is much closer to the experimental probability that we got from 1000 rolls of the die than that from 20 rolls of the die. Again, this was because of random chance affecting our results. Therefore, we can use probability to predict what might happen in similar situations, but we should make sure that we predict using a large number of data points. When we look at reasoning *with* the data, the sample size is something that we should reason *about* the data.

Misconceptions with data handling

We have discussed in detail in this chapter the notion of 'data handling' and the related area of probability. To gain further insight into these concepts, let us look at possible misconceptions involved with this area so that we are aware of possible problems when we are teaching the topic. Similar patterns to other areas of mathematics occur in children's difficulties with data handling. These mainly relate to misunderstandings with the mathematical language used or through their attempts to apply what they know from other contexts in some way. For example, with graphs, children's mistakes with graphical representation usually relate to one of the following misunderstandings (Ryan and Williams, 2007):

- *Seeing the graph as a picture* – this involves interpreting aspects of a graph iconically. A typical example would be interpreting a speed/time graph of a car accelerating and imagining that the slope of the graph is a hill or incline that the car was driving up.

- *Basing their interpretation on graphical prototypes* – this involves generalizing from earlier experiences, such as a inferring a one-to-one relationship from early work with pictograms with the number of items displayed, leading to a tendency to overlook the scale on an axis where one 'box' in a bar chart might represent 5 or 10 items. Issues with misinterpreting the scale on graphs are particularly common. Another issue that also occurs frequently is assuming that axes always start at zero.

Further difficulties include children finding it hard to interpret points on a graph which are not on grid intersections. This is similar to challenges to understanding in other areas of mathematics (such as not being able to give a decimal in between 1.4 and 1.5). Children also often misinterpret questions related to graphs and charts such as answering 'how many more did Billy get?' as simply 'how many did Billy get?' – this may either be

> **KEY POINT TO CONSIDER**
>
> Time should be allocated in our lesson planning for children to read a variety of graphs in order to become more proficient at both understanding questions relating to data and correctly interpreting the information gathered.

through a simple misreading of the question or because the task is too demanding for them to work out as a single step.

With probability, early research suggested that young children have little conception of it (Piaget and Inhelder, 1975; Shayer and Adey, 1981), but other studies indicate that early primary or elementary school children do have some intuitions about probability upon which further teaching can build. Falk *et al.* (1980) presented children with two sets, each containing blue and yellow elements. Each time, one colour was pointed out as the 'payoff' colour which provided a reward. The children then had to choose the set from which they would draw at random a 'payoff element' from which they could win. From the age of 6, children began to select the more probable set systematically. It was also found that the ability to choose a likely set correctly preceded the ability to explain or articulate these choices. It seems likely that the context helps to support children's understanding.

Older pupils can give correct examples for certain, possible and impossible events, although the concept of certainty is more problematic than 'possible' and 'impossible' (Fischbein and Gazit, 1984). However, children find it difficult to calculate the probability of events even after instruction on the procedure. That is partly because children at this age tend to create 'part–part' rather than 'part–whole' comparisons (e.g. 9 men and 11 women rather than 9 men out of a total of 20). Children also show some of the same misconceptions as older learners in this area (Ryan and Williams, 2007) such as being influenced by 'recency effects' and interpreting earlier occurrences as part of a pattern. For example, if a coin has come down heads five times, arguing it is more likely to be tails to redress the balance (negative recency) or arguing that if a coin has fallen 'heads tails heads tails, heads, tails' that the pattern will continue (positive recency). This kind of reasoning is also known as the 'Gambler's Fallacy' in trying to identifying patterns in random situations.

Communicating data handling

Following on from the misconceptions with data handling that we identified above, and also our previous discussion on data handling, we could say that one of the problems that children have is that we do not provide enough opportunities for them to reason with and about the data and to use different ways of representing the data. Therefore, when developing a strategy for teaching data handling, it is accordingly important to provide activities which provide this practice alongside the use of terminology as well. Children should be presented with problems or questions which through collaborative work lead them to determine the type of data, the recording and the presentation that is most appropriate. This also creates a real sense of purpose to the activity and children can see the relevance of this topic.

We saw earlier an approach to tackling problems suggested by Graham (1991) which included the following four stages:

- Pose the question
- Collect the data (collecting and recording)
- Analyse the data (processing and representing)
- Interpret the results.

We therefore need to begin by posing a problem. Data can then be collected and collated in a manageable and appropriate way, and discussion is a necessary part of this stage. Children should then be allowed to decide, through discussion, which is the most appropriate presentation of the data. At its simplest level, this can be by sorting and classifying a range of objects, for example buttons or leaves the results of which can be recorded in a Venn diagram using shape/colour/size, or, for simply recording two criteria at the same time as in a Carroll diagram. With younger children, pictograms can be introduced as another technique for recording data – for example, by finding out which is the favourite pet/most popular flavour of crisps/most popular fruit for the children in the class. This activity can be extended by comparing data from other classes and even extended to all classes in the school to see if there are any changes in the outcome.

Whatever the level of the problem, children should be encouraged from the onset to begin with such questioning and discussion as highlighted by Sutherland (2007):

- What is the important data to be collected?
- What is the function of the chart/graph?
- How useful is a particular chart/graph?
- What is the information collected?
- Who is it for?
- How is the information best organized?

The language development relating to handling data will come through the discussion, and an important role for the teacher is to encourage the use of correct terminology throughout the investigation. We can also see that we are encouraging reasoning with and about the data and different ways of representing the data.

Another activity which can be presented at different levels is 'How can we find out the number of each colour of sweets in a tube of Smarties?' At its simplest level, the children can count the different coloured Smarties in the tube and present the results as a bar chart. However, once this information is gathered and presented, the children might then consider its implications and pose further questions of their own such as: 'Does the most common colour in the Smartie tube coincide with the children's favourite colour?' A further class or school survey can be carried out following the same process as identified by Graham (1991) to establish what is the most popular colour, and whether this matches what the producers of Smarties think. We can see again that we are encouraging children to reason with the data that they obtain.

At a more sophisticated level, children can be involved in collecting and presenting information for a range of school projects. For instance, a plot of land has been allocated for a school garden for all the children to enjoy. Before any decision is made, it has to be clear what sort of garden the pupils in the school want. How is this information to be collected, and how and to whom does it have to be presented in order to move the project to take place? Presenting children with real life scenarios such as this allows for much cooperative work. Another problem to investigate is shown in Activity 10.1.

Activity 10.1 Save our playground!

There are threats to close the local playground. What can be done to prevent this? Decisions have to be made about what information has to be collected, how it is collected and what is the most appropriate format. For example, we could ask the questions:

- How many children frequent the playground?
- When is the area most used – time and days of the week?
- Which are the most popular playground activities?
- What would children like to see there?

The outcome needs careful analysis before the results can be presented to the most appropriate body (e.g. the local council).

This kind of activity lends itself to traffic surveys for having a zebra crossing with a lollipop lady outside the school gates, or refurbishing of the school library with the injection of the most popular new fiction and non-fiction books according to the children's preferences. Whatever the activity, we can see that we are encouraging children's representation and reasoning within data handling.

Over and above providing opportunites for data handling, the misconceptions section also highlighted that one cannot ignore the fact that children also need broader opportunities to interpret graphs and charts. This needs to be beyond just reading and responding to specific questions, as in Figure 10.19, for example. Instead, we could ask 'This graph shows a temperature change on Tuesday. Can you explain this?' This adds variety and interest and encourages the children to reason more with the data. We could make more use of everyday issues that appear as graphs or charts

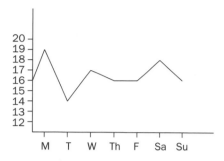

Figure 10.19 A simple interpretation of a graph

in magazines and newspapers, and as timetables/catalogues/travel brochures. This is not just in order to practise reading different and more interesting types of graphs, but to use them to encourage children to question the information presented to them and thus help them to reason about the data.

Moving on to probability, this concept is very much part of our everyday life so children will be familiar with the associated language from an early age. Decisions we make on a daily basis are often based on our experience of the likelihood of events actually happening. However, for very young children, the early ideas of probability can begin simply through the discussion of events in stories (Hopkins *et al.*, 1996). For example:

> What do you think happens to Goldilocks?
> Will Little Red Riding Hood see the wolf?

Hopkins *et al.* highlight a whole range of stories that can be used as a basis for the discussion of the likelihood of events happening, and which establishes quite early on a means of working with probability, and so developing a more confident use of the language through lively discussion.

The process can be developed throughout early primary or elementary school with simple activities based on a range of events familiar to the children. A 'washing line' is a useful tool:

Unlikely	....	Likely
Uncertain	....	Certain
Impossible	....	Possible

The children can place pegs along the line depending on how unlikely/likely, etc. they think the likelihood/certainty/possibility of a range of experiences:

> Seeing a lion on the way home
> Finishing school at 3.00
> Having sausages for tea
> Watching television tonight, etc.

Much lively discussion can ensue from discussing these possibilities, which can also be adapted for older children. The weather, for example, provides a suitable topic for constructing probability statements for which data can be collected and predictions analysed.

Games are a useful resource for introducing the concept of chance. Simple games like Snakes and Ladders can provide the opportunity for discussing the chances of throwing a six in order to commence the game. Children can then investigate the possibility of throwing a six – is it more difficult to get than any other number, or just as difficult? Children can explore a range of games to determine how fair or unfair they consider them to be, and why. They can record their results and discuss their decisions with one another as well as with the teacher, activities which provide further opportunities for developing their communication and language skills.

A challenge can be set for a group to design their own game, which can then be played by another group of children to determine how fair or unfair the game might be in relation to specific questions. Do all players have an equal chance of winning? If not, how can the game be adapted to ensure that it is fair for all players?

Because probability involves the concepts of chance and randomness (Askew, 1998) it is naturally associated with data handling, but it is also very much a part of our daily lives. It is accordingly important, therefore, that children are provided with a range of activities that are enjoyable and consolidate their knowledge and understanding of this aspect of handling data, while at the same time refining their command of the language associated with probability and so developing their communication skills.

Questions for discussion

1   In the past, pupils have often spent most of their time drawing graphs of data. Now, especially with the advent of computers, we can very quickly create these graphs. So what place does graph drawing have in a modern curriculum?

2   Should the focus of the data handling curriculum now be on analysing data rather than representing data, which can easily be undertaken accurately and quickly on a computer?

3   In your existing or potential role as a teacher, what data or graphs will you be required to collect, analyse, interpret and present? How can you enable others to reason with the data that you present? What issues may arise when you are reasoning about this data?

11

Problem solving

In this final chapter of the book we examine the concept of problem solving. It is debatable whether we should actually have this separate chapter, as there is a danger of treating problem solving as a separate 'topic' to the areas of mathematics we have already discussed. This is a criticism that has already been levelled by Schoenfeld (1992) at previous texts: 'In virtually all mainstream texts, "problem solving" is a separate activity and highlighted as such' (p. 354). We therefore emphasize that problem solving should not be seen as a 'topic', but rather as an approach to mathematics teaching that supports the aim of this book, that of developing understanding in primary mathematics. Lester and Lambdin (2004: 192) stated that:

> We believe that the primary goals of mathematics learning are understanding and problem solving, and that these goals are inextricably related because learning mathematics with understanding is best supported by engaging in problem solving. The connection between solving problems and deepening understanding is symbiotic . . . in order to become a good problem solver, you need to have sound understanding. Thus, understanding enhances problem solving.

Likewise, Hiebert *et al.* (1996) highlighted the following benefits of problem solving:

- Insights into the structure of the subject matter (i.e. relationships and connections between concepts);
- Develop strategies for problem solving;
- Develop dispositions (i.e. attitudes and beliefs) towards mathematics.

The first benefit is very much in line with our picture of understanding. Therefore, we can see that problem-solving activities can be seen as developing understanding in mathematics.

The reason we have included problem solving as a separate chapter is that when we examine what is entailed in the process, we see it as one of representing problem situations and reasoning our approaches to these. In fact, we will use our ideas of representation and reasoning to talk about approaches to problem solving. Therefore, we see problem solving as being in line with the approach to developing understanding in mathematics that we have discussed throughout the book. The discussion of problem solving is a fitting culmination in that it somewhat exemplifies the approaches towards mathematics that we have used in the

book. To open this chapter, as we have done throughout, we begin the discussion of problem solving by defining what we mean by the concept. We then move on to discuss what is involved in the process of problem solving, highlighting the representation and reasoning aspects of the process.

What is problem solving?  *definition of problem solving*

The National Council of Teachers of Mathematics (NCTM, 2000) in the US defines problem solving as 'engaging in a task for which the solution method is not known in advance' (p. 52). Likewise, Bell and Burkhardt (2002) state the definition for problem solving used by the Programme for International Student Assessment (PISA) project as follows: 'Problem solving is cognitive processing directed at achieving a goal when no solution method is obvious to the problem solver' (p. 2). Therefore, there is a consistent notion that problem solving involves not knowing the solution method. However, Bell and Burkhardt also provide their own definition of problem solving: 'Problem solving is the activity called into play when there is a demand to apply knowledge, skill and experience to unfamiliar situations' (p. 2). Again we have the unfamiliar or unknown method of approaching the problem. In addition though, we have the notion of applying our knowledge. Hiebert *et al.* (1996: 14) highlight this view of problem solving:

> The recent reform recommendations place a heavier emphasis on applications and connections of mathematics to the real-world . . . Mathematics acquired in these realistic situations, proponents argue, will be perceived by students as being useful. Rather than acquiring knowledge that is isolated from real situations, students will acquire knowledge that is connected to such situations, and they will be able to apply this knowledge to a range of real-life problems.

Therefore, another view of problem solving is in situations in which we have to 'apply' our knowledge, often in problems that are set in 'real-life' contexts. However, Hiebert *et al.* also warn that this view of problem solving results in a view that separates 'acquiring' knowledge and 'applying' it. If this is the case, then how do we reconcile this view of problem solving with the aim of developing understanding? For now, let us bear in mind this warning; we will return to this particular point in the discussion a little later on.

In defining what we mean by problem solving, we invariably end up looking at what we actually mean by a 'problem'. Mayer (1985) defines a problem as 'when you are confronted with a given situation – let's call that the *given state* – and you want another situation – let's call that the *goal state* – but there is no obvious way of accomplishing your goal' (p. 123; original emphasis). This obviously leads to the first view of problem solving given above. Likewise, Orton and Frobisher (1996: 25) define a problem as 'a situation in which an individual student:

(a) recognizes or believes that there exists a mathematical goal to be achieved, usually an answer of some kind;
(b) accepts the challenge to perform some mathematical task in order to reach the goal;
(c) has no readily known or recallable mathematical procedure available to enable the goal to be attained directly.'

In both cases, a problem has no obvious solution and also it has a 'goal' to be reached. Taking this view of a problem, it is interesting to consider the different types of problems that there are. Anghileri (2007) provides a range of problem types involving number. For example,

Missing numbers and missing operations:

$$170 + \square = 220 - \square$$
$$58 \; \square \; 26 = 84$$

Multi-step calculations:

Alice and Ben each buy a bicycle but they pay in different ways. Alice pays £179.99. Ben pays £8.62 every week for 24 weeks. Ben pays more than Alice. How much more?

Logical thinking:

Each missing digit in this sum is a 9 or a 1. Write in the missing digits.
$$\square\square + \square\square + \square\square = 201$$

Problems leading to algebra:

Riaz thinks of a number. He says 'Halve my number and then add 17. The answer is 23'. What is Riaz's number?

In each of the questions, we can say that the solution method is not obvious (in fact there may by more than one solution), but there is a goal to be achieved. Orton and Frobisher (1996) provide the contrast with other types of 'problems' that we may come across. For example:

How many more than 286 is 637?

They describe this as a 'routine problem' in that the problem simply involves a standard question 637 − 286 translated into words. From our definition, this is still a problem in that the child doing it needs to decide on the operation, and indeed there are different solution methods. Interestingly, Orton and Frobisher (1996) also discuss investigations such as 'explore square numbers'. Now with this open-ended question, we would argue that there is no particular goal here so we would say that investigations are distinct from problems. Therefore, we can be quite clear about what we mean by a problem. Interestingly, if we were to consider the 'real-life' view of problem solving, then we can see from the types of problems covered above that this view limits the types of problems we might use – for example, the logical thinking problem is anything but real-life. Also, when we talk about real-life problems, whose 'real-life' are we referring to? So, we would suggest that we need to maintain a broader perspective on problem solving than this.

What we have considered so far are situations that involve problem solving. However, we can view problem solving not just from the point of view of the situations but also the processes that the situations require when we actually problem solve. In the primary curriculum in England and Wales, problem solving comes under the strand of 'Using and applying mathematics'. Guidance notes provided by the Department for Education and Skills (DfES, 2006a) identifies five themes within this strand:

- Solving problems.
- Representing – analyse, record, do, check, confirm.
- Enquiring – plan, decide, organize, interpret, reason, justify.
- Reasoning – create, deduce, apply, explore, predict, hypothesize, test.
- Communicating – explain methods and solutions, choices, decisions, reasoning.

These themes are echoed in the research literature on what processes or activities are involved in problem solving. For example, Mayer (1985) identified the following factors as contributing towards problem solving performance:

- Practice in recognizing problem types.
- Practice in representing problems – whether concretely, in pictures, in symbols, or in words.
- Practice in selecting relevant and irrelevant information in a problem.

Orton and Frobisher (1996) identified the following processes within problem solving:

- Operational processes of collecting and ordering data.
- Mathematical process of searching for patterns.
- Reasoning processes of analysis and reflection.
- Communication processes in describing methods.

Perhaps the most famous 'processes' involved in problem solving were those described by Polya (1957):

- Understanding the problem, e.g. looking for unknowns or data.

- Devising a plan, e.g. looking for related problems, restating the problem in a different way.
- Carrying out the plan, in particular checking each step.
- Looking back, e.g. checking the result, obtain the result differently, use the result for other problems.

Therefore, trying to bring together these perspectives on the problem-solving process, we feel that there are two important elements to consider. First of all, there is 'representing problems' and second, there is 'reasoning with problems'. Of course, this relates to our view of developing mathematical understanding that has been an underlying theme of this book. Therefore, what we will do is concentrate on these two approaches to problem solving in the following sections. Within these sections, we will try and clarify how these two views cover the multitude of processes that we listed above.

Representing problems

> **KEY POINT TO CONSIDER**
>
> Representing and reasoning are important parts of the problem-solving process. There is a need to understand and address both aspects in our teaching in order to develop problem-solving skills that are transferable to all areas of mathematics.

When we talk about representing problems, we return to our views of representations highlighted at the start of the book. We may recall that we used Goldin's (1998) view of representations which included verbal representations, images, symbols and strategies. Therefore, we take a broad view of representations when it comes to relating it to problem solving.

Looking at the above problem-solving processes, some are directly related to 'representing' – for example, Mayer's suggestion that we practise representing problems in different ways, using concrete objects, symbols, pictures or words. We would also include Polya's suggestion of restating the problem. Other processes, however, can also be included within this representing theme. Take, for example, the solving problems theme in the 'using and applying' strand, or the practice in recognizing problem types as suggested by Mayer. The practice of solving problems allows us to relate a problem to a class of problems that we have done before, and therefore to strategies that we have used before. Therefore, what we are doing here is changing the representation of the problem type to a strategy representation. If we also think back to the last chapter on data handling, we categorized processes such as collecting and organizing data, and processing and interpreting data (for example looking for patterns within the data) as forms of 're-presenting' the information given. We would also include here the processes of picking out relevant information or restating the problem in terms of unknowns. Therefore, we feel that we can include much of what we do in problem solving under this broad view of representing the problem.

Can we be more specific then *why* representing problems is an important part of the problem-solving process? Heller and Hungate (1985) suggest that 'this representation mediates between the problem text and its solution'. Lesh *et al.* (1983) give an

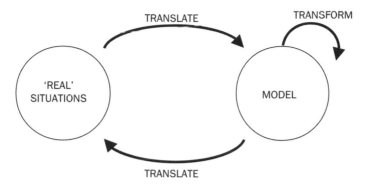

Figure 11.1 Lesh's conceptualization of the problem-solving process

example of this with a diagram representing the solving of a 'real-life' problem (Figure 11.1). If we have a real-life problem, or we would argue any other type of problem (as exemplified in the previous chapters), then translating the problem into a new representation, whether it is a model in the case of the situation, or a picture or symbols or whatever, provides us with something that we can then work with and transform into a solution. We then need to map the solution back to the original form of the problem so that the results 'fit' the original problem.

Let us provide another example of this process of representation, this time using a problem that we like to use with our own undergraduate student teachers. It comes from Geary (1994): 'Laura is 3 times as old as Maria was when Laura was as old as Maria is now. In 2 years Laura will be twice as old as Maria was 2 years ago. Find their present ages'. How can we solve this problem? One of the difficulties is that it is phrased in such a convoluted way that it is hard to understand exactly what is being said. In order to make sense of it, let us represent the problem as a diagram (see Figure 11.2). We have represented the passing of time implied in the problem as two lines – one for Laura and the other for Maria. All we have said is that Laura was born at some point, and then Maria was born at another point in time (we have assumed that Maria was the younger). We then have Laura and Maria at the present time. Now let us work with this representation. The first part of the problem is 'Laura is 3 times as old as Maria was . . .', so at some point in the past, Maria was a given age. Let us call this age x. And Laura right now is three times this age, so $3x$. Let us put this on the diagram as shown in Figure 11.3. The next part of the question is '. . . as Maria was when Laura

Figure 11.2 Representing the problem as a diagram

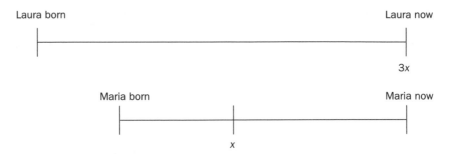

Figure 11.3 Adding the age that 'Maria was . . .'

was as old as Maria is now'. So, if we say Maria now is another age, say y, we can also show when Laura was this age (see Figure 11.4).

Now, what we would like is a relationship between the various ages. From Figure 11.4 we can see that the time from when Laura was y to now when she is $3x$ is the same as the time between when Maria was x to now when she is y. Representing this relationship symbolically:

$$3x - y = y - x$$

Rearranging this equation:

$$3x + x = y + y$$
$$4x = 2y$$
$$x = y/2$$
$$3x = 3y/2$$

If we relate this back to our original problem, the last equation tells us that Laura's age now is one and a half times Maria's age now. Therefore, by representing the problem as a diagram, and working with the diagram, this has helped to clarify what is happening in the problem.

However, we have still not finished the problem. We still do not know Laura's and Maria's ages. However, we have not used the last part of the problem: 'In 2 years Laura will be twice as old as Maria was 2 years ago'. To solve this part, let us produce a table for Laura's and Maria's present ages to see which values fit this condition (see

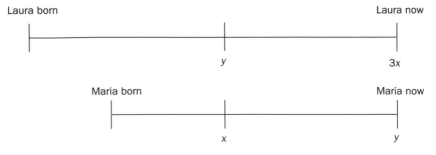

Figure 11.4 Adding the age that 'Maria is now . . .'

Table 11.1 Table of possible ages for Maria and Laura

Maria's age now	Laura's age now (1½ times Maria's)	Maria's age two years ago	Two times Maria's age two years ago	Laura's age in two years' time
1	1½	-1	-2	3½
2	3	0	0	5
3	4½	1	2	6½
4	6	2	4	8
5	7½	3	6	9½
6	9	4	8	11
7	10½	5	10	12½
8	12	6	12	14
9	13½	7	14	15½
10	15	8	16	17
11	16½	9	18	18½
12	18	10	20	20
13	19½	11	22	21½
14	21	12	24	23
15	22½	13	26	24½

Table 11.1). The table provides another representation showing clearly the relationship between Laura's and Maria's ages. The ages that fit the last condition are when Maria's and Laura's ages are 12 and 18 respectively. So this seems to be the solution. Let us relate this back to the original problem to see if it fits. 'Laura is 3 times as old as Maria was when Laura was as old as Maria is now. In 2 years Laura will be twice as old as Maria was 2 years ago. Find their present ages'. Maria is 12 now. When Laura was 12 (i.e. 6 years ago), Maria was 6. Laura is 3 times this age which is 18, which indeed is the case.

We have therefore solved this problem. Looking back at the process, we can see that representing the problem in different ways has clarified it and helped us see what needed to be done. One therefore cannot 'jump' to the solution of a problem. We need to look for alternative representations which mediate between the problem and the solution. Of course, the difficulty is to come up with helpful representations, and this may be partly through experience and partly through trial and error. The neat solution provided above to the problem has in fact gone through a process of refinement to reach its present state. What we want to emphasize, though, is looking for alternative representations at the outset is an important part of the problem-solving process.

> **KEY POINT TO CONSIDER**
>
> Representing a problem in different ways clarifies the problem and helps us to see what needs to be done – alternative representations 'mediate' between the problem and the solution.

Reasoning with problems

In addition to representing problems, the other process we put forward earlier as being important for problem solving was that of reasoning with problems. Let us examine this idea in detail here.

Looking back at the variety of processes that we identified in the literature concerning problem solving, we can see that some of these relate very obviously to reasoning. For example, there is a reasoning theme within the definition given in the 'using and applying' strand for England and Wales. This includes processes such as deducing and predicting. Within the enquiring theme, we have interpreting, reasoning, justifying, and within the communicating theme, we have explaining methods and solutions, choices, decisions and reasoning. Even within the representing theme, we have checking and confirming which we would count as reasoning (in fact, we feel that these themes within the Using and applying strand are rather mixed up and could be set out more clearly – however, we can still identify the elements of representing and reasoning within these). In the research literature, we have from Orton and Frobisher the reasoning processes of analysis and reflection, and also the communicating of methods. We do see this latter process as being 'reasoning' in that it is about making clear and justifying your methods. From Polya, we have the checking of each step (i.e. justifying each step), and looking back and checking the result, in other words looking at the reasoning used throughout the problem-solving process. Therefore, we can identify 'reasoning with problems' as being an important part of the problem-solving process.

As we did with the idea of representing problems, can we go into more detail as to why this reasoning process is so important? We can turn to the research literature again for some answers. Hiebert *et al.* (1996) describe the American philosopher and educationalist John Dewey's views of problem solving. Within this view, 'reflective inquiry' is seen as a key part of the problem-solving process:

> The importance of this claim for Dewey lay not only in the fact that problems trigger reflective inquiry but also in the proposition that those who engage in reflective inquiry look for problems. They problematize their experiences in order to understand them more fully.
>
> (p. 15)

In the context of problem solving, if we reflect on the methods we have used, the links we have made and the reasoning we have used, and we call these into question (i.e. **problematize** them), this encourages us to develop new and stronger links, and therefore develops our understanding of the concept we are looking at.

But how do we know whether to do this and how to do this? Schoenfeld (1992) uses the concept of **metacognition** to describe a number of processes related to this question. Metacognition involves:

- Self-regulatory procedures, including monitoring and 'on-line' decision making.
- Individuals' knowledge about their cognitive processes.
- Beliefs and affects.

We interpret these in the following way. The first process is related to that of 'reflective inquiry' in that you are reflecting on how well you are completing the problem:

> You keep tabs on how well things were going. If things appeared to be proceeding well, you continue along the same path; if they appeared to be problematic, you took stock and considered other options. Monitoring and assessing progress 'on-line', and acting in response to the assessment of on-line progress, are the core components of self-regulation.
>
> (Schoenfeld, 1992: 355)

However, we have seen from Dewey's view of problem solving that reflective inquiry is more than this – it is also about actively calling into question what you are doing and looking for alternatives. We would include this view under the second and third of Schoenfeld's metacognitive processes. We need to know that problem solving is not just about getting the right answer – we have to have the view and the belief that problem solving is more than that. We need to know that our

KEY POINT TO CONSIDER

It is important to question ourselves and 'problematize' our mathematics. In doing so, we strengthen our reasoning and develop our understanding through alternative views of the same problem and linking to different areas of mathematics.

understanding is developed if we try and use alternative representations and we call into question the reasoning that we use linking the different stages of the problem (again, different representations if you like). Therefore, we need to have this broader view and this broader knowledge about problem solving and understanding so that we can approach problems in the most effective way.

In order to illustrate the reasoning processes that might be entailed in tackling a problem, let us look at a specific example. Another problem that we like to use with our undergraduate students is the following. We show the picture seen in Figure 11.5

Figure 11.5 Picture for problem-solving activity

on a screen for 5 seconds. We then blank the screen and ask students to try and calculate the total number of spots in the picture. We do give some clues:

- All the dominoes are flat on the table, i.e. not on top of each other.
- All the dominoes are close together so that they are touching other dominoes.
- Some dominoes go off the edge of the screen.
- The highest number of spots on these dominoes is 18 (a 'double 9').
- The relative sizes of one domino to the full picture is as shown in Figure 11.6.

So how can we solve this (without looking at the original picture!)? Let us try one solution method. In Figure 11.6, the area of the domino is 0.8cm × 1.7cm = 1.36cm². The area of the picture is 6.4cm × 8.5cm = 54.4cm². Therefore, the number of dominoes that could fit in the picture is 54.4 ÷ 1.36 which is 40 dominoes.

Now, how many spots might be on these 40 dominoes? Well, we could calculate the average number of spots on each domino and multiply by 40. We can write out all the possible combinations of spots, as shown in the table in Figure 11.7. We have filled in all of the table because we are assuming that we need to double-count dominos (i.e. there are two 0/1 dominos etc.) except in the case of doubles (1/1, 2/2, etc.). Adding all these combinations up, we have a total of 900 spots over 100 combinations. The average number of spots is therefore 900 ÷ 100 = 9. Over 40 dominoes therefore, we would expect 9 × 40 which is 360. So we would suggest that there would be 360 spots.

Let us now consider this answer. More specifically, let us look back at the reasoning we used to get this answer. In the first step, we worked out the area of the domino and the area of the picture and found how many dominos could fit into the picture. But this would be the case when they are pushed together perfectly with no spaces –

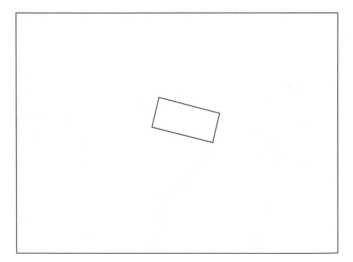

Figure 11.6 Relative size of one domino to the picture

	0	1	2	3	4	5	6	7	8	9
0	0	1	2	3	4	5	6	7	8	9
1	1	2	3	4	5	6	7	8	9	10
2	2	3	4	5	6	7	8	9	10	11
3	3	4	5	6	7	8	9	10	11	12
4	4	5	6	7	8	9	10	11	12	13
5	5	6	7	8	9	10	11	12	13	14
6	6	7	8	9	10	11	12	13	14	15
7	7	8	9	10	11	12	13	14	15	16
8	8	9	10	11	12	13	14	15	16	17
9	9	10	11	12	13	14	15	16	17	18

Figure 11.7 Possible combinations of spots

we need to account for these spaces. So we can already see that we might have overestimated the number of spots. We then need to think of ways to resolve this problem of accounting for places. We could guess that there is a certain proportion of space in the picture. Or we could experiment with actual dominos and see what amount of space we get. In either case, we would again need to reason whether the approach we are taking is reasonable. Likewise, in the second step of the problem, we decided to double-count the dominos. But is this right? Again, we might need to check this with a box of dominos.

In actual fact, the important thing here is not about getting the right answer![1] What is important is that in looking at the reasoning that we have used, we start to make other links, perhaps to other areas of mathematics, or even to carrying out experiments or to find out about the manufacture of dominos! Therefore, we can see that we are developing our understanding by problematizing our approach, and we need to see that it is beneficial that we do so. Therefore, we can see that reasoning about the problem is an important part of developing our understanding through problem solving.

Communicating problem solving

In communicating to children about problem solving in the classroom, we have already highlighted the need to be clear what we mean by terms such as problem solving, problems and investigations. For example, 'problems' are more than just 'real-life' situations or, as are commonly used in the classroom, word problems. For example, 'On the first day of an eight day trip we travelled 424 km. On the second day we travelled 586 km, on the third 489 km and on the fourth 386 km. If the total distance we need to travel was 3,000 km, how may more kilometres did we have to travel?'

---

[1] However, for those that have to have an answer, we think the number is about 271.

Problem : time consuming + needs creativity

Time is often spent on teaching children how to deal with such word problems – underlining key words, etc. As isolated activities, children can find these activities meaningless and uninteresting. Rather, it is important to plan for activities that are richer and more enjoyable and that also extend the knowledge and experience of the children and allow them to question them-selves and others (including the teacher). As we have seen previously, this requires a par-ticular view of problem solving and its role in developing understanding. Children need to be exposed to a classroom environ-ment that supports and encourages a positive attitude to problem solving and investigations, and provides adequate time for such activities. Activities 11.1 and 11.2 provide examples of problems and activities that we could use in the classroom.

Activity 11.1 Making up numbers

Using only the number 4 and the four operations (+, −, ×, ÷), can we make all the numbers 0 to 20?

Activity 11.2 A broken 6

The 6 button on your calculator is broken. How can you find the answers to these calculations below? Compare strategies with others in your group. Make some more up for others to solve.

48×6

$126 - 58$

$32 + 16$

$146 \div 7$

The difference between 76 and 263

62×16

$263 \div 62$

Problem solving and investigations which allow children to discuss their own ideas in describing and explaining their current thinking, as well as listening to the thoughts of others, will promote reasoning and therefore greater understanding. It is also helpful to create an interactive maths display to which the children can add on a daily basis or when any new solutions or examples arise – e.g. 'my Dad thought of another example'. These types of activities are also essential in that they can be tackled by children of different abilities and involve all children in their own learning, thus developing self-esteem and confidence. It is often surprising what children labelled as 'low attainers' can contribute.

Creativity is an important factor in teaching and learning mathematics and is particularly relevant to problem solving and investigations. In planning maths activities, teachers can be both imaginative and creative and still achieve the learning objectives. For example, take the learning objective of 'Identify and use appropriate operations to solve word problems involving number and quantities'. An activity for older primary children could be planning and organizing an infant party or designing a new school playground. For younger children, it could be organizing a teddy bears' picnic or tea party. In both instances there are many issues that need discussing prior to preparations, such as:

- What will be the theme of the party?
- What food will be needed and how much?
- What jobs need to be done and when?
- Who will do what?
- What music shall we play?
- What size/area do we need and what venue?
- What decorations do we need?

As we can see, these activities can also provide a more integrated way of working across the curriculum. However, we can also approach more 'standard' topics in a more creative way. See Activity 11.3, for example. Another example is simply 'The answer is 24. What is the problem?' Of course, activities need not be just associated with number – indeed, the point about problem solving and investigations is that they can and should cover all areas of mathematics. For example, Activity 11.4 uses shape.

Activity 11.3 The nine times table

Take a look at the nine times table:

$1 \times 9 = 9$
$2 \times 9 = 18$
$3 \times 9 = 27$

What do you notice about the table so far? Can you see a pattern? Can you explain the pattern? Can we predict what will happen next?

Activity 11.4 Five squares

How many shapes can you make using five squares?

Can the shapes that you make fit together to make a rectangle? Is there only one way of doing this?

Questioning has an important role in the problem-solving process in terms of promoting 'reflective enquiry'.

In addition to choosing or creating appropriate actives for problem solving and investigations, there is an important role for questions and questioning in problem solving specifically for promoting the 'reflective inquiry' and the reasoning that we highlighted earlier in the chapter. Questions or statements such as:

Tell the others how this works.
What made you think of that?
I had not thought of that. Could you explain it to me?
How did you work this out?
Did Tony use the same method?
What do you think?

The questions are therefore not about testing knowledge. Rather, what is important is to plan for and use a range of open questions that promote discussion and reasoning. Likewise, working in groups or pairs in solving problems or investigations can provide opportunities for children to share and communicate ideas and ultimately develop a deeper understanding of the mathematical concepts involved.

Misconceptions and misunderstandings about problem solving

Knowledge of specific areas of mathematics should be developed alongside that of problem-solving skills. Also, it is important that we develop children's beliefs about mathematics in order to incorporate the problem-solving view of mathematics.

Let us now examine some of the misconceptions that children have about problem solving in mathematics. In doing so, let us draw together the ideas that made up this chapter, and indeed that have made up the approach to mathematics in this book.

Children's difficulties with problem solving in mathematics relate directly to their general understanding about the nature of mathematics and to their specific conceptions about the different areas of mathematics presented in the earlier chapters. So any of the specific difficulties about understanding of fractions or decimals or about shape or measures will apply to problem solving, where these topics are part of a problem-solving situation. In addition, the specific details of the problem-solving task and in particular the language used and the choice of representation that they adopt will also significantly affect how successful they are in tackling a problem (Cummins, 1991).

As they progress though school children develop beliefs about mathematics that affect their approach to different tasks and their performance (Schoenfeld, 1985). As children mature, they tend to think that mathematics has practical, everyday uses but to consider it more important for society than for them personally (Brown *et al.*, 1988). Some of the research on mathematical problem solving has included investigations of the beliefs learners hold about the nature of mathematics (Schoenfeld, 1985, 1989a, 1989b, 1992). These studies indicate that learners see mathematics as governed by rules rather than involving processes of investigation; that they consider that mathematics is an unchanging discipline that is not related to solving problems from their own experience; and that memorization is more important than understanding in learning mathematics. Such profound beliefs about mathematics are difficult to change.

Typical beliefs about mathematics (Schoenfeld, 1985, 1989a, 1989b) are:

- There is only one correct way to solve any mathematics problem.
- Mathematics problems have only one correct answer.
- Mathematics is done by individuals in isolation.
- Mathematical problems can be solved quickly or not at all.
- Mathematical problems and their solutions do not have to make sense.
- Formal proof is irrelevant to processes of discovery and invention.

It is therefore important that these deeper misunderstandings about the nature of mathematics are tackled systematically as children develop their knowledge and understanding of the subject. Research has also been undertaken into children's beliefs about themselves and their ability and attainment in mathematics (e.g. Skaalvik and Hagtvet, 1990; Muijs, 1998). This research suggests that children who are relatively low attaining at a young age will make less progress than other pupils and will develop negative beliefs about mathematics or a disposition which will be increasingly difficult to change. Early success in mathematics is therefore essential to develop skills and understanding effectively.

It is also vital that children are able to choose the best representation for a particular problem. Cummings (1991) investigated children's interpretations of standard arithmetic word problems and the factors that influence their interpretation of what was required mathematically. The children were asked to solve a series of problems and then to draw and select pictures that represented the problem structures. Success was found to be directly related to the nature of the representations chosen or drawn but the crucial factor in their success was the interpretation given to particular phrases used in the problems.

Misconceptions and misunderstandings result from a number of different causes

(Ryan and Williams, 2007) and have been classified in different ways (Radatz, 1979; Confrey, 1990). It is found that children:

- Have difficulties with language and informal meanings (words such as 'difference' or 'multiply' have general meaning as well as particular meanings in mathematics);
- Tend to over-generalize (such as when applying rules or when thinking about properties of shapes and numbers);
- Often try something which works in another context (such as applying the wrong rule or using an inappropriate procedure);
- Have a gap between their formal and informal knowledge (such as being able to describe a rule in number patterns, but not be able to translate this into a formal expression).

We also know that misunderstandings and misconceptions are inevitable and remarkably difficult to overcome (Confrey, 1990). However, the mistakes that children have should be seen as providing an important teaching opportunity, rather than as unfortunate errors to be corrected quickly (Williams and Ryan, 2000). They can also be seen by the pupils themselves as a learning opportunity rather than something they have done wrong. The role of mathematical representations and explicit articulation of pupils' thinking plays a key role in an approach to teaching which incorporates mistakes and misconceptions. Without knowing what children think in terms of how they are seeing what they do and reasoning about what they think, it is difficult to address their mathematical difficulties.

Therefore, the approach to understanding that we have taken in this book, incorporating the ideas of representations and reasoning, is integral to how we approach the learning of mathematics, for example through problem-solving activities. The identification of how children represent and reason is also integral to the identification of misconceptions among children. As identified by Schoenfeld above, we believe that having this clear view of what it means to do and understand mathematics is essential for developing our practice as teachers and improving the mathematical experience of children in the primary or elementary classroom.

Questions for discussion

1   Problem solving is not a topic but an approach to mathematics. To what extent is this correct or incorrect?

2   Is tackling all topics in mathematics through a problem-solving approach a viable way of developing the mathematics curriculum?

3   How does the view of mathematics presented in this chapter, in particular that of problem solving, differ to that which you have seen in school?

4   What is the implication of applying this view of problem solving to any of the mathematics that we do in school, even 'straightforward' number calculations?

Glossary

Algorithm A precise prescription of a general solution to a *problem* set out as a step-by-step description. A sequence of unambiguous instructions for solving a problem. The word 'algorithm' derives from the name of a Persian mathematician, Abu Ja'far Muhammad ibn Musa Al-Khwarizmi (circa 825).

Array A rectangular arrangement of objects in equal rows or columns. Used to represent a multiplicative relationship between the rows, columns and total number of objects. It can be organized with gaps or colours to enable easier recognition of the numbers representing their products.

Axioms A universally accepted principle or rule. In mathematics an axiom is a proposition that is assumed without proof in order to study the consequences which follow.

Base-10 The numbering system we commonly use in which different symbols (the ten digits) are used for ten distinct values (0–9) and where each place to the left or right represents a power of 10. Sometimes called the denary system, it can be contrasted with binary (base-2) and hexadecimal (base-16).

Binary Involving two elements. Therefore, a binary operation involves two inputs.

Capacity The capacity of an object can be defined as how much it can hold (e.g. the capacity of a bottle is the maximum amount of liquid inside it). This is as opposed to the volume of a solid object which is the space that it takes up.

Cardinal number The aspect of the quantity or the numerousness of elements in a mathematical set; the quantity rather than the order. See also *ordinal number*.

Chunking Method of division calculation, based on the idea of division as repeated subtraction, but grouping (chunking) the amounts to be subtracted to make the calculation more efficient.

Commutativity The property of being able change the order of something without changing the end result.

Concept An abstract idea or a *generalization* which brings different elements into a basic relationship on the basis of a key principle. A characteristic aspect of a class of objects, relations or things.

Conservation That a property remains unchanged in terms of factors that have no bearing on the property. For example, the order in which we count a group of objects, or whether we measure the height of a room from top to bottom or bottom to top.

Continua Continuous series of things, no part of which is noticeably different from its adjacent parts. The numerical continuum (singular) is the series of real numbers; the linear continuum is the series of points on a geometrical line.

Coordinate system A system used to assign numbers to describe points in space.

Decimal A decimal number is an extension of the base-10 system in order to express rational numbers.

Denominator The quantity on the bottom of a fraction. It represents the number of equal-sized parts into which a whole or group has been split. See also *numerator*.

Dependent variable When we observe how one quantity changes with another quantity that we can control, the quantity we observe changing is called the dependent variable.

Derived fact A fact obtained by rearranging known facts. For example, we can derive the fact that 13 + 15 is 28 from adding 2 to the know fact 13 + 13 = 26.

Discretizing The process of making things discrete or separate. Identifying the separate parts of a whole.

Distributivity The property of being distributive. Multiplication is distributive over addition so that $2 \times (1 + 3) = (2 \times 1) + (2 \times 3)$.

Dividend The number to be divided in a division problem. For example, in the equation, $8 \div 2 = 4$, the number 8 is the dividend. See also *divisor* and *quotient*.

Divisor The number you are dividing by in a division problem. So, for example, in the equation, $8 \div 2 = 4$, the number 2 is the divisor. Otherwise, 8 is called the dividend and 4 is the quotient. See also *dividend* and *quotient*.

Equivalent fractions See *fraction – equivalent*.

Fraction In everyday language, a small part forming a piece of a whole. Mathematically, it a ratio of two integers, the *numerator* and the *denominator*, usually written one above the other and separated by a horizontal line (vinculum) or a slash (solidus). Common or vulgar fractions (e.g. ½) are distinguished from decimal fractions (e.g. 0.5).

Fraction – equivalent Equivalent *fractions* show the same ratio between the parts and the whole (e.g. ½ = ¾ or ⅖ = ⁴⁄₁₀).

Fraction – improper A *fraction* is described as improper when the *numerator* is greater than or equal to the *denominator* (e.g. ³⁄₂ or ¹²⁄₅) as these forms can be expressed as mixed numbers (i.e. 1½ and 2⅖ respectively). This is as opposed to 'proper' fractions where the *numerator* is smaller than the *denominator*.

Fractional measure One of the uses of rational number, denoting how much we have of a quantity out of a whole unit of that quantity.

Frequency The rate at which something happens or a measure of the number of occurrences of a repeating event in a specified time period.

Generalization The process of forming general ideas or *concepts* by abstracting common properties of instances. Generalization is a key feature of logic and *reasoning*. It implies the existence of a domain or set of elements with common characteristics shared by those elements. It is the basis of all deductive thinking and inference. The process of *proof* or verification is needed to decide whether a generalization holds true for any given situation.

Grouping/quotative situations Division situations involving the removal of equal groups of a quantity. For example, a certain number of sweets can be given to each person, and we can find how many people we can repeat this for.

Improper fraction See *fraction – improper*.

Independent variable When we observe how one quantity changes with another quantity that we can control, the quantity we control is called the independent variable.

Inter-quartile range The range between the upper and lower quartiles of a distribution (i.e. the middle 50%); it is equal to the difference between the 75th and the 25th percentile; a measure of variability.

Investigation A mathematical inquiry usually with an open-ended focus. As well as exploring mathematical content, students often have to pose questions and decide which route to follow to find a solution or solutions. This active involvement with an explicit focus on mathematical thinking is often for an extended period of time in order to provide an opportunity for students to learn to persist and sustain their engagement in a mathematics task.

Known fact A relationship which we have memorized, rather than needing to derive. For example, the times tables, number bonds to 10 or doubles of numbers.

Linear coordinate One of the uses of rational number, denoting a number in between whole numbers on a linear measure or number line.

Mean A descriptive statistic used to measure the average or central tendency. To calculate the mean, all the values of a variable are added and then the sum is divided by the number of values totalled. For example if a group of children were aged 5, 6, 6, 9, 10, 11 and 12 their mean age would be 8.4 years. See also *median* and *mode*.

Measure numbers Numbers used in conjunction with the amount of a given physical property. Related to cardinal numbers in that they constitute a 'quantity', but they differ in that they indicate a physical property other than numerousness.

Median A descriptive statistic used to measure the average or central tendency. The median is the value that is the middle value of a set of values; 50% of the values lie above the median, and 50% lie below the median. For example, if a group of children were aged 5, 6, 6, 9, 10, 11 and 12 their median age would be 9 years. See also *mean* and *mode*.

Mental representations An internalized (in the mind) representation of a mathematical concept.

Metacognition Thinking about one's own thinking processes. It has to do with the active monitoring and regulation or deliberate control of one's thinking and reasoning.

Misconception A naive or incorrect conception of an idea or *concept*. Referred to in a variety of ways in the research literature (preconceptions, conceptual primitives, emerging conceptions and alternative conceptions) they relate to the development of a more complete understanding which can be influenced by a learner's existing ideas and understanding.

Mode A descriptive statistic that is a measure of the average or central tendency. The mode is the value that occurs most frequently in a set of data. For example, if a group of children were aged 5, 6, 6, 9, 10, 11 and 12 their modal age would be 6 years. See also *mean* and *median*.

Modelling The act of representing something (usually on a smaller or simplified scale) in order to understand it. A number line is a model or *representation* of the relative or relational value of numbers. An *array* is a model of multiplication and division.

Multiplicand A number that is to be multiplied by another (the *multiplier*).

Multiplier The multiplying number or the number by which a *multiplicand* is multiplied.

Numerator The quantity of a *common fraction* written above the line which indicates the number of fractional parts of the whole that are included. See also *denominator*.

Operation A mathematical calculation (such as addition, subtraction, multiplication or division).

Operator One of the uses of rational number, denoting a transformation, such as a magnification by 2.5 times.

Ordinal number Numbers referring to their position or order: first, second, third, etc. See also *cardinal number.*

Parallelogram A *quadrilateral* in which both pairs of opposite sides are parallel. The opposite sides of a parallelogram are equal in length, and the opposite angles of a parallelogram are congruent. A square and a rectangle are examples of special parallelograms whose angles are the same (all 90°).

Partitioning The act of dividing or separating into distinct groups. More precisely, the partitioning of a set is the division of the set into non-overlapping parts which include all of the original set, such that they are collectively exhaustive and mutually exclusive.

Pictograph A form of bar graph with the bars replaced by rows or columns of symbols, also sometimes called a pictogram.

Polygon Three or more line segments joined together to form a closed shape or figure. Triangles, quadrilaterals and pentagons are all examples of polygons.

Probability The likelihood that an event will occur.

Problem A question to be answered; a school task such as a word problem in mathematics where an answer is required. In mathematics, problem solving is the application of mathematics to find a solution to a puzzling or problematic situation where the solution method is unclear.

Problematize To make into or to regard as a problem; to create or pose problems in order to understand a situation or idea.

Proof In mathematics, a proof is a convincing demonstration that some mathematical statement is necessarily true, according to accepted standards. Proofs result from deductive *reasoning*, rather than from inductive or empirical arguments. A proof must show that a statement is true in all cases, without a single exception.

Proportion A quantity of something that is part of the whole amount, or the relation of one part to another or to the whole with respect to magnitude, quantity or degree. Also referred to as 'part/whole' situations.

Quadrilateral A four-sided *polygon*; examples include a square, rectangle, *parallelogram*, kite, trapezium, etc.

Quanta The plural of quantum, indivisible parts or units of a given quantity.

Quotient The result when one number (the *dividend*) is divided by another (the *divisor*). For example, in the calculation $8 \div 2 = 4$, 8 is the *dividend*, 2 is the *divisor* and 4 is the *quotient*. It is more commonly referred to as the answer of a division calculation.

Range The difference between the maximum and the minimum of a given set of numbers.

Reasoning Engaging in a process of thinking which leads to a conclusion or inference using known facts or assumptions. Two main forms of reasoning are deductive reasoning and inductive reasoning. Formal and mathematical logic is deductively based. The study of inductive reasoning is generally described as informal logic or critical thinking.

Ratio A measure of the comparative relationship between two different quantities. For example, having two boys to every three girls (or a ratio of 2:3) in a class.

Rate The relationship between two quantities to give a new quantity. Most often used in physical measurements such as speed (the relationship between distance travelled and time) or density (the relationship between the mass and the volume of a material).

Repeated addition Viewing multiplication as a process of repeatedly adding a quantity. For example, seeing 5×3 as adding 3 lots of 5.

Repeated subtraction Viewing division as a process of repeatedly subtracting a quantity from an initial total. For example, seeing 15 ÷ 3 as how many times we can subtract 3 from 15. This way of viewing division follows directly from grouping or quotative situations.

Representation A figure, image or symbol which is a substitute for another idea or *concept*. In mathematics a representation contains some features or properties which can be systematically related to what is being represented. So, for example, a 0–100 number line is a representation of the *ordinal* properties of number and where aspects of the *base-10* system are also shown (usually indicating ten and multiples of ten by size, colour or by length of the lines or by indicating decades with different colours or shading).

Sample In the context of statistics, a sample is a part of the population we are looking at. For example, the four authors of this book are a sample of the people that work at Durham University.

Sequence A serial arrangement in which things follow in logical order or follow a recurring pattern. It is like an ordered list of things. Like a collection or set, it contains members (also called elements or terms), and the number of terms is called the length of the sequence (though this may be infinite). Unlike a set the order matters, however, and is a predictable pattern.

Sharing/partitive situations Division situations involving the equal sharing of a quantity. For example, sweets can be shared by giving one to each person, and finding how many times this process can be repeated.

Symmetry A figure has symmetry if it has parts which correspond exactly with each other in terms of size, form and arrangement. Line symmetry is the exact matching of parts on either side of a straight line and is sometimes called mirror symmetry or bilateral symmetry. A figure has rotational symmetry when it can be rotated around a central point, or turned less than 360° and still be identical to the original figure.

Transformation A systematic change to a shape such as reflecting, rotating, scaling or shearing.

Transitivity A relation between three things so that if there is a relationship between the first and second and the second and third it also applies between the first and third. So, if 10 is greater than 5 and 5 is greater than 3, then 10 must be greater than 3.

Translation A form of transformation in geometry, where an object is moved in space.

Unary Involving one element. Therefore, a unary operation involves one input.

Variable A quantity which changes in a mathematical expression, or the symbol (such as x or y) which is used to represent a quantity which varies or changes.

References

Ainley, J. (1991) Is there any mathematics in measurement? in D. Pimm and E. Love (eds), *Teaching and Learning School Mathematics*. Sevenoaks: Hodder & Stoughton Ltd, pp. 69–70.

Anghileri, J. (1989) An investigation of young children's understanding of multiplication, *Educational Studies in Mathematics*, 20: 367–85.

Anghileri, J. (2007) *Developing Number Sense*. London: Continuum.

APU (Assessment of Performance Unit) (1980) *Mathematical Performance: Primary Survey Report No. 1*. London: HSMO.

Ashlock, R. D. (1990) *Error Patterns in Computation*. New York: Macmillan.

Askew, M. (1998) *Teaching Primary Mathematics*. London: Hodder & Stoughton.

ATM (Association of Teachers of Mathematics) (1991) *Language of Mathematics*. Derby: ATM.

Ausubel, D. P., Novak, J. D. and Hanesian, H. (1978) *Educational Psychology: A Cognitive View*, 2nd edn. New York: Holt, Rinehart and Winston.

Bailey, A., Townsend, L. and Wilkinson, W. (1990) *Practical Guides – Maths*. Leamington Spa: Scholastic Publications.

Baroody, A. and Standifer, D. J. (1993) Addition and subtraction in the primary grades, in R. J. Jensen (ed.), *Research Ideas for the Classroom: Early Childhood Mathematics*. New York: Macmillan, pp. 72–102.

Behr, M., Erlwanger, S. and Nichols, E. (1980) How children view the equal sign, *Mathematics Teaching*, 92: 13–15.

Behr, M. J., Lesh, R., Post, T. P. and Silver, E. A. (1983) Rational-number concepts, in R. Lesh and M. Landau (eds), *Acquisition of Mathematics Concepts and Processes*. New York: Academic Press, pp. 91–126.

Beishuizen, M. (1993) Mental strategies and materials or models for addition and subtraction up to 100 in Dutch second grades, *Journal for Research in Mathematics Education*, 24(4): 294–323.

Bell, A. and Burkhardt, H. (2002) Domain frameworks in mathematics and problem solving. Paper presented at the annual meeting of the American Educational Research Association, New Orleans. Available at: www.nottingham.ac.uk/education/MARS/papers (accessed 25 September 2008).

Benenson, W., Harris, J. W., Stocker, H. and Lutz, H. (2000) *Handbook of Physics*. New York: Springer-Verlag Inc.

Blöte, A., Klein, A. S. and Beishuizen M. (2000) Mental computation and conceptual understanding, *Learning and Instruction*, 10: 221–47.

Briars, D. and Siegler, R. S. (1984) A featural analysis of preschoolers' counting knowledge, *Developmental Psychology*, 20: 607–18.

Brissenden, T. (with the Lakatos Primary Mathematics Group) (1988) *Talking about Mathematics: Mathematical Discussion in Primary Classrooms*. Oxford: Basil Blackwell.

Brousseau, G., Brousseau, N. and Warfield, V. (2007) Rationals and decimals as required in the school curriculum Part 2: from rationals to decimals, *Journal of Mathematical Behavior*, 26: 281–300.

Brown, M. (1981) Number operations, in K. M. Hart (ed.), *Children's Understanding of Mathematics: 11–16*. London: John Murray, pp. 23–47.

Brown, J. and Van Lehn, K. (1982) Towards a generative theory of 'bugs', in T. P. Carpenter, J. Moser and T. Romberg (eds), *Addition and Subtraction: A Cognitive Perspective*. Hillsdale, NJ: Lawrence Erlbaum Associates, pp. 117–35.

Brown, C., Carpenter, T., Kouba, V. et al. (1988) Secondary school results from the fourth NAEP mathematics assessment: algebra, geometry, mathematical methods, and attitudes, *Mathematics Teacher*, 81(5): 337–47.

Burger, W. F. and Shaughnessy, J. M. (1986) Characterising the van Hiele levels of development in geometry, *Journal of Research in Mathematics Education*, 17(1): 31–48.

Canobi, K. H. (2005) Children's understanding of addition and subtraction, *Journal of Experimental Child Psychology*, 92: 220–46.

Carpenter, T. P. and Moser, J. M. (1983) The acquisition of addition and subtraction concepts, in R. Lesh and M. Landau (eds), *Acquisition of Mathematical Concepts and Processes*. New York: Academic Press, pp. 7–44.

Carpenter, T. P. and Moser, J. M. (1984) The acquisition of addition and subtraction concepts in grades one through three, *Journal for Research in Mathematics Education*, 15(3): 179–202.

Carpenter, T. P., Moser, J. M. and Bebout, H. C. (1988) Representation of addition and subtraction word problems, *Journal of Research in Mathematics Education*, 19(4): 345–57.

Carpenter, T. P., Fennema, E., Franke, M. L., Levi, L. and Empson, S. B. (1999) *Children's Mathematics: Cognitively Guided Instruction*. Portsmouth, NH: Heinemann.

Chapman, C. R. (1995) *How Heavy, How Much and How Long? Weights, Money and Other Measures Used by our Ancestors*. Dursley: Lochin Publishing.

Clausen-May, T. (2005) *Teaching Maths to Pupils with Different Learning Styles*. London: Paul Chapman Publishing.

Clement, J. (1982) Students' preconceptions in introductory mechanics, *American Journal of Physics*, 50(1): 66–71.

Clements, D. H. (1999) Teaching length measurement: research challenges, *School Science and Mathematics*, 99(1): 5–11.

Clements, D. H. and Battista, M. T. (1992) Geometry and spatial reasoning, in D. Grouws (ed.), *Handbook of Research on Mathematics Teaching and Learning*. New York: MacMillan, pp. 420–64.

Clements, D. H. and Sarama Meredith, J. (1993) Research on Logo: effects and efficacy, *Journal of Computing in Childhood Education*, 4(4): 263–90.

Clements, D. H., Swaminathan, S., Hannibal, M. A. Z. and Sarama, J. (1999) Young children's concepts of shape, *Journal for Research in Mathematics Education*, 30(2): 192–212.

Clements, D. H., Wilson, D. C. and Sarama, J. (2004) Young children's composition of geometric figures: a learning trajectory, *Mathematical Thinking and Learning*, 6(2): 163–84.

Cockburn, A. D. (1999) *Teaching Mathematics with Insight*. London: Falmer Press.

Collins English Dictionary (2004) 1st edn. Glasgow: HarperCollins.

Confrey, J. (1990) A review of the research on student conceptions in mathematics, science, and programming, *Review of Research in Education*, 16: 3–56.

Cummins, D. D. (1991) Children's interpretations of arithmetic word problems, *Cognition and Instruction*, 8(3): 261–89.

Dantzig, T. (2007) *Number: The Language of Science*. New York: Plume.

Davis, R. B. (1984) *Learning Mathematics: The Cognitive Approach to Mathematics Education*. London: Croom Helm.

Dehaene, S. (1997) *The Number Sense*. New York: Oxford University Press.

Devlin, K. (1994) *Mathematics: The Science of Patterns*. New York: Scientific American Library.

Devlin, K. (1998) *The Language of Mathematics*. New York: W.H. Freeman and Company.

DfEE (2000) *Mathematical Vocabulary*. London: DfEE Publications.

DfES (2006a) *Primary Framework for Literacy and Mathematics – Guidance Papers – Using and Applying Mathematics*. Available at: www.standards.dfes.gov.uk/primaryframework/downloads/PDF/using_appliying_guid_paper.pdf (accessed 19 August 2008).

DfES (2006b) *Primary Framework for Literacy and Mathematics: Core Position Papers Underpinning the Renewal of Guidance for Teaching Literacy and Mathematics*. Norwich: DfES.

Dickson, L., Brown, M. and Gibson, O. (1984) *Children Learning Mathematics: A Teacher's Guide to Recent Research*. London: Cassell Education Ltd.

English, L. D. and Warren, E. A. (1998) Introducing the variable through pattern exploration, *The Mathematics Teacher*, 91(2): 166–70.

Falk, R., Falk, R. and Levin, I. (1980) A potential for learning probability in young children, *Journal for Research in Mathematics Education*, 11: 181–204.

Falkner, K. P., Levi, L. and Carpenter, T. P. (1999) Children's understanding of equality: a foundation for algebra, *Teaching Children Mathematics*, 6: 232–6.

Fischbein, E. and Gazit, A. (1984) Does the teaching of probability improve probabilistic intuitions? *Educational Studies in Mathematics*, 15: 1–24.

Fischbein, E., Deri, M., Nello, M. and Marino, M. (1985) The role of implicit models in solving verbal problems in multiplication and division, *Journal for Research in Mathematics Education*, 16: 3–17.

Flegg, G. (1983) *Numbers: Their History and Meaning*. New York: Schocken Books.

Frobisher, L. (1999) Primary school children's knowledge of odd and even numbers, in A. Orton (ed.) *Pattern in the Teaching and Learning of Mathematics*. London: Cassell, pp. 31–46.

Frobisher, L. and Threlfall, J. (1999) Teaching and assessing patterns in number in the primary years, in A. Orton (ed.), *Pattern in the Teaching and Learning of Mathematics*. London: Cassell, pp. 84–103.

Fuson, K. C. (1986) Teaching children to subtract by counting up, *Journal for Research in Mathematics Education*, 17: 172–89.

Fuson, K. C. (1988) *Children's Counting and Concepts of Number*. New York: Springer-Verlag.

Fuson, K. (1992) Research on whole number addition and subtraction, in D. Grouws (ed.), *Handbook of Research on Mathematics Teaching and Learning*. New York: MacMillan, pp. 243–75.

Fuson, K. C. and Kwon, Y. (1991) Learning addition and subtraction: effects of number words and other cultural tools, in J. Bideaud, C. Meljac and J. P. Fischer (eds), *Pathways to Number*. Hillsdale, NJ: Erlbaum, pp. 283–302.

Fuson, K., Richards, J. and Briars, D. (1982) The acquisition and elaboration of the number word sequence, in C. Brainerd (ed.), *Progress in Cognitive Development Research Vol. 1: Children's Logical and Mathematical Cognition*. New York: Springer Verlag, pp. 33–92.

Fuys, D., Geddes, D. and Tischer, R. (1988) *The van Hiele Model of Thinking in Geometry Among Adolescents*. Reston, VA: National Council of teachers of Mathematics.

Gates, P. and Griffin, P. (1988) *Preparing to Teach Angles*. Milton Keynes: Centre for Mathematics Education, Open University.

Geary, D. C. (1994) *Children's Mathematical Development*. Washington, DC: American Psychological Association.

Gelman, R. and Gallistel, C. (1978) *The Child's Understanding of Number*. Cambridge, MA: Harvard University Press.

Ginsburg, H. (1977) *Children's Arithmetic: How They Learn it and How You Teach it*. Austin, TX: Pro-Ed.

Goldin, G. A. (1998) Representational systems, learning and problem solving in mathematics, *Journal of Mathematical Behaviour*, 17(2): 137–65.

Goldin, G. A. and Shteingold, N. (2001) Systems of representation and the development of mathematical concepts, in A. A. Cuoco and F. R. Curcio (eds), *The Roles of Representation in School Mathematics [2001 Yearbook of the National Council of Teachers of Mathematics]*. Reston, VA, National Council of Teachers of Mathematics, 1–23.

Graeber, A. O. and Tirosh, D. (1990) Insights fourth and fifth graders bring to multiplication and division with decimals, *Educational Studies in Mathematics*, 21(6): 565–88.

Graeber, A. O., Tirosh, D. and Glover, R. (1989) Preservice teachers' misconceptions in solving verbal problems in multiplication and division, *Journal for Research in Mathematics Education*, 20(1): 95–102.

Graham, A. (1991) Where is the 'P' in statistics? in D. Pimm and E. Love (eds), *Teaching and Learning School Mathematics*. Sevenoaks: Hodder & Stoughton Ltd, pp. 97–108.

Gravemeijer, K. (1994a) Educational development and developmental research in mathematics education, *Journal of Research in Mathematics Education*, 25(5): 443–71.

Gravemeijer, K. P. E. (1994b) *Developing Realistic Mathematics Education*. Utrecht: CD-B Press.

Greer, B. (1992) Multiplication and division as models of situations, in D. Grouws (ed.), *Handbook of Research on Mathematics Teaching and Learning*. New York: MacMillan, pp. 276–95.

Hand, D. J. (2004) *Measurement Theory and Practice: The World Through Quantification*. London: Arnold.

Hanna, G. (2000) Proof, explanation and exploration: an overview, *Educational Studies in Mathematics*, 44(1/2): 5–23.

Hannula, M. S. (2003) Locating fraction on a number line, in N. A. Pateman, B. J. Dougherty and J. Zilliox (eds), *Proceedings of the 27th Conference of the International Group for the Psychology of Mathematics Education*, 3: 17–24.

Hansen, A. (2005) *Children's Errors in Mathematics*. Exeter: Learning Matters Ltd.

Hapkiewicz, A. (1992) Finding a list of science misconceptions, *MSTA Newsletter*, 38: 11–14.

Hart, K. M. (ed.) (1981) *Children's Understanding of Mathematics: 11–16*. London: John Murray.

Haylock, D. (2006) *Mathematics Explained for Primary Teachers*. London: Sage.

Heller, J. I. and Hungate, H. N. (1985) Implications for mathematics instruction of research on scientific problem solving, in E. A. Silver (ed.), *Teaching and Learning Mathematical Problem Solving: Multiple Research Perspectives*. Hillsdale, NJ: Lawrence Erlbaum Associates, pp. 83–112.

Hershkowitz, R. (1990) Psychological aspects of learning geometry, in P. Nesher and J. Kilpatrick (eds), *Mathematics and Cognition*. Cambridge: Cambridge University Press, pp. 70–95.

Hewson, M. G. (1985) The role of intellectual environment in the origin of conceptions: an exploratory study, in L. West and A. Pines (eds), *Cognitive Structure and Conceptual Change*. New York: Academic Press, pp. 153–62.

Hiebert, J. (1984) Why do some children have trouble learning measurement? *Arithmetic Teacher*, 32: 19–24.

Hiebert, J. (ed.) (1986) *Conceptual and Procedural Knowledge: The Case of Mathematics*. Hillsdale, NJ: Lawrence Erlbaum Associates, Inc.

Hiebert, J. and Carpenter, T. P. (1992) Learning and teaching with understanding, in D. A. Grouws (ed.), *Handbook of Research on Mathematics Teaching and Learning*. New York: Macmillan, pp. 65–97.

Hiebert, J. and Wearne, D. (1986) Procedures over concepts: the acquisition of decimal number knowledge, in J. Hiebert (ed.), *Conceptual and Procedural Knowledge: The Case of Mathematics*. Hillsdale, NJ: Lawrence Erlbaum Associates, Inc, pp. 199–223.

Hiebert, J., Wearne, D. and Taber, S. (1991) Fourth graders' gradual construction of decimal fractions during instruction using different physical representations, *The Elementary School Journal*, 91(4): 321–41.

Hiebert, J., Carpenter, T. P., Fennema, E. et al. (1996) Problem solving as a basis for reform in curriculum and instruction: the case of mathematics, *Educational Researcher*, 25(4): 12–21.

Hopkins, C., Gifford, S. and Pepperell, S. (1996) *Mathematics in the Primary School: A Sense of Progression*. London: David Fulton Publishers.

Hughes, M. (1986) *Children and Number*. Oxford: Blackwell Publishers.

Ifrah, G. (1985) *From One to Zero: A Universal History of Numbers*. New York: Viking.

Kaput, J. (1992) Technology and mathematics education, in D. A. Grouws (ed.), *Handbook of Research on Mathematics Teaching and Learning*. New York: NCTM, pp. 515–50.

Kerslake, D. (1986) *Fractions: Children's Strategies and Errors*. London: NFER Nelson.

Kieran, C. (1989) The early learning of algebra: a structural perspective, in S. Wagner and C. Kieran (eds), *Research Issue in the Learning and Teaching of Algebra*. Reston, VA: NCTM, pp. 33–56.

Kouba, V. (1989) Children's solution strategies for equivalent set multiplication and division word problems, *Journal for Research in Mathematics Education*, 20(2): 147–58.

Kouba, V. and McDonald, J. (1991) What is mathematics to children? *Journal of Mathematics Behaviour*, 10: 105–13.

Krutetskii, V. (1976) *The Psychology of Mathematical Abilities in School Children*. Chicago: University of Chicago Press.

Leinhardt, G., Zaslavsky, O. and Stein, M. K. (1990) Function, graphs, and graphing: tasks, learning, and teaching, *Review of Educational Research*, 60(1): 1–64.

Lesh, R., Landau, M. and Hamilton, E. (1983) Conceptual models and applied mathematical problem-solving research, in R. Lesh and M. Landau (eds), *Acquisition of Mathematics Concepts and Processes*. Orlando, FL: Academic Press, pp. 263–343.

Lester, F. K. and Lambdin, D. V. (2004) Teaching mathematics through problem solving, in B. Clarke, D. Clarke, G. Emanuelsson et al. (eds), *International Perspectives on Learning and Teaching Mathematics*. Gothenburg, Sweden: National Center for Mathematics Education, pp. 189–203.

Lewis, A. (1994) *Starting from Scratch: Shape and Space*. London: BEAM.

Long, K. and Kamii, C. (2001) The measurement of time: children's construction of transitivity, unit iteration, and conservation of speed, *School Science and Mathematics*, 101(3): 125–31.

Lucas, J. R. (2000) *The Conceptual Roots of Mathematics*. London: Routledge.

Ma, L. (1999) *Knowing and Teaching Elementary Mathematics: Teachers' Understanding of Fundamental Mathematics in China and the United States*. Mahwah, NJ: Lawrence Erlbaum Associates.

Mack, N. (1993) Learning fractions with understanding: building on informal knowledge, *Journal for Research in Mathematics Education*, 21(1): 16–32.

Magina, S. and Hoyles, C. (1997) Children's understandings of turn and angle, in T. Nunes and P. Bryant (eds), *Learning and Teaching Mathematics: An International Perspective*. Brighton: Psychology Press, pp. 99–114.

Markovits, Z. and Sowder, J. (1991) Students' understanding of the relationship between fractions and decimals, *Focus on Learning Problems in Mathematics*, 13(1): 3–11.

Martinez, J. G. R. and Martinez, N. C. (2007) *Teaching Mathematics in Elementary Middle School – Developing Mathematical Thinking*. New Jersey: Pearson Education.

Mason, J. (2001) Questions about mathematical reasoning and proof in schools, in J. Abramsky (ed.), *Reasoning, Explanation and Proof in School Mathematics and their Place in the Intended Curriculum: Proceedings of the QCA International Seminar*. London: QCA, pp. 11–23.

Mayer, R. E. (1985) Implications of cognitive psychology for instruction in mathematical problem solving, in E. A. Silver (ed.), *Teaching and Learning Mathematical Problem Solving: Multiple Research Perspectives*. Hillsdale, NJ: Lawrence Erlbaum Associates, pp. 123–38.

Menninger, K. (1969) *Number Words and Number Symbols: A Cultural History of Numbers*. Cambridge, MA: MIT Press.

Miller, K. and Gelman, R. (1983) The child's representation of number: a multidimensional scaling analysis, *Child Development*, 54: 1470–9.

Mitchelmore, M. C. and White, P. (1996) Young children's interpretations of physical angle situations, in P. C. Clarkson (ed.), *Proceedings of the 19th Annual Conference of the Mathematics Education Research Group of Australasia, Melbourne*, pp. 383–9.

Mitchelmore, M. C. and White, P. (1998) Recognition of angular similarities between familiar physical situations, in A. Olivier and K. Newstead (eds), *Proceedings of the 20th International Conference for the Psychology of Mathematics Education, Stellenbosch*, 3: 271–8.

Mitchelmore, M. C. and White, P. (2000) Development of angle concepts by progressive abstraction and generalisation, *Educational Studies in Mathematics*, 41(3): 209–38.

Mokros, J. and Russell, S. J. (1995) Children's concepts of average and representativess, *Journal for Research in Mathematics Education*, 26(1): 20–39.

Muijs, R. D. (1998) The reciprocal relationship between self-concept and school achievement, *British Journal of Educational Psychology*, 67(3): 263–776.

Munn, P. (1994) The early development of literacy and numeracy skills, *European Early Childhood Education Research Journal*, 2(1): 5–18.

NCTM (National Council of Teachers of Mathematics) (2000) *Principles and Standards for School Mathematics*. Reston, VA: NCTM.

Nesher, P. (1987) Towards an instructional theory: the role of students' miscon- ceptions', *For the Learning of Mathematics*, 7(3): 33–40.

Nunes, T. and Bryant, P. (1996) *Children Doing Mathematics*. Oxford: Blackwell.

Orton, A. and Frobisher, L. (1996) *Insights into Teaching Mathematics*. London: Cassell.

Orton, J., Orton, A. and Roper, T. (1999) Pictorial and practical contexts and the perception of pattern, in A. Orton (ed.), *Pattern in the Teaching and Learning of Mathematics*. London: Cassell, pp. 121–36.

Piaget, J. and Inhelder, B. (1975) *The Origin of the Idea of Chance in Children*. London: Routledge & Kegan Paul.

Pimm, D. (1987) *Speaking Mathematically: Communication in Mathematics Classrooms*. London: Routledge & Kegan Paul.

Polya, G. (1957) *How to Solve it*. New York: Doubleday Anchor Books.

Pritchard, C. (ed.) (2003) *The Changing Shape of Geometry: Celebrating a Century of Geometry and Geometry Teaching*. Cambridge: Cambridge University Press.

Radatz, H. (1979) Error analysis in mathematics education, *Journal for Research in Mathematics Education*, 10(3): 163–72.

Radford, L. (2003) Gestures, speech, and the sprouting of signs: a semiotic–cultural approach to students' types of generalization, *Mathematical Thinking and Learning*, 5(1):37–70.

Resnick, L. (1983) Mathematics and science learning: a new conception, *Science*, 220: 477–8.

Roche, J. J. (1998) *The Mathematics of Measurement: A Critical History*. London: Athlone Press.

Ryan, J. and Williams, J. (2007) *Children's Mathematics 4–15: Learning from Errors and Misconceptions*. Maidenhead: Open University Press.

Schoenfeld, A. (1985) *Mathematical Problem Solving*. New York: Academic Press.

Schoenfeld, A. (1989a) Explorations of students' mathematical beliefs and behavior, *Journal for Research in Mathematics Education*, 20: 338–55.

Schoenfeld, A. (1989b) Problem solving in context(s), in R. Charles and E. Silver (eds), *The Teaching and Assessing of Mathematical Problem Solving*. Reston, VA: National Council of Teachers of Mathematics, pp. 82–92.

Schoenfeld, A. H. (1992) Learning to think mathematically: problem solving, metacognition, and sense making in mathematics, in D. A. Grouws (ed.), *Handbook of Research on Mathematics Teaching and Learning*. New York: Macmillan, pp. 334–70.

Shaughnessy, J., Garfield, J. and Greer, B. (1996) Data handling, in A. Bishop, K. Clements, C. Keitel, J. Kilpatrick and C. Laborde (eds), *International Handbook of Mathematics Education (Part 1)*. Dordrecht: Kluwer, pp. 205–37.

Shayer, M. and Adey, P. S. (1981) *Towards a Science of Science Teaching*. London: Heinemann.

Sierpinska, A. (1994) *Understanding in Mathematics*. London: The Falmer Press.

Skaalvik, E. M. and Hagtvet, K. A. (1990) Academic achievement and self-concept: an analysis of causal predominance in a developmental perspective, *Journal of Personality and Social Psychology*, 58(2): 292–307.

Skemp, R. (1989) *Mathematics in the Primary School*. London: Routledge.

Smith, J. P., diSessa, A. A. and Roschelle, J. (1993) Misconceptions reconceived: a constructivist analysis of knowledge in transition, *The Journal of the Learning Sciences*, 3(2): 115–63.

Sowder, J. (1992) Making sense of numbers in school mathematics, in G. Leinhardt, R. Putnam and R. Hattrup (eds), *Analysis of Arithmetic for Mathematics Teaching*, Hillsdale, NJ: Lawrence Erlbaum Associates, pp. 1–51.

Stacey, K. and MacGregor, M. (1997) Ideas about symbolism that students bring to algebra, *Mathematics Teacher*, 90(2): 110–13.

Stacey, K., Helme, S., Archer, S. and Condon, C. (2001) The effect of epistemic fidelity and accessibility on teaching with physical materials: a comparison of two models for teaching decimal notation, *Educational Studies in Mathematics*, 47: 199–221.

Steffe, L. P. (1988) Children's construction of number sequences and multiplying schemes, in M. Behr and J. Hiebert (eds), *Number Concepts and Operations in the Middle Grades (Research Agenda for Mathematics Education)*. Reston, VA: National Council of Teachers of Mathematics, pp. 119–41.

Steffe, L. P. and Cobb, P. (1988) *Construction of Arithmetic Meanings and Strategies*. New York: Springer-Verlag.

Steinle, V. (2004) Changes with age in students' misconceptions of decimal numbers. Unpublished doctoral thesis, University of Melbourne. Available at: http://eprints.unimelb.edu.au/archive/00001531/ (accessed 10 September 2008).

Sutherland, R. (2007) *Teaching for Learning Mathematics*. Maidenhead: Open University Press.

Swan, M. (1983) *Teaching Decimal Place Value: A Comparative Study of 'Conflict' and 'Positive Only' Approaches*. Nottingham: Shell Centre for Mathematical Education.

Thompson, I. (1997) The role of counting in derived fact strategies, in I. Thompson (ed.), *Teaching and Learning Early Number*. Buckingham: Open University Press, pp. 52–62.

Thompson, I. (1999a) *Issues in Teaching Numeracy in Primary Schools*. Buckingham: Open University Press.

Thompson, I. (1999b) Mental calculation strategies for addition and subtraction: Part 1, *Mathematics in School*, 28(5): 22–5.

Thompson, I. (2000a) Mental calculation strategies for addition and subtraction: Part 2, *Mathematics in School*, 29(1): 24–6.

Thompson, I. (2000b) Place value: time for a reappraisal? *Educational Review*, 52(3): 291–8.

Thompson, I. (2008) Addressing errors and misconceptions with young children, in I. Thompson (ed.), *Teaching and Learning Early Number*, 2nd edn. Maidenhead: Open University Press, pp. 205–13.

Threlfall, J. (1999) Repeating patterns in the early primary years, in A. Orton (ed.), *Pattern in the Teaching and Learning Of Mathematics*. London: Cassell, pp. 18–30.

Tirosh, D. (2000) Enhancing prospective teachers' knowledge of children's conceptions: the case of division of fractions, *Journal for Research in Mathematics Education*, 31(1): 5–25.

Treffers, A. and Beishuizen, M. (1999) Realistic mathematics education in the Netherlands, in I. Thompson (ed.), *Issues in Teaching Numeracy in Primary Schools*. Buckingham: Open University Press, pp. 27–38.

Van Hiele, P. (1986) *Structure and Insight*. Orlando, FL: Academic Press.

Vergnaud, G. (1983) Multiplicative structures, in R. Lesh and M. Landau (eds), *Acquisition of Mathematics Concepts and Processes*. New York: Academic Press, pp. 127–74.

Watson, J. M. and Moritz, J. B. (2001) Development of reasoning associated with pictographs: representing, interpreting, and predicting, *Educational Studies in Mathematics*, 48: 47–81.

White, R. and Gunstone, R. (1992) *Probing Understanding*. London: The Falmer Press.

Wilder, R. L. (1968) *Evolution of Mathematical Concepts*. Milton Keynes: The Open University Press.

Williams, J. and Ryan, J. (2000) National testing and the improvement of classroom teaching: can they co-exist? *British Educational Research Journal*, 26(1): 49–73.

Yackel, E. (2001) Perspectives on arithmetic from classroom-based research in the United States of America, in J. Anghileri (ed.), *Principles in Arithmetic Teaching: Innovative Approaches for the Primary Classroom*. Buckingham: Open University Press, pp. 15–32.

Zacharos, K. (2007) Prevailing educational practices for area measurement and students' failure in measuring areas, *Journal of Mathematical Behavior*, 25: 224–39.

Index